Eccentric and
Bizarre Behaviors

Eccentric and Bizarre Behaviors

Louis R. Franzini, Ph.D.
John M. Grossberg, Ph.D.

JOHN WILEY & SONS, INC.
NEW YORK • CHICHESTER • BRISBANE • TORONTO • SINGAPORE

Credits

The authors gratefully acknowledge permissions to reprint the following material:

Pages 47–48, 52: From Fogel, G. I. and Myers, W. A., *Perversions and Near-Perversions in Clinical Practice* (New Haven: Yale University Press). Copyright © 1991. Used by permission of the publisher.

Pages 112–115: From Money, John; Wainwright, Gordon; Hingsburger, David, *The Breathless Orgasm: A Lovemap Biography of Asphyxiophilia* (Buffalo, NY: Prometheus Books). Copyright © 1991 by John Money, Gordon Wainwright, and David Hingsburger. Used by permission of the publisher.

Pages 181–183: From Viscott, David S., "A Musical Idiot Savant," *Psychiatry* (New York, NY: Guilford Press). Copyright © 1970. Used by permission of the publisher.

Pages 197–199: From Ilan, E. and Alexander, E., Eyelash and eyebrow pulling (Trichotillomania), *The Israel Annals of Psychiatry and Related Disciplines*, 3, pages 267–281. (Jerusalem, Israel: Gefen Publishing House). Copyright © 1965. Used by permission of the publisher.

Library of Congress Cataloging in Publication Data:

Franzini, Louis R.,
    Eccentric and bizarre behaviors / Louis R. Franzini, John M. Grossberg.
       p.   cm.
    Includes index.
    ISBN 0-471-54520-1 (paper : acid-free paper)
    1. Psychology, Pathological. 2. Psychology, Pathological—Case studies.   I. Grossberg, John M.   II. Title.
    RC454.F68   1994
    616.89—dc20   94-36298

Printed in the United States of America

10 9 8 7 6 5 4

Preface .

Nothing is as inspiring, as tragic, as sensational, as captivating, or as powerful as *real life*. The stories in this book are all true and are about real people. However, they are real with a crucial difference—their behavior can be so extreme that it is sometimes hard to believe we all belong to the same species. In fact, most of the time their behavior is so unusual that these individuals are labeled "mentally ill" or worse, such as "perverse," "inhuman," or "animalistic."

We believe that such labeling interferes with, rather than helps, our understanding of these individuals. What motivates them? How did they get that way? Can they ever change and conform to the larger society? Should they? Are they truly fundamentally different from the rest of us?

These unanswered questions demonstrate that our knowledge of the human species is far from complete. There are major gaps in our psychological understanding. Such strange and exotic behaviors also reveal the shortcomings of the professionals' rather simple attempts to standardize the behavior disorders, such as the ponderous official Diagnostic and Statistical Manual (DSM) published by the American Psychiatric Association.

The behavior of the unusual people described in this book reminds us of how society has contained us within the very narrow margins of the domain of social acceptability. We humans are allowed to meet our most basic needs, such as the way we express love and our universal craving for intimacy and understanding, in only certain circumscribed and "approved" forms. Radical departures from the acceptable may make us uneasy by confronting us with some of our own deep and hidden desires. We all seem to go to great lengths to deny the dark side within ourselves.

Finally, such strange behavior patterns remind us how essential it is to study *all* human actions in their sociocultural context to obtain a more complete psychological understanding. Actions and beliefs which are isolated from their natural settings may well strike the outsider as strange or repulsive because we are ignorant of the laws, customs, and deeply held beliefs about normal behavior in that particular society.

In this book we will portray a dozen of the rarest and most intriguing human behavior disorders, and everything that is currently known about them. In each instance, we define and describe the disorder, with special reference to its historical background. Then we present a brief theoretical explanation from the perspectives of modern psychiatry and psychology. Throughout, each disorder will be illustrated by actual case histories.

Above all, we have tried to emphasize that you will be reading about *human beings,* not "patients" or "cases" or "diagnoses." We have much to learn from these people, and we believe sincerely that what we learn can also help them. According to the teachings of Buddha, for a person to become perfect, there are two qualities which must be developed equally: compassion and wisdom. These qualities are inseparably linked. We would hope that reading *Eccentric and Bizarre Behaviors* will be a first step toward increasing these qualities in our readers, and ultimately toward alleviating the suffering of the unfortunate individuals we describe.

Louis R. Franzini and John M. Grossberg

Acknowledgments

This book is the result of a close collaboration between two inquisitive investigators who are endlessly fascinated by the often puzzling complexities and variations of human behavior. As a joint effort, authorship of our first collection of unusual psychological rarities was decided alphabetically.

We gratefully acknowledge the publishers (Yale University Press, Prometheus Books, Guilford Press, and Gefen Publishing House, Jerusalem, Israel) and authors who granted permission to quote from their works.

We gratefully acknowledge the conscientiousness and hard work of our unpaid student research assistants; Kathleen Ellard, Ron Hasbrooke, Candace Milow, Heidi Schlodtfelter, and Sunny Sipes. The staff of the Interlibrary Loan Office of San Diego State's Love Library provided outstanding skill and perseverance in locating our many obscure primary sources. We are also grateful to our editor, Herb Reich, who shared our enthusiasm for illuminating the darker aspects of human behavior. Finally, we owe much to our many colleagues and students, whose intense curiosity about unusual tastes in psychological subject matter reinforced our conviction that this project was indeed worthy and of educational value to the broader reading public.

Contents

CHAPTER 1

Erotomania
Obsessive Loving

To be pursued by a seemingly insatiable female who will not take no for an answer sounds like the answer to the *Penthouse* male's dream. Flowers and expensive gifts arrive at his office, some including a hotel room key or a fragrant undergarment. Frequent phone calls and letters describe in delicious detail exactly how she will extract the last drop of pleasure from his quivering, satiated body. She lives only for him, a toy, a love slave, his perfect partner. Yet somehow, almost unbelievably, at some point the unquenchable hunger and need beneath her aggressive pursuit begins to trigger little warning signals in his brain. He decides to slow things down a bit and keep the courtship at a distance. He explains that he is married, or that there is too big an age difference, or that affairs of state have replaced affairs of the heart in his aging body. No matter, the fervent admirer will not be deterred. She knows his wife is just a political convenience, she knows that he is mad for her. Or she knows that their exchange of glances at the water fountain mean that, deep down inside, he returns her love. Her letters express the certainty that these little obstacles are merely tests—the greater the barrier, the better to prove the strength of her love. Now, however, when her letters and love tokens are returned unopened, undelivered, and her phone calls are unanswered, her letters and calls turn nasty, the tone becomes harsh and threatening. "Are you some impotent sissy, afraid of that ugly cow

1

you supposedly married? Perhaps if we get her out of the way you won't be afraid to acknowledge our great passion."

We have been describing a psychological disorder called *erotomania*, perfectly portrayed in the movie *Fatal Attraction*. At this point there are three different directions the fantasy relationship may take. In the pattern just described, the rejected lover's intense love is replaced by intense hatred, her letters are laced with accusations of betrayal, cowardice, and broken promises. Threats replace compliments, and the spurned lover may turn violent and try to attack the love object, those close to him, or the buffer persons who try to protect the victim. Some of the most widely publicized attacks on celebrities and other public figures illustrate such a furious reaction to rejection. Many domestic relations tribunals have found it necessary to install metal detectors and bulletproof barriers in courtrooms where divorce and custody cases are tried.

Dr. Park Dietz, a well-known forensic psychiatrist and the country's foremost authority on violent erotomanics, analyzed personal letters sent to celebrities and politicians. Of the 214 letters to celebrities, 16% showed erotomanic delusions and 11 of the writers actually believed they were married to their phantom lovers. Of the 100 people who wrote to legislators, 5 had erotomanic delusions and 2 believed that they were married. Although Dr. Dietz estimates that only 5% of erotomanics are violent, the erotomania behavior pattern is so widespread nationally that tens of thousands of women and a smaller number of men are at risk for harassment and worse.

In the second and most frequent scenario, the ardent admirer, when faced with consistent nonresponse, will gradually give up. The calls, letters, gifts, and threats will taper off over the course of a year or two. Then the erotomanic customarily repeats the pattern by selecting other new imaginary lovers, one after the other, in a chronic and virtually unbreakable chain.

The third pattern is typical of those who suffer from severe preexisting mental illness. The erotic delusions constitute merely one of the many secondary symptoms whose specific nature and content are determined by the type and severity of the underlying mental illness. In these cases the patient may hallucinate a successful outcome of the pseudo-affair, perhaps a secret marriage to the loved one or, for a woman, that she is carrying his baby. Often a patient may believe that they share their great love through telepathic communication or coded newspaper messages.

Erotomania is not confined to any one group, country, society, race, or gender. Published cases have been reported in Canada, France, Italy, Russia, Saudi Arabia, Singapore, Tanzania, the United Kingdom, and the United States. Modern interest in erotomania was stimulated by the French psychiatrist Gaetane de Clérambault, who fascinated mental health professionals with a series of five dramatic cases reported in 1921. For this pioneering work, the disorder he described is sometimes called "de Clérambault's syndrome," rather than erotomania. De Clérambault himself called this rare disorder *psychose passionelle,* or passionate insanity, to differentiate it from the more common paranoid states such as delusions of persecution or grandeur. He also distinguished between pure erotomania and a secondary form, the latter being just one of the possible symptoms of some other severe underlying primary mental disorder, such as schizophrenia. The pure form described in the classic 19th century cases was characterized by its sudden explosive onset—obsessive love at first sight, if you will—which differentiated it from more commonplace fixed delusions. The patient is usually described as an unattractive and sexually inexperienced woman. Often her erotomania is initiated by some trigger event, such as a chance sighting of a celebrity departing at the airport, which is immediately interpreted by the smitten erotomanic as preordained. At long last she has met her soul mate, the one perfect person who will make her complete.

De Clérambault went on to describe the fundamental postulate forming the basis of the entire disorder, a conviction that one is in amorous communication with a person of much higher status or rank. There is a precise and sudden onset. The patient firmly believes that this famous personage fell in love first and made romantic overtures to him or her. Patients frequently believe they can never again experience real joy in life without the love object. All obstacles to eventual union, such as a wife and family, status difference, or the other person's high office, are dismissed as trivial or easily overcome. They believe that other people approve of the relationship. Even the loved one's outright rejection or consistent failures to respond to repeated overtures are rationalized as mere pretense for public consumption, or tests of the strength of the patient's devotion. The object of affection is continuously observed and magically protected by the wooer, who often collects photos, recordings, newspaper clippings, and other such memorabilia associated with the loved one. Erotomanic delusions are remarkably resistant to change, in the majority of instances persisting for years or even decades. Psychiatrists Enoch and Trethowan in their classic text, *Uncommon Psychiatric Syndromes,* cite a case reported by Dr. de Clérambault which illustrates the major themes characterizing the pure form of the disorder:

> A 53 year old fashionable dressmaker with a paranoid disorder of ten years duration was convinced that King George V of England was madly in love with her. Fortunately for her, she knew that the soldiers and sailors and tourists she ran into on the streets were really his emissaries, sent by the king to proclaim his love for her. Prior to this royal romance, she had been convinced that King Edward VII was in love with her, and his predecessor in turn had been an American general. She pursued the unfortunate King George from 1918 onwards, paying several visits to England hoping to get together. She frequently waited for him outside Buckingham Palace. Once she saw a curtain move in one of the palace windows and of course interpreted it as a signal from the king. She claimed that all Londoners knew of their royal affair. She vividly summarized her passion for him as follows;
>
> "The king might hate me but he can never forget. I could never be indifferent to him, nor he to me. . . . It is in vain that he hurts me. He is the most distinguished of men. . . . I was attracted to him from the depths of my heart. I wished to live under the same heaven as he and in the midst of his subjects. If I have offended him I have suffered in my heart."

In our effort to construct a coherent picture of the human mind, rare and bizarre behavior disorders generate a great deal of professional attention. Are we truly seeing something altogether new and exotic here, or is the case at hand merely a variation on some older theme? And if we are dealing with a new disorder, what are the possible causes, symptoms, and eventual outcomes? In the case of erotomania there is a long medical tradition, going back to Greek and Roman times, warning of the excesses of carnal love as potentially dangerous to one's physical and mental health. In fact, the Greeks often visited the love-stricken person, bringing gifts and earnest hopes that their friend would soon recover from love and return to his senses. The Roman physician Soranus sternly advised against allowing the mentally ill to indulge in love's pleasures, since such strong emotion would no doubt make them worse: "Some have imagined themselves descending into Hades for the love of Proserpine; some have believed they were favored by a promise of marriage to a goddess." Cicero went so far as to declare, "Of all the emotions there is none more violent than love. Love is a madness."

For centuries the theory prevailed that love was not only a *form* of insanity, but frequently the *cause* of it as well. By the end of the eighteenth century, however, amorous disturbances were generally regarded as an effect or symptom of some severe mental illness. Doctors also believed a majority of the afflicted were women, the weaker, gentler sex. As such, their disorder was not regarded as serious. The unfortunate patients were described by contemporary medical authorities as persons "sentimental, chaste, using modest language," who approached their love objects with respect, and who "never pressed the limits of propriety." Even before Freud, Victorian physicians attributed women's erotic illness to some variation of either not getting enough sex, or degenerate sexual obsession, masturbation, and licentiousness, a transparent version of the Woman as Virgin/Whore duality so prevalent in patriarchal societies. As delicately phrased by the contemporary psychiatrist Bianchi in his 1906 psychiatry textbook, erotomania occurred "in individuals of defective sexual life, not much inclined to copulation, in old maids. . . ." Coincidentally, in the same year (1921) that de Clérambault published his influential series of five erotomania cases, Dr. Bernard Hart included a chapter entitled "Old Maid's Insanity" in his psychiatry text.

Case examples of de Clérambault's "pure" form of erotomania have proven to be elusive. As published cases accumulated, psychiatrists estimated that some 20% to 30% were of males. Perhaps the number of males would be larger if we surveyed the populations of jails and mental institutions. In the largest diagnostic survey of 62 erotomanics, 43% were diagnosed as schizophrenic, 25% were classified as having delusional disorders, 7% were manic depressives, and 25% diagnosed as "Other," a category that included many cases of brain diseases. An investigating psychiatrist, Dr. Jonathan Segal, of Harvard University and Massachusetts General Hospital, concluded that there were many different causes for erotomania, rather than a single cause producing a pure form of the disorder.

Today authorities describe two separate forms of the disorder, "fixed" and "recurrent" erotomania. The fixed form is chronic and the much more serious type. The delusion is rigid and unshakeable and may well last the lifetime of the patient, despite repeated confrontations with reality. The typical sufferer is a timid and dependent woman with little sexual experience. The object of the patient's devotion is usually some modest local authority figure, such as a minister or a doctor. In such cases the passion could be a defense against low self-esteem and unconscious sexual and aggressive impulses. Psychiatrists generally assign these individuals a primary diagnosis of schizophrenia, a severe, chronic mental disorder.

Those with recurring erotomania are somewhat better adjusted psychologically, but this is not necessarily a good thing. It means that they will be more ingenious in tracking their victims and evading authorities. Their delusions are certainly intense and colorful, but in some cases tend to be short-lived. They are obsessed with a fancier class of victims, singling out celebrities and the spectacularly rich and famous. For example, one of Madonna's most diligent pursuers, insisting that he is her husband, has been apprehended many times climbing the wall around her home. David Letterman, the late-night talk show host, has had his home invaded repeatedly by 41-year-old Margaret Ray, who claims to be his wife. Another erotomanic actually succeeded in invading Queen Elizabeth's bedroom in Buckingham Palace. Rebecca Schaeffer, a popular 21-year-old sitcom starlet, was shot to death by her stalker. Former U.S. Senator Robert Krueger (D., Texas) and his wife, Kathleen, have been harassed by a former employee for the past eight years.

Recurrent erotomanics are more sexually experienced and aggressive, but, if thwarted consistently, sometimes will temporarily abandon their delusion or even switch to another phantom lover. Recurring erotomania in some cases may be a way of denying unconscious homosexual wishes. In other cases it is evident that there is a psychological identification with the powerful phantom lover, enabling the patient to incorporate the loved one's power and success into his or her own self-image.

The unusual amount of professional concern regarding the precise diagnostic classification and description of erotomanic symptoms stems from the legal difficulties that are generated by the obsessive lover's harassment tactics and potential for violence. Is ardent pursuit and persistence in the love quest a form of mental illness? In the words of the poet Alexander Pope, "Is it, in Heav'n, a crime to love too well?" The legal system and the courts are still unable to deal with this issue in a consistent manner, as we will see in the markedly different outcomes of the trials of John Hinckley, Jr., and Prosenjit Poddar.

Three recent developments have combined to push erotomania to the forefront of public consciousness. First and foremost was John Hinckley's attempted assassination of President Reagan as a love offering to the actress Jodie Foster. Second, the California Supreme Court, following the murder of a Berkeley student by her rejected suitor, ruled that therapists now have a legal duty to warn potential victims of a patient's violent impulses. Third was the enactment of antistalking laws, the culmination of a long struggle by women's groups to curtail the victimization of women whose admirers refuse to take no for an answer.

Today we are no longer comfortable viewing the typical erotomanic as female, or as the harmless spinster who is just a chronic crank, that is, de Clérambault's "pure" variety. According to Dr. Dietz, more celebrities and public figures, male and female, have been attacked in the last 10 years than in all previous U.S. history. Although erotomania is directed at both men and women, Dr. Dietz maintains that more men than women are likely to act upon their delusions, often in a violent manner. The many erotomanic men now single out as targets prominent women, such as Madonna. As a function of the increasing power and prominence of women over the last 30 years, the successful women of today make much more worthy objects of males' grandiose fantasies and romantic obsessions. At the same time, the women must also bear the brunt of the low-status male's hostility and resentment. Meanwhile, the general level of violence in our society has increased enormously, so that erotomania is much more likely to produce violence.

Two remarkable cases, those of John Hinckley, Jr., and Prosenjit Poddar, have commanded national attention and provoked intense ongoing debate about the legal and mental status of the erotomanic. Hinckley, in love with the movie star Jodie Foster, but unable to attract her attention despite a barrage of letters and phone calls, decided to kill the president of the United States as a unique love offering and desperate attempt to achieve immortality. Poddar, also a rejected lover, believed that he was being ridiculed because of his failure to win the heart of a young woman whom he mistakenly believed returned his love. In a rage, he shot and stabbed her to death. Although the erotomanic delusions of both Hinckley and Poddar led to violence and bloodshed, it is hard to imagine two young men from such radically different backgrounds.

Hinckley was the youngest of three children born to a well-to-do Colorado couple and enjoyed a privileged upbringing. Throughout adolescence he was markedly withdrawn, depressed, unhappy as a schoolboy, and in and out of college several times. Impressed by the Beatles and sure that he had musical talent, he made vague plans to get formal training so as to make it big in Hollywood. As his unhappiness and lack of focus became more evident to his family, they were able to persuade him to consult a psychiatrist. The doctor did not believe John was severely mentally disturbed, but instead saw him as spoiled, immature, and overdependent on family handouts. The doctor insisted that John move out on his own, find a job, and rent his own apartment. During the several months that he was seeing the psychiatrist, but unknown to his doctor and the family, John was flying back and forth across the country in pursuit of Jodie Foster, then a 20-year-old actress enrolled at Yale University in New Haven, Connecticut. Consumed with passion, he tried calling her at all hours and wrote her notes, poems, songs, and love letters, which he slipped under the door of her dormitory room. Frustrated and furious that she never acknowledged any of his advances, he plotted bizarre stunts to get her attention. Many of his written fragments and scribbled plans were discovered by the FBI and the Secret Service in his hotel room after his attempted assassination of President Reagan. In one plan he was going to hijack an airliner. Another note told of his intention to shoot himself on Valentine's Day in front of the Dakota Hotel on the very spot where his idol, John Lennon, had been murdered. In this note he said:

Jodie, after tonight John Lennon and I will have a lot in common. It's all for you, Foster.

On a postcard picturing President and Mrs. Reagan, he detailed his grandiose ambition as follows:

"Dear Jodie,
Don't they make a darling couple? Nancy is downright sexy. One day you and I will occupy the White House and the peasants will drool with envy. Until then, please do your best to remain a virgin. You are a virgin, aren't you?"

The following letter was an explanation of his motives, written in case he was killed. It appeared in John's parents' book, *Breaking Point:*

Dear Jodie,
There is a definite possibility that I will be killed in my attempt to get Reagan. It is for this very reason that I am writing you this letter now. As you well know by now, I love you very much. The past seven months I have left you dozens of poems, letters and messages in the faint hope you would develop an interest in me.

Although we talked on the phone a couple of times, I never had the nerve to simply approach you and introduce myself. Besides my shyness, I honestly did not wish to bother you. I know the many messages left at your door and in your mailbox were a nuisance, but I felt it was the most painless way to express my love to you.

I feel very good about the fact that you at least know my name and how I feel about you. And by hanging around your dormitory I've come to realize that I'm the topic of more than a little conversation, however full of ridicule it may be. At least you'll know that I'll always love you.

Jodie, I would abandon this idea of getting Reagan in a second if I could only win your heart and live out the rest of my life with you, whether it be in total obscurity or whatever. I will admit to you that the reason I'm going ahead with this attempt now is because I just cannot wait any longer to impress you. I've got to do something now to make you understand in no uncertain terms that I am doing all of this for your sake. By sacrificing my freedom and possibly my life I hope to change your mind about me. This letter is being written an hour before I leave for the Hilton Hotel.

Jodie, I'm asking you to please look into your heart and at least give me the chance with this historical deed to gain your respect and love.

I love you forever.
John Hinckley

After Hinckley was found not guilty by reason of insanity, he was committed to St. Elizabeth's federal mental hospital. He immediately wrote a long letter to a *New York Times* reporter, purportedly a speech he intended to deliver if found guilty. He said that his horrendous deed was planned to be a true measure of the strength of his love for Jodie Foster. It said, in part:

> The shooting outside the Washington Hilton Hotel was the greatest love offering in the history of the world. I sacrificed myself and committed the ultimate crime in hopes of winning the heart of a girl. It was an unprecedented demonstration of love. But does the American public appreciate what I've done?

It went on to say:

> At one time Miss Foster was a star and I was the insignificant fan. Now everything is changed. I am Napoleon and she is Josephine. I am Romeo and she is Juliet. I am John Hinckley, Jr., and she is Jodie Foster. I may be in prison and she may be making a movie in Paris or Hollywood but Jodie and I will always be together, in life and in death.

So, in his deranged way Hinckley did indeed accomplish his mission. He forged an eternal bond between him and his innocent victim, not one of love as he had hoped, but one of notoriety. He had gotten away with stealing a part of Jodie Foster's identity. She may well be forever linked to him and his terrible crime. However, to end on a hopeful note we present John's 1985 message to the public:

> I overcame the obsession with Jodie Foster through intense therapy, medication and a lot of love from the people around me. . . . I now cherish my life and believe that everyone's life is sacred and precious. I will never again harm another human being.

We would like to believe that treatment is helping John Hinckley, Jr., but we are not encouraged by the negative outcomes in similar cases. The common pattern in violent borderline erotomania is assault, followed by protestations of remorse, and then more violence.

A tragic murder at the University of California at Berkeley resulted in far-reaching changes in therapist-patient confidentiality. The incident is discussed in detail in Winslade and Ross; *The Insanity Defense:*

Twenty-five-year-old Prasenjit Poddar was an Indian graduate engineering student at the University of California at Berkeley. He grew up amidst grinding poverty in a tiny rural village in India. As if that wasn't enough of a handicap, he was a member of the Harijan or "Untouchable" caste. His early environment was so poor that an Indian friend and mentor at Berkeley, Farrokhg Mistree, had to teach him how to use plates and how to eat with a knife, fork, and spoon. Many considered Poddar to be a genius in overcoming such a background, winning a rare Indian government fellowship for study in the United States, and then excelling in his graduate studies of electronics and naval architecture. After two years of unrelenting devotion to his work, however, he was ready to take Mistree's advice about all work and no play. He began attending weekly folk dances sponsored by the International Student Organization.

Here he was attracted to Tanya Tarasoff, a lively, outgoing 20-year-old American student. Although she continued to chat and dance with other young men, she included Poddar in her circle of admirers, occasionally even visiting him in his room to continue their conversations. Poddar had never before been involved with a woman, and he was completely baffled by her friendly interest. Mistree, his more worldly friend, correctly saw that Tanya was no more nor less friendly to Poddar than to any of her other foreign student friends, and told Poddar she was only being sociable. However, a New Year's Eve party found Poddar and Tanya momentarily alone together in an elevator, and she impulsively reached out and kissed him for the New Year. For one glorious moment the Untouchable was Touchable, his first kiss. He was ecstatic, convinced now that she had at last revealed her true loving feelings for him.

However, in subsequent months she behaved as before. Sometimes she stood him up, danced with others, and talked openly in his presence of her intimate involvement with other men. At other times she enjoyed conversations with him as before. Baffled by her mood changes, he began tape-recording their talks in his room. Then he would spend long hours brooding over every word of their conversations. He began to skip meals, and then classes, and soon had to withdraw altogether from winter quarter classes completely. Mistree persuaded Poddar that it was essential to make a clean break from the fickle Tanya and return to his studies. This plan was successful for several months—until she called, saying she missed his friendship. Now he was drawn back under her spell once more. He became more determined than ever to discover her true feelings, endlessly playing his tapes and even splicing them to make her voice express great love for him. In desperation, one day he suddenly proposed marriage to a very startled Tanya, who turned him down. Now the distraught Poddar became convinced that everyone was laughing at him behind his back.

"Even you, Mistree, laugh at my state. But I am like an animal. I could do anything, I could kill her. If I killed her, what would you do?" In reply Mistree said, "I would tell the truth." To this Poddar said, "Then I would have to kill you too."

Relenting later, Poddar sought out his friend that evening and warned him that he was out of control. After that, Mistree slept with a chair wedged against his door.

Mistree was alarmed by Poddar's' escalating threats of violence and persuaded him to seek psychological counseling at the U.C. Health Service. Dr. Stuart Gold, a staff psychiatrist, examined him and told him he was seriously disturbed. Dr. Gold prescribed antipsychotic drugs and scheduled him for weekly appointments with Dr. Lawrence Moore, the staff psychologist. Poddar did not think his secrets were safe with Dr. Moore, so while he continued to repeat his violent threats, he never revealed the identity of his intended victim. After 10 sessions, he abruptly terminated therapy and told Mistree of plans to buy a gun. When Mistree told the doctors, they wrote to the campus police describing the danger and recommending hospitalization for Poddar. Armed with this information, the police warned Poddar to stay away from Tanya, but took no further action. Meanwhile, Poddar thoroughly frightened Tanya by following her around campus and loitering around her house. He decided to confront her with his pain and humiliation one last time. She met him in the doorway of her home and told him to leave, but he pushed his way inside. She ran; he ran after her and suddenly shot her, then stabbed the dying woman numerous times as she fell.

Just as there were vast differences in the backgrounds of these disturbed young men, so too were the outcomes in the legal proceedings of these cases. Hinckley's trial resembled a psychiatric circus, in which opposing psychiatrists took turns declaring Hinckley's mental illness and denying it. He was found not guilty by reason of insanity and committed to St. Elizabeth's Hospital until such time as he is judged to be no longer a danger to himself or others. Poddar was convicted of second degree murder and served five years in prison in California before his sentence was reversed, on appeal, by the California Supreme Court. Rather than try the case again, a plea bargain was struck and Poddar was deported to India. He reportedly married a lawyer and resumed his life there.

Modern female erotomanics have also shown an alarming tendency toward aggression and violence. Recall that the prototype of de Clérambault's "pure" erotomania was the virginal old maid imagining she possessed a secret amorous connection with some rich and powerful prince who loved her madly. Contrast this description with Marie Brenner's sensitive and insightful account of the life and times of one highly publicized modern erotomanic, Diane Schaefer, described in the September 1991 issue of *Vanity Fair* magazine. Ms. Brenner interviewed Schaefer and her friends, therapists, lawyers, judges, and victims, and provides the detailed and extensive account of female erotomania in the 1990s which follows:

> Ms. Diane Schaefer is a 41-year-old freelance medical writer and peep-show model, and most recently the nemesis of one Dr. Murray Brennan, head of cancer surgery at prestigious Sloan Kettering Memorial Hospital in Manhattan. Ms. Schaefer is currently serving a two-year prison sentence for harassing Dr. Brennan. She is an intelligent, attractive, and well-educated person. For the previous eight years she trailed Dr. Brennan to medical conferences all over the world, using computer skills learned while a travel agent to book adjoining hotel rooms and seats on airplanes. At airports she frequently attempted to force her way into taxis with him. She called his office so frequently, using so many aliases and disguised voices, that his frantic office staff often snarled and hung up on genuine patients. She left obscene messages on his hospital answering machine. She bombarded him and his family with letters and notes. Finally, in 1990, she wrote him nine letters, the legal basis for a nine-count harassment indictment. When [she was] arrested, police searched her purse and found numerous airline frequent-flier cards and club memberships, Dr. Brennan's detailed travel itinerary, per-

sonal data about his family, friends, and staff, including their un-listed phone numbers, a box of expensive stationery, and a rubber glove. Other ruses included calling Dr. Brennan's college in New Zealand, posing as a reporter composing his obituary and asking for transcripts and personal information.

Although she was interested in a medical career while attending high school in an affluent New York suburb, her application to Sarah Lawrence's human genetics and physiology master's program was rejected. Nevertheless, she began passing herself off as a phy-sician, frequently reading medical books and journals even between sets as a nude dancer at the Honey Buns club. In fact, she became so knowledgeable in medicine that she was able to earn money oc-casionally as a medical writer and freelance medical researcher. She somehow obtained a medical ID, wore a white coat, and ate in the hospital cafeteria. Sometimes she succeeded in smuggling herself into grand rounds and Dr. Brennan's colorectal case conferences, coming to be known as the "colorectal groupie."

Throughout the years during which she pursued Dr. Brennan, she steadfastly held to her delusional belief that they had once been lovers, portraying herself as the other woman in his life, puzzled and heartbroken by his rejection. Just as consistently, Dr. Brennan up-held his innocence, supported by Schaefer's long history of erotic delusional attachments. Predictably, Schaefer had become infuriated when her advances were consistently rejected or ignored. Dr. Bren-nan recorded her calls, which became increasingly threatening.

These threats directed at him and especially at his children finally persuaded Dr. Brennan to take strong legal action. After several false starts Ms. Schaefer was indicted on nine counts of harassment. As is common in erotomania, when arrested for harassing Brennan, she apparently found room in her affections to include both the DA's prosecuting attorney and the trial judge. The judge at first refused to appreciate the potential distress posed by unwanted sexual pursuit, especially by a bright and attractive woman. According to Linda Fairstein, Chief of Sex Crimes in the Manhattan district at-torney's office, the harassment and stalking which almost defines erotomania is a tricky legal problem in many jurisdictions. "How do you get rid of a nuisance before it escalates into violence? These cases are often treated in the courts as complete garbage." The judge changed his mind quickly when Ms. Schaefer, posing as a divorced reentry student, alarmed his wife, a professor at Fordham University, with intense detailed questions about where she and the judge lived. Soon the judge began to notice Schaefer following him, sometimes appearing in the same subway car. She also wrote him many erotic letters.

For her court hearing, Schaefer, always in impeccable taste, appeared in Manhattan criminal court wearing handcuffs and Chanel pumps, a Cartier watch, Norell perfume, and a simple but elegant black sheath. When her female lawyer offered to buy her makeup for the court appearance, she snapped, "You wouldn't know what to do at a Chanel counter."

Schaefer refused to let her attorney use a psychiatric defense, fearful that she would be forced to take mind-numbing drugs. She also insisted on testifying on her own behalf, without success. After a brief trial she was sentenced to two years in prison. Dr. Brennan, who had been reluctant to seek criminal prosecution, probably spoke for most people when he said, "A woman like that doesn't belong in jail." However, when restraining orders and mandated psychiatric treatment fail, there really are no alternatives.

As we have seen in this case, the usual remedies, such as psychotherapy and legal restraints, are ineffectual. Even direct confrontation, with overt rejection by the target person, not only is unsuccessful but sometimes intensifies the erotomanic's passion.

Unfortunately, the most dangerous and the most numerous kind of erotomanics are to be found in that larger group called stalkers. They are rarely jailed or given therapy. Even when jailed or treated, they typically continue their terroristic tactics upon release. According to the Threat Management Unit of the Los Angeles Police Department, 9.5% of stalkers are delusional erotomanics, and the great majority of other stalkers are either rejected ex-lovers, former employees, or harassing attention seekers.

In order to understand the large number of nondelusional violent stalkers, Dr. J. Reid Meloy, chief of Forensic Mental Health Services of San Diego County, introduced the concept of "borderline erotomania." In his important article on unrequited love and the wish to kill, he defines borderline erotomania as "an intense and tumultuous attachment to an unrequited love." It is quite different from the pure erotomania described by de Clérambault. In de Clérambault's classical cases, some homely, shy, and unloved woman suddenly singles out a prominent stranger and worships him from afar, spinning out elaborate romantic fantasies. Contact, if any, is limited to letters and phone calls. In contrast, Dr. Meloy regards borderline erotomania as a variant of pathological morbid jealousy. For such individuals rejection produces "abandonment rage," which frequently results in severe psychological and physical damage to the target, as in the movie *Fatal Attraction.* Meloy explains:

> These individuals are remarkable for their initial idealization, and then rageful devaluation, of the love object, and the tenacity of their approaches in the face of treatment intervention or legal sanction.

In other words, their initial infatuation swiftly turns to rage upon rejection, and they are not deterred by therapy, arrest, or imprisonment. They follow what one judge called "the classic stepping stones of stalking": first, harassing calls, followed by notes, vandalism, and then violence. In 1990 California became the first of 42 states to make a crime of stalking, defining it as, "willful and malicious following and harassing and a credible threat of violence."

California State Senator Edwin R. Royce's sponsorship of the new law was initiated when stalkers murdered five women in Orange County, despite the fact that all the men were under restraining orders and all the victims had told the police of their fear of imminent harm. Royce's bill was reinforced by a U.S. Department of Justice study reporting that fully 30% of all murdered women in the United States are the victims of either present or former spouses or boyfriends. According to Dr. Meloy, there are literally tens of thousands of such cases of nondelusional but potentially violent individuals with distorted love relationships. Many of these individuals resort to retaliatory harassment, intimidation, domination, and physical attacks in an attempt to force reconciliation, to prevent abandonment, or to restore self-esteem. Newspapers almost daily document the beatings, suicides, and homicides that all too frequently are the outcomes of this condition. Most of the perpetrators are not delusional in the sense that they believe the prominent love object really does return their affections. However, they grossly distort reality with the fantasy that they can force the loved one to return their affections. For example, John Hinckley believed that his desperate attack on President Reagan would win Jodie Foster's love.

THEORETICAL VIEWS

None of the causal explanations for erotomania are widely accepted, perhaps because there are too few published investigations or case studies in depth. In the Victorian era erotomania was attributed to sexual frustration in virginal spinsters with moist Cinderella dreams of a secret admirer. This view gradually evolved into an emphasis on the lonely, isolated, and unrewarding lives of the afflicted persons. Erotomanic delusions, it was thought, served to bolster their sense of personal worth, value, and purpose. The frustrated-spinster theories gave way to Freudian psychoanalytic theories, which provide a rich and fanciful feast, best appreciated, we believe, when accompanied by a mild suspension of belief.

Psychoanalytic View

Analysts tend to attribute the cause of erotomania to the loss of the father figure early in life, termed "object loss." The loss does not have to be a literal one, as through death or desertion. More often it is symbolic, perhaps represented by an abusive or alcoholic father, or one who is absent emotionally. This loss is a shattering blow to self-esteem, because the person interprets it as rejection and abandonment. The individual feels unloved and unlovable, and unconsciously yearns for a better, more loving father figure. Since these longings have incestuous implications, they are projected onto the father figure: "I don't love and desire him, he desires me." For men, a homosexual element remains. Therefore the male erotomanic unconsciously substitutes the love of a woman: *she* loves him. Finally, to restore self-esteem, the love object who desires the person must be a famous and powerful individual. In sum, the wish to be loved is replaced by the delusion that one is loved, and by a highly desirable and eminent person. This delusional transformation serves an adaptive and restorative function.

Dr. Meloy has offered a somewhat different psychoanalytic theory. He attributes borderline erotomania to profound childhood neglect and rejection, which causes severe disruption of bonding and affectional attachment. Borderline erotomanics are not insane and, in fact, have often had prior contact with the loved one. That contact could be an actual failed relationship, an impersonal autographed publicity photograph, or a casual wave of the hand in a concert hall. After continual rebuffs, the borderline erotomanic experiences "abandonment rage," a reopening of the old childhood rejection wounds. The person formerly loved and adored is now ragefully devalued. The sought-after person is unconsciously divided into a "good loved one" and a "bad loved one," through a mechanism that the Freudians call "splitting." As passionate love turns to hatred, the good/bad lover now becomes a target. Revenge fantasies replace the former daydreams of lifelong bliss.

Sociobehavioral View

The behavioral perspective offers no new analysis of erotomanic behavior beyond explanations in terms of the functional value of symptoms for the patient. For example, activities such as pestering a desirable but initially aloof woman with frequent love notes and extravagant gifts of flowers and candy could become a habitual practice if rewarded by even an occasional successful courtship or intermittent attention.

Several investigators have offered simple commonsense explanations of erotomania that avoid the heavy-handed pronouncements of psychoanalysis. For example psychiatrists Hayes and O'Shea of St. Brendan's Hospital, Dublin, showed that erotomanic behaviors may serve a useful function in helping the patient adapt to stressful situations.

A devout 44-year-old married Roman Catholic woman suddenly fell in love with a priest at the Lourdes shrine. She was convinced that he returned her love telepathically, even though he made no overt signs of affection. She became obsessed with sexual fantasies involving him, and masturbated frequently in a vain effort to forget him. Her psychiatrist noted that her invalid husband had been unable to perform sexually for 10 years. He interpreted her symptoms as a response to the burden of caring for her husband, her lack of a more satisfying sex life, and financial insecurity. The psychiatrist prescribed psychoactive medication and arranged for housekeeping help and a part-time job. Best of all, a local nursing home agreed to take her husband once a year to allow her a two-week vacation. She gave up her obsession and was able to live a more gratifying life.

There is another sociological interpretation that seems to fit well with Dr. Meloy's category of violent borderline erotomania. According to this view, the man's victimization of the love object reflects our larger society's devaluation of the woman's worth. In earlier times, women were treated as possessions who were expected to endure exploitation and maltreatment at the hands of a spouse or other male authority figure. Divorce, separation attempts, or rejection of the man were regarded as escape maneuvers, and for these actions society sanctioned strong punishments ranging from ostracism to beatings and worse. With the recent increase in the empowerment of women through lawsuits, social protests, and education, women have enjoyed considerable success in extending the protection of the state to themselves. However, male social attitudes have lagged behind, with large numbers of traditional males reluctant to relinquish their traditional power and privilege, often supported by orthodox religion and custom. Harassment and obsessive possessiveness may then be regarded as the combined outcome of cultural lag plus male insecurity, fear of abandonment, and fragile masculine ego.

SURVIVING A STALKER

According to Dr. Michael Zona, forensic psychiatrist for the Los Angeles police department, 51% of stalking victims are ordinary citizens. Of these, 13% are former employers of the stalkers. Of the remaining victims, 17% are high-profile celebrities and 32% are lesser-known public figures. For the average victim seeking to stop a stalker, the first step is to notify the police immediately. It is surprisingly difficult to persuade victims to do, since many are either afraid of retaliation or believe that the stalker will eventually become discouraged or listen to reason. Next, the person should get some sort of court-sanctioned restraining order.

Unfortunately, many victims have found that such a paper cannot stop bullets, but if their state has an antistalking law, violation of the protection order will frequently trigger prompt arrest and longer prison sentences.

The victim should give a picture of the stalker to the police, relatives, friends, and employers. The victim should also obtain the phone number of an officer who can be contacted directly. She (or he) should try to deal with the same officer all the time so that she will be perceived as a real person rather than just another case. Every contact with the stalker should be reported in order to build up a substantial case file. It is also useful for the victim to keep a diary. Victims should request periodic police drive-bys and install a home security system and a car telephone. It is also helpful for the victim to avoid being alone, as much as possible, both for moral support and as a deterrent. Joining a support group can often help in dealing with the devastating fear, anger, and frustration experienced by victims.

None of these measures is foolproof. When there is an actual threat to life, sometimes there is no realistic remedy other than moving to another community and adopting a new identity. Violent erotomania is only now receiving serious scientific and legal scrutiny. We hope that future research will provide more hopeful and optimistic recommendations. Meanwhile, antistalking laws should afford some breathing room for victims by authorizing more arrests, more vigorous prosecution, and longer prison terms.

Suggested Further Readings

Brenner, M. (1991 Sept.) Erotomania. *Vanity Fair, 54,* #9, 188–195, 256, 258–260, 262–265.

Enoch, M., & Trethowan, W. (Eds.). (1991) *Uncommon psychiatric syndromes.* (3rd ed.). Oxford: Boston: Butterworth-Heinemann.

Goldstein, R. (1978) de Clérambault in court: A forensic romance. *Bulletin of the American Academy of Psychiatry and the Law, 6,* 36–40.

Lovett-Doust, J., & Christie, H. (1978) The pathology of love and some clinical variants of de Clérambault's syndrome. *Social Science and Medicine, 12,* 96–106.

Meloy, J. (1989). Unrequited love and the wish to kill. *Bulletin of the Menninger Clinic, 53,* 477–491.

CHAPTER 2

Munchausen's Syndrome by Proxy
The New Form of Child Abuse

Baron Karl Friedrich Heironymus von Munchausen was a cavalry officer in service to eighteenth-century Russia. After retiring from the military, he amused his friends by telling outrageous stories about his prowess as a soldier and athlete. His fame was facilitated by a popular book by Rudoph Raspe and the 1989 movie *The Adventures of Baron Munchausen*. The Baron's main legacy, though, is not the fanciful musings of an eccentric Pinnochio. Rather, he has become eponymous; that is, in a bizarre twist the Baron's name is remembered as that of a strange medical-psychological disorder.

Munchausen syndrome patients actually fake their illnesses by describing or creating unusual and perplexing patterns of symptoms. For example, they may take massive quantities of unrelated medications; they may inject themselves with saliva or urine; they may deposit blood or feces in samples of their own urine submitted for laboratory tests. Their ingenuity in inventing symptoms is itself worthy of acclaim, but not of approval.

A classic case was Leo Lamphere, who claimed to be a professional wrestler—"the Indiana Cyclone." In addition to having a history of many hospitalizations and surgeries, Mr. Lamphere was able to spit up blood as needed for attention in emergency rooms. Later it was discovered that he carried the blood in a concealed pouch in his mouth, which he bit and spit as needed.

Munchausen patients usually have considerable familiarity with medical terminology and hospital routines. They present symptom patterns that are difficult for conscientious physicians to diagnose, such as vague abdominal pains and unexplained fever. Consequently, many expensive, and often painful, diagnostic tests are ordered for these complex and suffering patients. Such individuals are doctor and hospital shoppers who, when they fail to receive what they judge to be adequate treatment, will move on angrily to the next medical setting and begin the process anew.

Munchausen's syndrome is estimated to affect as many as 12,000 Americans and to cost taxpayers well over $40 million a year. The disorder, which appears worldwide, was first named by English physician Richard Asher in 1951. The syndrome is regarded as *factitious,* which means that its physical and psychological symptoms are invented by the patient.

The case of Wendy Scott of Scotland illustrates how extensive the career of a Munchausen patient can be. Her disorder began at age 16, and over the next 12 years she was admitted to 385 hospitals and received 38 operations. When she eventually had a genuine medical problem, a fistula (an abnormal passageway leading from an internal abscess to the skin surface), the suspicious medical community (finally) ignored her pleas for treatment. She did not die, as she was eventually treated, but there are other cases on record in which death did occur before the doctors realized this time, there really was a "wolf."

Other patients have developed serious medical problems as a result of their many exploratory surgeries and other diagnostic tests. Gangrene and other infections have forced amputations of limbs. One man developed leukemia, presumably as a result of having been subjected to hundreds of unnecessary X-rays. His doctors, unaware of this patient's medical history, were trying to obtain an accurate diagnosis of his unexplainable symptoms. These patients come to doctors' offices or hospital emergency rooms with grandiose stories, bizarre and dramatic descriptions of symptoms, and outright lies about their histories. They are likely to be extremely compliant and cooperative at first, but when no illness can be found or a psychiatric referral is suggested, they become hostile, belligerent, and occasionally violent.

Classic Munchausen patients typically undergo a number of painful, and even dangerous, medical procedures and treatments. Yet the situation is clearly self-induced and self-maintained. Whatever pain or risks such individuals experience, ultimately, these results are of their own doing, and so other people may be less inclined to be sympathetic or compassionate to them.

For a more complete account of Munchausen's syndrome, we recommend the recent book *Patient or Pretender* by Alabama psychiatrists Marc Feldman and Charles Ford with Toni Reinhold.

Beyond the bizarre Munchausen syndrome is an even more incomprehensible disorder known as *Munchausen syndrome by proxy* (MSP). MSP typically involves a parent, almost always the mother, who actually creates symptoms in her child. These symptoms can be painful, debilitating, and dangerous. Estimates are that nearly 10% of such children die. If they are not killed by the parent's behavior, they end up being subjected to an exhaustive array of risky and aversive diagnostic procedures performed by concerned medical personnel. The symptoms usually baffle pediatricians and other clinicians because they are not characteristic of known diseases. It usually takes quite a long time for unsuspecting doctors to even consider that the child's condition may have been deliberately induced by a seemingly loving and protective mother.

The techniques used to create symptoms in children are as varied as they are cruel. For example, some children have been secretly injected with feces, urine, or saliva or have had fecal flora and vaginal microbes introduced into their intravenous (IV) tubes. Some children have simply been poisoned with arsenic, rat poison, Epsom salts, ipecac syrup (an over-the-counter remedy designed to induce vomiting), mineral oil, Ex-Lax, insulin, prescription tranquilizers and sedatives, table salt, pepper, sugar, and even massive quantities of water. One study of 48 MSP children, 8 of whom ultimately died, listed 27 *different* poisons that had been administered to them.

Direct physical attacks on a child's body have included jabbing pins into the face and body to create bleeding, digging out facial lesions with an instrument or fingernail, and suffocation by placing a hand or pillow over an infant's face. Deliberate underfeeding in a home environment of extreme filth and mounds of rubbish, and inducing "epilepsy" or unconsciousness by applying pressure on a key artery in a child's neck also constitute physical attacks that are equally dangerous and repulsive.

A more indirect technique used by some MSP parents is to contaminate specimens that are to be submitted for laboratory analysis. Since many MSP mothers have had some nursing training, they are often entrusted to obtain these samples from their own children. Thus, they have the opportunity to add bits of feces, blood, or sugar to the urine, to substitute their own urine or blood, and even to alter the actual lab test reports. One mother substituted the sputum of an actual cystic fibrosis patient to simulate signs of cystic fibrosis in her own son.

Dr. Donna Rosenberg of the University of Colorado Health Sciences Center summarized the four chief identifying characteristics of MSP:

1. The child's illness has been simulated and/or produced by a parent or caregiver.
2. The child has been presented for medical evaluation and treatment, usually repeatedly.
3. The perpetrator denies knowing the cause of the child's illness.
4. The acute symptoms abate when the child is separated from the perpetrator.

Rosenberg reviewed 117 cases of MSP in the professional literature. Her summary conclusions are worth noting and may help in understanding this strange syndrome. The child victims are equally likely to be boys or girls. MSP occurs in all socioeconomic classes. All the perpetrators were the mothers or other female caregivers. In 25% of the cases the physical symptoms were only simulated (faked); in 50% symptoms were directly produced (in 95% of those cases the illness was produced while the child was already in the hospital); and the final 25% of cases included both the simulation and the production of symptoms. Of course, because of the need for doctors to conduct a variety of diagnostic tests, the physicians were involved in producing pain and other symptoms in 100% of the children.

Sometimes the damage is permanent disfigurement or permanent impairment of function. In addition, multiple abdominal surgeries, which were later determined to be unnecessary, were themselves likely to predispose those children to future medical problems.

In Rosenberg's review 10 of the children had died, representing a mortality rate of 9%, all of whom were less than 3 years of age. It is especially tragic that in 20% of these cases, the parents had been confronted with the MSP diagnosis, but the child was sent home with them anyway, only to die later.

One woman in Texas killed five of her own children and the daughter of a cousin. She also is suspected in the death of another of her own children. Licensed vocational nurse Genene Jones, also in Texas, was probably responsible for 15 or more children's deaths while they were under her care. She was charged with and convicted of only two murders and received a prison sentence of 60 years.

Marybeth Tinning of Schenectady, New York, was convicted of causing the death of two of her children, but authorities believed that she was responsible for the deaths of all *nine* of her children. None lived to the fourth birthday. It is common that many abuse-related deaths go unreported as such or are classified as nonhomicides. Of course, all child-abuse deaths are not MSP deaths.

NAMING THE SYNDROME

Sometimes MSP is referred to as *Polle syndrome.* According to legend, the elderly (age 74) Baron von Munchausen married a 17-year-old woman, Bernhardine Brun, but she danced with another on their wedding night. Within a year a boy was born, and friends of the family predicted that he would not live long because they suspected that the Baron was probably not the boy's father. Sure enough, the son, Polle, died mysteriously within a year. Thus, the folktale emerged that somehow the Baron caused the death of Polle. Drs. David Burman and David Stevens of Bristol, England, in 1977, suggested the term "Polle syndrome—a child of a Munchausen whose life expectancy is liable to be short."

Seven years later Drs. H. Strassburg and W. Peuckert corrected Burman and Stevens. The child in question was a girl, and Polle was the name of the home *village* of Bernhardine. The Baron did deny paternity. The official cause of death of the child was seizures, and the Baron was in no way involved.

Being the first to name a syndrome in the professional literature can become a matter of inordinate personal pride. Of course, it is advisable to be accurate in historical facts, as in the case of the misnamed Polle syndrome. Who coined the term "Munchausen syndrome by proxy"? Nearly all researchers credit pediatrician Roy Meadow of St. James Hospital in Leeds, England, in his 1977 paper. Psychologist John Money of Johns Hopkins University, though, bothered to note in print that he and June Werlwas first used the term "Munchausen's syndrome by proxy" in their 1976 report on folie à deux in the child-abusing parents of children who became dwarfs (see page 32–33).

In any case, the experts in this area all seem to recognize the relation of MSP to the adult Munchausen syndrome. Drs. Neel Ackerman, Jr. and Cory Strobel, U.S. Air Force pediatricians, treated a 34-month-old girl for chronic diarrhea, whose mother had given her laxatives. The mother herself described her own chronic bloody diarrhea, which was later learned to have been fabricated. The doctors concluded from their case and their literature review that "Munchausen will beget Polle."

Conversely, Drs. Tona McGuire and Kenneth Feldman, of the University of Washington School of Medicine, note the multigenerational features of the syndrome: "The child victims of Munchausen syndrome by proxy become adult Munchausen patients."

Thus, the two syndromes seem able to follow each other in either order. This confusion simply reflects our incomplete understanding of these bizarre phenomena of illness fabrication.

An interesting example of the interrelationship of the syndromes is offered by child psychiatrist David Waller. His patient, 2-year-old Robert, had been admitted to the hospital because of easy bruising, vomiting, coughing up blood, blood in his urine, and bloody stools. All of these symptoms were reportedly appearing at the same time. Even though only age 2, when asked by a nurse how the blood got into his urine bag, Robert answered, "Mommy put it in there."

The medical staff scheduled an appointment with Robert's mother to confront her with their suspicions and evidence of MSP. Rather than keep that appointment, the mother checked herself into a neighboring hospital, convinced a surgeon that she had appendicitis—despite having no fever and a normal blood count—and received an operation. The removed appendix was normal.

MSP AND CHILD ABUSE

Munchausen's syndrome by proxy plainly is child abuse. The professional literature refers to these children as "chemically abused" or "bacteriologically battered." This form of child abuse is not very well known by either the public or the medical professionals having contact with these patients. There have been only about 200 documented cases of MSP in the United States since Dr. Roy Meadow's report of 1977. It is vital that all healthcare professionals become aware of this bizarre syndrome, because it indeed can be a matter of life and death. The true prevalence of MSP is unknown, as it is frequently missed by diagnosticians who are desperately trying to help a hurting child with serious symptoms. Even when MSP is suspected, healthcare professionals are reluctant to undertake the frustrating and time-consuming task of reporting their concerns to legal and social agencies who, in turn, are likely to be totally ignorant of this syndrome.

SUBTYPES OF MSP

Drs. Judith Libow and Herbert Schreier of Children's Hospital Medical Center in Oakland, California, have provided a useful system of classifying MSP according to three types of parents or caregivers:

1. *Help Seekers.* These cases only superficially look like those of MSP. Typically, there is just a single episode of factitious complaints rather than an extended series of medical contacts. When confronted, the mother reacts with relief and cooperation rather than hostility and denial. The deception serves to permit her to pursue medical attention for herself. It legitimizes her own need for psychological help through the medium of her "sick" child.

2. *Active Inducers.* These are the *prototypical* MSP cases in which a parent directly and actively produces symptoms in the child through suffocation, injections, or poisoning. What is disarming is that these mothers are extraordinarily cooperative and continually grateful to the medical staff. They are seemingly ideal, loving parents.

3. *Doctor Addicts.* In these MSP cases the deception is confined to the false reporting of the child's history and symptoms. There is no direct production of symptoms. This is a more passive form of abuse. Of course, the false reports result in many unnecessary and painful tests for the child, which are delivered by medical personnel. The mothers are convinced that their children are genuinely ill and are distrustful and angry with doctors who do not confirm their beliefs. The children in this category tend to be older than those in the other groups. Their mothers tend to be more hostile, paranoid, and demanding in their interactions with the doctors to whom they are "addicted."

Social worker James Masterson and his Denver colleagues point out a subtle variant of MSP in which there really is a clinically verified disease, but to only a mild degree, in a child. Therefore, the possibility of MSP may be missed by a medical staff because of the positive results from standard lab tests. They refer to this subtype of MSP as "illness exaggeration" by the child's mother. According to her, every headache must mean a brain tumor; every pimple must be skin cancer; every twinge must signal a heart condition.

Other than including a real organic basis for the child's symptoms, this category is similar to that of the doctor addicts. In both types there may be excessive school absences, a preoccupation with illness, heavy reliance on medications, family refusal to accept the psychosocial aspects of chronic illness, either neutral or overtly negative reactions to a physician's report of improvement in the child's condition, and frequent disagreements with and changes of the primary care physician.

THE MSP MOTHER

What kind of parent would deliberately inflict such painful treatment on a son or daughter? It is emotionally wrenching for most parents to see their child ill or being subjected to medically necessary injections, invasive diagnostic procedures, or major operations. In cases of MSP the parent either produces painful symptoms directly or manipulates the healthcare system to obtain a variety of seemingly necessary tests and treatments.

The MSP parent is almost always the mother. There is one case in the literature in which the father was the perpetrator and another in which both parents seemed to be equally involved. We discuss the father's role later.

The MSP mother typically is a fairly well educated and articulate woman. She often has had medical or nursing training, although not necessarily to completion of a formal degree. She is fascinated by medicine and enjoys watching medical shows on TV and reading technical medical literature and dictionaries. She is comfortable in the hospital setting, cooperative and friendly with staff, and soon becomes a trusted reporter of symptoms. Nurses and doctors are often astounded once the correct MSP diagnosis is achieved, because the mother seemed to be a "perfect" example of a loving and concerned parent.

The mother's more pathological side, though, is her paranoid thinking, her delusion that her child is indeed ill, and sociopathy (a character disorder in which a charming and manipulative style enables a person to exploit others by violating social and legal standards without guilt or remorse). An example of such sociopathy is shown by a mother who forged a letter from another physician, attesting to the presence of illness in her child. The letter was then given to the child's current physician. Other examples of deliberately deceptive acts include the mother who disconnected her child's IVs of antibiotics and the one who withdrew blood from her son and gave it to him to drink (so that lab tests would suggest that he was bleeding internally).

Drs. Libow and Schreier describe the psychological characteristics of the MSP (active inducer type) mother:

> The most consistent picture emerging is of an anxious and depressed mother who uses an extreme degree of denial, dissociation of affect, and paranoid projection. The medical staff's appreciation of these mothers as outstanding caretakers is the most apparent secondary gain in conjunction with their simultaneous enactment of a controlling relationship with the treating physicians.

Because of the obvious priority to focus care on the child in question, MSP mothers have not been adequately studied psychologically. As a result of interviews, mothers have been labeled by various physicians as exhibiting hysteria, sociopathy, narcissistic personality disorder, borderline personality disorder, paranoid grandiosity, and as suffering from feelings of low self-worth and insufficient attention to themselves. They are thought to need a sense of power and accomplishment.

Dr. Elaine Leeder, a social worker by training, describes the personality of the MSP mother from a feminist perspective:

> She has a problem with empathy in that her own emotional needs are far more important to her than the very health of her child. She seeks and receives the attention she needs vicariously through her child; constantly seeking admiration and attention, her self-esteem is fragile and dependent on how she is regarded by the medical staff.
>
> This is a mother who is well trained and competent at mothering. She is nurturing, loving and caring, and has been well socialized into the role of motherhood. Her main identity comes from caring for an ill child and receiving praise and confirmation for herself as a person from highly respected social authorities, for example, the medical establishment. It appears to me that this syndrome is actually a predictable outgrowth of the dominant patriarchal social order and its training of women. . . . Motherhood is not the work of choice or reinforcing enough [for the woman's identity].

Many MSP mothers have a history of Munchausen syndrome themselves. Dr. Randell Alexander and his colleagues studied five families with "serial MSP"; that is, families in which more than one child was victimized. They found that 80% of their MSP mothers at some point in the past had fabricated their own medical symptoms. In serial MSP it is interesting that typically only one child at a time is the target. However, Dr. Deborah Lee in England reported a case of MSP in 4-month-old twins who allegedly were vomiting blood. Luckily, an alert hospital nurse detected a diaper pin hidden in their mother's hand, which had been used to puncture the baby boy's lower lip. (The pin was suspicious because the hospital routinely used self-adhesive diapers, which did not require pins.)

Without detection and subsequent treatment MSP mothers tend to continue their deception. In fact, they may intensify the creation of symptoms in subsequent cases. Dr. Carol Rosen and her colleagues in the Department of Pediatrics at Baylor College of Medicine described a case of siblings, a 7-month-old girl and a 4-year-old boy, who suffered from repeated episodes of cardiorespiratory arrest. Their mother was eventually discovered, by a hidden videotape camera, to be inducing the cessation of breathing and then skillfully resuscitating the hospitalized baby. The tape clearly showed the mother placing her right hand over the child's face for a full 90 seconds. When the mother was confronted with the staff's MSP diagnosis for this child, no more episodes ever occurred in either child.

ROLE OF FATHERS IN MSP

Nearly all cases of MSP identify the mother or a foster mother as the perpetrator. The role played by the father remains much more mysterious. The father is most commonly described as absent from the home or exhibiting such a "low profile" that he is effectively absent. Of course, his noninvolvement gives more freedom to the mother to produce symptoms without interference. When the mother is confronted, however, the father typically becomes very supportive of her and may even confirm her fabrications. Thus, he becomes a tacit facilitator or enabler of her behavior. In one case, while the hospital staff was confronting the parents with their suspicions that their child's "bleeding" had been factitious, the father began a diversionary conversation, which freed the mother to escape from the hospital with the child. A father functions most frequently as an accessory to a mother's MSP behavior.

Pediatrician Adel Makar and nurse Paula Squier of St. Joseph Mercy Hospital in Mason City, Iowa, reported a case of MSP that is unique in two respects: (1) the child involved is the youngest one we are aware of in the professional literature (8 days old), and (2) the father was the perpetrator. After a normal birth, the baby girl was brought to the family physician following two episodes of cessation of breathing (apnea) resulting in bluish coloration (cyanosis). The father was present and claimed to have revived her by shaking until her breathing resumed. The baby was referred and admitted to the local medical center's apnea detection program. Many diagnostic tests were performed there and at the university hospital. Even though all heart and respiratory test results were normal, the father reported that the baby had had three seizures one night while he stayed with her in the room. Continuous electronic monitoring revealed no seizure activity. Nevertheless, to our amazement, the child was given phenobarbital for a seizure disorder.

Four days after discharge the father brought the child back to the hospital, reporting that she had had a major epileptic seizure, as well as bright red blood in her stools. All hospital tests continued to be negative, including tests for blood in the stool. *In the hospital* three episodes of apnea occurred and triggered alarms by the electronic monitoring system. In all occurrences the father was present in the room or had reached the child before the staff arrived. The dosage of the phenobarbital was increased. Because the medication increase was ordered, it is unclear whether or when the staff became suspicious. The child was moved, however, to a room adjacent to the nurses' station where direct observation of the infant would be very easy.

After three days in the hospital, a nurse unexpectedly entered the child's room. The door had been closed, the curtains on the observation window from the nurses' station were drawn, and the lights had been turned off. The nurse observed the father with his left hand on the back of the baby's head, pressing her face against the mattress. The monitors had been turned off, and the mother was not in the room.

Fortunately, no permanent damage was done. The infant was discharged from the hospital to foster parents, and no further episodes occurred. She eventually lived with her grandmother and developed normally.

Two cases (out of the 50 they had seen) of *abuse dwarfism* reported by Dr. John Money and his colleagues at Johns Hopkins University involved the father as an equal "colluder" with the mother in MSP. Money points out:

> [Abuse dwarfism is] also known as psychosocial dwarfism. This syndrome is characterized by extreme failure of growth in stature, intellect, and sociobehavioral status. All three components of growth failure persist and eventually become irreversible, unless the child is rescued from the abusive environment, usually the parental home, where he/she has been the victim of multiple practices of child abuse

and neglect. The earlier the rescue, the greater the amount of physical, mental, and social catch-up growth that can be achieved. . . .

After a century of neglect, when child abuse was rediscovered under the name of the battered child syndrome, it became a sexist vogue to exonerate mothers. Along with their children, they were considered victims of the brutality of their child-abusing husbands. Now, however, it is known that the mother herself may be the instigator of child abuse. Her husband acquiesces in what is, in effect, a folie à deux—a conspiracy or collusion to abuse.

MOTIVES OF THE MSP MOTHER

What is "in it" for the mother who endangers her child by creating symptoms and making up false medical histories? Some children die, and some are left permanently damaged with mental retardation, seizures, or destructive joint changes resulting in a limp. Even the child may become convinced that he or she truly is ill, when this is not so.

The explanation agreed upon by most experts can be summed up in a single word—"attention." The misguided effort by the mother is sometimes elaborated as a maladaptive way to relieve boredom and loneliness. The presentation of a sick child with perplexing symptoms draws the interest of a multitude of hospital staff members and, often, a flurry of professional activity to help the child. All of this action allows the mother to assume the patient role in the manner of a surrogate.

In cases in which she has performed life-saving CPR on a child who had stopped breathing, the loving mother receives much praise for her efforts. The rewards are obvious. One mother was actually receiving public funds to pay for hospital services for her child. She was bold enough to ask for a car (at public expense) in order to take the child for treatments and a color TV for their viewing pleasure. Again, the advantages are obvious.

Attacks on a child, which can be fatal, are sometimes interpreted as vicarious attacks on the father. Perhaps the father is emotionally distant or physically absent, and the distressed marriage becomes the motivation for the mother to obtain revenge on the father via hurting the child.

SPECIAL VARIATIONS OF MSP

The prototypical picture of MSP is a mother who falsifies or induces serious symptoms in her child, takes the child for medical attention, and fulfills certain of her own needs in the process. We have discovered two cases that are extraordinary exceptions of MSP.

Dr. Mircea Sigal and colleagues in Israel reported a case in which a 34-year-old *man* abused two *adult women,* one of whom died. First, he feared that his wife would leave him. So he put sleeping pills into her coffee and then injected her with gasoline. She lost weight, and unusual abscesses appeared all over her body. She weakened progressively despite her husband's spending endless hours at her bedside, lovingly caring for her. The medical and nursing staff of the hospital greatly admired and respected his devotion. Her death, however, ruined this valuable vehicle for obtaining their high praise for his being an exemplary husband. Three years later this perpetrator had a new girlfriend, whom he subjected to the same "treatment" of gasoline injections in the neck, the breasts, and the backside. The girlfriend survived but became paraplegic. Although he regarded his own actions as loving and not criminal, the police did not agree. He was convicted in court and is presently serving a 46-year sentence in prison. Sigal labeled this variation "Munchausen syndrome by adult proxy."

A case reported by social worker N. J. Smith and psychiatry consultant M. H. Ardern in London extended MSP to the elderly. A 55-year-old former nurse presented her 69-year-old male friend to 25 different medical teams over a 4-year-period. The most prominent symptoms reported for him were rectal bleeding, blood in the urine, and memory loss. Whenever testing proved negative, this woman would routinely come up with a new symptom or suggestion for a different diagnostic procedure for her friend. She had a very extensive medical history of her own, which also contained elements of probable Munchausen syndrome.

Not only has MSP been extended to an old man in this case, but additional details indicate that this former nurse eventually involved her pet dog. She took her dog to a series of veterinarians, citing the problem of his continual mounting of legs, both animate and inanimate. No vet was of much help with this "problem," despite the accumulation of some major bills for service. To our knowledge, this is the first recorded case of MSP with an animal victim.

PSYCHODYNAMIC THEORIES OF MSP

Psychiatrist M. Lesnik-Oberstein of the Free University in Amsterdam reviewed an MSP case in which a mother, a nurse, had repeatedly inflicted vaginal and rectal injuries on her 3-year-old child. From this case and the literature, he theorized, "The Munchausen-by-proxy mother's childhood is characterized by severe emotional deprivation. . . . The child is caused to be hospitalized in order to provide for mother the vicarious satisfaction, by proxy, of her emotional needs which are also more directly met through mother's involvement in the pediatric ward. The painful and dangerous consequences for the child of mother's behavior are dealt with by denial."

When MSP results in a child's death, some psychoanalysts suggest that the family dynamics illustrate the classic *Medea complex*. In the original myth, Medea vented her rage toward her husband, Jason, by killing the children he loved and valued. Such a case of "spouse revenge" and this Medea complex interpretation are described by psychiatrists Shirley Lansky and Harold Erickson, Jr., at the University of Kansas Medical Center. Although in this case the 3½-year-old child did not die, she endured 27 hospital admissions over a period of 20 months. The child was treated for burns of the esophagus, which were probably caused by a common oven cleaner. Overall, she underwent multiple surgeries and numerous tests of blood and urine, electroencephalographic studies (EEGs), and spinal taps. Then, *while in the hospital,* the child was poisoned by a nearly lethal dose of chloral hydrate. (Chloral hydrate was stored in large bottles on an open shelf in an easily accessible location near the child's room.)

Lansky and Erickson believe that the mother poisoned the child in a desperate effort to win back the affection of her husband by eliminating her competition. The father openly degraded his wife by publicly calling her "stupid" and a "fat-assed old broad." In contrast, he stated frequently that he loved his daughter more than any other human being.

BEHAVIORAL THEORIES OF MSP

The behavioral view, in general, seeks to identify the reinforcers for MSP mothers, which serve to create and then to maintain this bizarre and socially disapproved behavior pattern—that of putting an innocent child through unnecessary pain and often at risk for death. In various cases discussed earlier we have seen the extreme value to these mothers of getting attention for themselves via their children's illnesses. If they have saved a child through CPR, they very clearly achieve heroic status in everyone's eyes. They appear to be loving and very attentive to their child's physical needs and are praised by health professionals for their alert and valid reporting (when, in fact, the opposite is true). Another possible reinforcer for such perpetrators' behavior is the joy of defeating doctors and the medical establishment in a bizarre game of diagnostic and therapeutic challenges.

An MSP woman treated with interpretive psychotherapy by Dr. A. R. Nicol in England illustrated these points well. She explained, with insight, "I liked the sympathy, I needed my daughter to be ill so that I was important. I felt I was *somebody* in the ward." Nicol and colleague M. Eccles noted, "She derived much pleasure from the contact with the doctors. 'They were intelligent, I liked to feel that I was being considered by intelligent people.' She also described far less complimentary feelings—she had found the doctors dithering and took considerable pleasure in having outwitted them for so long."

Dr. John Money ties the concept of atonement for sin to the *disease* of MSP, while incorporating a behavioral perspective as well. He suggests that when a forbidden and repugnant behavior is practiced, such as those involved in MSP, there has been a complete reversal of negative into positive values, which is accompanied by corresponding neuro-chemical changes in the brain. Money introduces the controversial concept of *addiction to abuse,* which presumably happens with child victims of MSP. These children, he theorizes, become addicted to the abuse of symptom creation—and even seek it out. (Incidentally, Money relies on the same concepts to understand the Stockholm syndrome, which we discuss in detail in Chapter 5.)

RECOMMENDATIONS AND THERAPY FOR MSP

Pediatrician Basil Zitelli, social worker Miriam Seltman, and nurse Rose Mary Shannon of Children's Hospital in Pittsburgh have provided some useful suggestions for medical teams that suspect or have confirmed cases of MSP. Of course, the first priority is to treat the child in whom symptoms have been created. All unnecessary medical tests should be stopped. Psychological evaluation and psychotherapy for the mother should be ordered. Moreover, the psychological well-being of the child should not be forgotten, because this entire experience can produce genuine emotional trauma in the victim who has been deliberately harmed by someone whom he or she trusted. Two additional specific suggestions by this team may help to prevent the spread of MSP: (1) establish a statewide registry (why not national?) of MSP patients, and (2) include MSP formally as part of hospital discharge diagnoses.

Dr. Roy Meadow, mentioned earlier as one of the first to describe MSP, adds that it is crucial to separate the child victim from the mother to prevent ongoing abuse. If the patient is not carefully monitored, symptoms usually continue even after the child has been hospitalized. Lab specimens must be protected against tampering. A mother's reports of both her own and her child's medical histories must be verified independently. Despite their familiarity with medical terminology and hospital routines, the MSP mothers' descriptions of events simply cannot be trusted.

Drs. Paul Robins and Robin Sesan, psychologists in Wilmington, Delaware, recommend that MSP women be treated in accord with the assumptions and tenets of feminist therapy:

> Included in these principles are (a) recognizing the harmful effects of sexism in society; (b) exploring costs, consequences, and contradictions in prescribed sex roles for women; (c) valuing and supporting women's inner resources and their capacity for nurturance and healing; (d) maintaining a nonsexist frame of reference; (e) demystifying the power relationship in therapy; (f) encouraging women to look elsewhere for help, for example, support groups; and (g) using social change as a source of empowerment for women.

We really do not know accurately just how prevalent MSP is. Although the youngest child victim we know of was just 8 days old, undoubtedly there have been even younger victims. What about the cases of women knowingly taking narcotics or amphetamines when pregnant? Could they constitute cases of MSP or child abuse by legal definitions?

The more medical personnel, law enforcement officers and judges, and informed citizens know about MSP, the better our health and legal systems will be able to identify child victims early and to minimize the harm done to them. The more psychology and psychiatry can learn about MSP perpetrators and how to treat them, the sooner we can begin to *prevent* MSP in high-risk parents.

In considering this syndrome, as well as all the other bizarre disorders discussed in this book, we are guided by the words of Goethe: "We only see what we know."

Suggested Further Readings

Brodeur, A. E., & Monteleone, J. A. (1995). *Child Maltreatment: A Clinical Guide and Reference.* St. Louis: Mosby.

Eggington, J. (1990). *From Cradle to Grave: The Short Lives and Strange Deaths of Marybeth Tinning's Nine Children.* New York: Jove Books.

Kellerman, J. (1993). *Devil's Waltz.* New York: Bantam.

Rosenberg, D. (1987). Web of deceit: A literature review of Munchausen syndrome by proxy. *Child Abuse and Neglect, 11,* 547–563.

Schreier, H. A., & Libow, J. A. (1993). *Hurting for Love: Munchausen by Proxy Syndrome.* New York: Guilford Press.

CHAPTER 3

Frottage
A Touch of Love

Have you ever been riding a crowded subway train and been bumped from behind? Was that bump not exactly a rough jolt, but rather a more sensuous contact, with someone who held that contact with your buttocks, gently swaying with the movement of the train? Perhaps you had just met a frotteur. A *frotteur* seeks out strangers to rub against for his own sexual gratification. Is the act of frottage abnormal? Why would anyone rub and touch people he has never met? In this chapter we discuss this bizarre behavior pattern and whether frotteurs should receive therapy for their unusual interests.

The touch of another human being is actually necessary for life, just as much as food or water or oxygen. Infants who do not receive a basic minimum of tactile stimulation, holding and caressing, fail to thrive. Indeed, they will begin to waste away physically and, if they do survive, inevitably suffer from intellectual deficiencies. Until this need for vital human contact was recognized, newborns and young children who were confined to institutions, such as orphanages and impersonal hospitals, frequently died prematurely following a stunted developmental course.

We adults appreciate the touch of another human as a sign of caring, as an expression of a variety of positive emotions, and as a critical part of sex play and lovemaking. We have learned the desirability of touching in human relationships. We have felt the pleasure of touching and being touched. Even petting our dogs is now known to be therapeutic in terms of forming bonds of companionship and even as a vehicle for lowering our blood pressure without drugs.

Yet the experience of touch can be distorted. A number of authorities and laypersons would even use the term "perverted." Some people, mostly men, will touch others, mostly women, without their permission and, sometimes, even without their awareness. Why? For those people (technically called "frotteurs") that anonymous touching is a means of sexual stimulation and a bizarre expression of love. The true purpose of the act is secretive (because it can appear accidental); it is exciting (because of the ever-present possibility of getting caught); and it is socially deviant (because it is an indirect and uninvited way of making contact with an adult woman).

Of course, the female may not always be an adult. Novelist Vladimir Nabokov provided an erotic literary description of frottage, without naming it as such, in his account of one of Humbert Humbert's contacts with the 12-year-old Lolita:

> The impudent child extended her legs across my lap. By this time I was in a state of excitement bordering on insanity; but I also had the cunning of the insane. Sitting there on the sofa, I managed to attune, by a series of stealthy movements, my masked lust to her guileless limbs. It was no easy matter to divert the little maiden's attention while I performed the obscure adjustments necessary for the success of the trick.
>
> Talking fast, lagging behind my own breath, catching up with it, mimicking a sudden toothache to explain the breaks in my patter— and all the while keeping a maniac's inner eye on my distant golden goal, I cautiously increased the magic friction that was doing away, in an illusional, if not factual, sense, with the physically irremovable, but psychologically very friable texture of the material divide (pajamas and robe) between the weight of two sunburnt legs, resting athwart my lap, and the hidden tumor of an unspeakable passion. . . .
>
> Her legs twitched a little as they lay across my live lap; I stroked them; . . . and every movement she made, every shuffle and ripple, helped me to conceal and to improve the secret system of tactile correspondence between beast and beauty—between my gagged,

bursting beast and the beauty of her dimpled body in its innocent cotton frock. . . . Her young weight, her shameless innocent shanks and round bottom, shifted in my tense, tortured, surreptitiously laboring lap; and all of a sudden a mysterious change came over my senses. I entered a plane of being where nothing mattered, save the infusion of joy brewed within my body. What had begun as a delicious distension of my innermost roots became a glowing tingle which *now* had reached that state of absolute security, confidence and reliance not found elsewhere in conscious life. With the deep hot sweetness thus established and well on its way to the ultimate convulsion, I felt I could slow down in order to prolong the glow. . . .

Everything was now ready. The nerves of pleasure had been laid bare. The corpuscles of Krauze were entering the phase of frenzy. The least pressure would suffice to set all paradise loose. . . . I was a radiant and robust Turk, deliberately, in the full consciousness of his freedom, postponing the moment of actually enjoying the youngest and frailest of his slaves.

Humbert Humbert was indeed a frotteur. Of course, he may also have qualified as a pedophile. At the very least, he sensitized us to the joys of the touches of love. For that we remain grateful.

Society has rules about touching. No one posts these rules, but we must learn them nevertheless. Who can touch whom? Where? When? When is the touching *sexual* and when is it not, even when the same body parts are touched? How do we give permission to be touched? Is it ever OK to touch without permission?

All of these issues mark tactile stimulation as a very touchy subject. Complicating it all are the cultural variations in acceptable forms of touching. For example, the friendly native Italian who reaches out and pinches the butt of the unsuspecting female American tourist may be engaging in a very socially acceptable form of personal introduction in Rome. If that Roman, while visiting America, tries the same behavior, he may well find himself under arrest for assault and battery, at worst, or verbally chastised at best.

Different countries and subcultures have their own rules and standards for greeting by kissing and same-sex hugging and hand-holding. Americans abroad often experience discomfort during the social rituals of arrival and departure and when encountering men who flirt by touching.

Unwelcome touching can be a crime or even a type of mental illness. Psychiatrists and psychologists have identified a bizarre disorder of inappropriate touching and rubbing, which they refer to as a type of paraphilia. A *paraphilia* is technically defined as a sexual behavior pattern which runs counter to a culture's social norms and which is antibiological, that is, a sexual behavior that is something other than male-female vaginal intercourse. This definition provides one of the few examples in which psychiatry is in harmony with the position of the Roman Catholic Church.

The *Diagnostic and Statistical Manual of Mental Disorders* (DSM) is the bible of psychiatry. The current edition lists eight paraphilias plus a final category to include any paraphilias not otherwise specified. These behavior patterns become disorders, because the accompanying sexual urges and fantasies are both intense and required for sexual satisfaction. An official diagnosis is to be made only if the person has acted on such urges or is "markedly distressed" by them. The urges must be of at least six months' duration. When other humans are involved, they are either children or nonconsenting adults. Otherwise, most of the behaviors involved might be accepted as legitimate forms of expression by sexually liberated individuals, a notion we discuss later.

There is a distinct sex difference among the paraphilias. The DSM estimates that for Sexual Masochism the sex ratio is 20 males to one female. For all other paraphilias, females are "practically never diagnosed." This imbalance in the relative frequency of diagnosis, however, may be due more to social and cultural considerations than to actual prevalences within the population. As a result, men with paraphilias definitely get into more trouble. Women with paraphilias may be less numerous than men, but they do exist; they just are not reported or caught as often.

The diagnosis of paraphilia as a sexual disorder creates a very interesting, blurred boundary between what is normal sexual responsiveness and what is a bizarre deviation. Much of the older writings by mental health specialists and theologians refer to these interests with the loaded term "perversions." Yet even the DSM allows for sexual arousal in "normal" heterosexual men by objects that could be considered fetishistic, such as bras and panties, and by looking at a female undressing.

Does it matter whether a person only fantasizes about these unusual interests? Must he actually act them out to be abnormal? What if these interests appear only occasionally in his sexual life? What if his partner is fully consenting?

How should we regard a man who chooses a career in which he necessarily will be able to carry out his paraphilic interests as "just part of the job"? Some possible examples might be, although not necessarily so, of course, the women's shoe salesman, the doctor who must perform breast or vaginal examinations, and the erotic magazine photographer. When one's job choice has such multiple determinants, would there still be a diagnosable disorder?

Frotteurism or *frottage* occurs when a person derives sexual satisfaction from rubbing against unsuspecting strangers in public places. Common crowded settings include subways, elevators, happy hours in bars, and anywhere else many people congregate in large numbers. The physical contact is designed to appear accidental, and that may indeed be a reasonable conclusion, given the crowded conditions and possible jarring caused by a moving train, for example. The individuals being touched may or may not acknowledge the contact. Some men, also known as "frictionists," frequently report reaching orgasm while rubbing against an unknown woman's legs or buttocks. Both people remain fully clothed. One variation of frottage is *toucheurism,* in which the individual actually reaches out and touches someone with his hand, a degree of fondling probably not intended by the phone company's persuasive advertising.

In toucheurism, when one squeezes a stranger's breast or feels another's genitals, the behavior is more obvious and could be considered a form of physical assault and, therefore, a prosecutable criminal act. However, with the other paraphilias, excepting sexual contact with children, a genuine issue arises as to whether these behavior patterns should ever be formally diagnosed and treated. If one has a consenting adult partner who accommodates or tolerates these preferences as in sexual masochism, why should mental health professionals intervene to label the individual, to prescribe potent drugs, to require intensive psychotherapeutic self-examination, to hospitalize, to deliver aversive stimuli such as electric shock, or otherwise try to remedy this behavior?

The available statistics on the prevalences of these paraphilic behavior patterns unquestionably underestimate how frequent they are in our society. In addition, who can monitor the fantasy lives of citizens who may, in their overt behavior, be conforming to legal and mentally healthy ideals? Sexologist Paul Gebhard suggests that "the impulse to pinch a well-rounded buttock . . . involve[s] millions of U.S. males." If so, a mental health professional could diagnose them with DSM disorder Code No. 302.89, *Frotteurism.*

Oregon psychologists Terrel Templeman and Ray Stinnett sampled sexual histories and arousal patterns in 60 normal men, with an average age of 21.5 years, attending a small college in eastern Oregon. Their sexual behavior data were gathered via questionnaires and individual face-to-face interviews. Even in this nonanonymous setting, 21 of the men (35%) admitted to having tried touching and rubbing up against women in crowds for sexual purposes. As many as 65% had engaged in some form of sexual misconduct, which also included voyeurism, obscene telephone calling, exhibitionism, contact with underage girls, and coercive sex.

Frotteurism can be a form of erotic distancing, even though, by definition, there is body contact. Of course, it is clothed contact, and the two individuals may never speak or meet again. The arousal and even occasional orgasm for the frotteur are achieved anonymously and with no need for further commitment.

As an enlightened society we should prepare to debate and consider the wisdom of retaining all of our sex laws as they now stand. It has been just a few years since homosexuality was included in the DSM as one of the paraphilias. Oral sex, anal sex, and even interfemoral (between the legs) and intermammary (between the breasts) intercourse not long ago were regarded as "paraphilic expedients" by leading psychoanalytic theorists. For example, Dr. Benjamin Karpman pointed out that these activities do not have a "biological aim." Although orgasm would indeed seem to be a biological aim, as well as a tension-releasing event, Dr. Karpman's concern was that none of those frequently practiced pleasures could lead to procreation. Now, in the age of AIDS, perhaps we should be vigorously publicizing our recommendations of interfemoral and intermammary intercourse as safe sex alternatives.

Some of the paraphilias described in the DSM do not involve intimate sexual contact. Therefore, those behavior patterns and preferences are called *parasexual* activities. Examples include voyeurism, exhibitionism, and frottage. Looking at the genitals of another or having your own looked at could be sexually arousing, but there is no direct sexual contact involved. Frottage, even toucheurism, in which the other person's body is touched, squeezed, or fondled, is still considered a parasexual behavior.

Of course, reaching out and touching someone who has not consented to that contact and who may not even know the toucher is clearly an aggressive act, if not one that is intimately sexual. The question arises as to whether the toucher is dangerous and liable to commit a further assault or even to attempt rape. Although there are cases in which such attacks do follow frottage, they are very rare. Much more commonly, the man scurries away as rapidly as he can, fearing possible arrest and probably fearing a direct confrontation with the woman. If she were to approach him sexually, he most likely would retreat instantly.

Personality studies of frotteurs typically find that these men have long-standing difficulties in their relationships with women. They have active fantasy lives and indulge those fantasies during masturbation. However, they do not seem to be able to initiate or carry on mature interpersonal or sexual relationships with women.

The frottage behavior is usually quite intermittent and not a dominating force in the man's life. Yet, when motivated by distressing feelings of loneliness, anxiety, depression, or irritability, he may act out via frottage. The touching behavior can then assume a compulsive quality. He becomes preoccupied and *must* do it. The compulsion then leads to risk taking. The pressure to touch and rub strangers for sexual gratification increases and puts him at greater and greater risk of being detected and identified. Loss of self-control is frequently helped by the use of alcohol. Any social drinker can confirm that alcohol in moderate quantities functions as a social lubricant. Alcohol can help lower behavioral inhibitions of the frotteur, who may then aggressively seek out targets to touch.

RESEARCH STUDIES WITH FROTTEURS

Dr. Ron Langevin and his colleagues at the Clarke Institute of Psychiatry in Toronto have conducted extensive research on the interests and behaviors of a variety of paraphilic patients. Very little formal research has ever been conducted with frotteurs, which makes the Clarke group's work all the more valuable.

Dr. Langevin points out: "Too often sexual anomalies have been viewed as distortions of conventional heterosexuality rather than as behaviors in their own right." He suggests that most people engage in a variety of sexual behaviors for a variety of reasons, such as curiosity, availability or deprivation, and tradition. He believes it is critical to examine a person's *erotic preferences,* that is, the most desired stimuli and responses that lead to sexual arousal and climax.

His group of heterosexual transvestites were significantly more likely to peep, to expose themselves, to molest females with their hands, and to rub against them in crowds, than were the comparison group of homosexual transsexuals. Actually, the differences in sexual orientation itself can probably account for the interest of the transvestites in touching and rubbing women. Dr. Langevin was surprised at the degree of toucheurism and frottage among the transvestites, because he presumed that they were "more feminine gender identified." We are not particularly surprised that a group of heterosexual men, even though they cross-dress at times, will engage in heterosexual behaviors.

The frotteur is not likely to submit himself to a therapist voluntarily. He is more likely to come to the attention of the legal system eventually, which might "encourage" him to seek professional help.

Therapy is unlikely to be successful when the patient is coerced into treatment, whether by a spouse, a parent, or a judge. Often it is a judge who imposes that requirement on a frotteur who has been arrested. Since the victim is not physically harmed, the legal charge is usually some form of "indecent assault."

CASE REPORTS

Dr. Benjamin Karpman reported a case originally described by the well-known sexologist Krafft-Ebing:

> For some time he had attracted attention in churches, because he crowded up behind women, both old and young indifferently, and toyed with their 'bustles.' He was watched, and one day he was

arrested in the act. . . . For two years he had been subject to the unhappy impulse to go in crowds of people—in churches, at box-offices of theatres, etc.—and press up behind females and manipulate the prominent portion of their dresses, thus producing orgasm and ejaculation.

Psychiatrist Wayne Myers associates the paraphilia of frottage with the atypical paraphilia of telephone scatalogia (making obscene calls for sexual gratification). Although at first glance they may not seem related, both of these unusual behavior patterns are "parasexual" in that they do not involve genital intercourse. Myers described a case of a man (Mr. A) who practiced these two separate "perverse" acts (an interesting adjective for Myers to use in the 1990s). The following excerpt from the case history of Mr. A is perhaps the most complete description of frottage available in the clinical literature.

In discussing his wife, he frequently complained about her housekeeping and about her own heavy dependence on alcohol. The aura that pervaded his discussions of all these people was one of disappointment and a touch of bitterness, as if they had all hurt him in some rather profound way and his aloofness was a way of getting even with them. . . .

He disclosed his tendency to make late-night obscene phone calls to women when his wife was away or was too intoxicated to interact with him. In these calls he usually pretended to be taking a survey of female attitudes on a variety of subjects. If the women answered his initial questions and remained on the phone, he quickly steered the inquiries to matters concerning their sexual practices and desires. The longer he could keep a woman on the phone in such a call, the more aroused he would become. As he at the same time masturbated to orgasm, he would verbalize aloud his desire to "eat" the woman until he had "sucked her dry" or to "fuck" her into "oblivion."

Thus the wish to "suck dry" the women he was calling could be seen as expressing his desire to obtain the nourishment from the mother that he originally felt deprived of after the birth of his younger brother. . . . The call constituted an undoing of the trauma involved in the birth of the younger sibling and the concomitant expulsion from the parental bedroom. . . .

Mr. A began to express curiosity as to what I might be doing with my female patients during sessions. When questioned about this, his associations quickly turned to speculations about his wife's interactions with her previous lovers and then to thoughts about his parents' sexual activities in the bedroom during the years he had shared the room with them.

This mechanism of turning passive into active, an identification with the aggressor, was also a major part of the other perverse sexual practice he revealed to me at this time, the act of frotteurism. In this ritual, he would ride the subway home from work during the evening rush hour. If he spotted a woman alone standing with her back to him, he would inch his way along the crowded car until he was stationed right behind her. Then he would let the crush of the people on the subway car carry him and his erect penis against her buttocks. He would not move at first, in order to allay any fear or anger the woman might feel at the presence of his penis against her buttocks. Then, when he felt more secure in her lack of verbal response, he would press closer to her and begin to move his penis against her gluteal region until he had an orgasm.

Occasionally a woman would scream out or would attempt to hit him, and he would pretend that she was imagining the assault on her. This tactic inevitably worked in the crowded subway cars, as most of the passengers were essentially disinterested in the machinations of their fellow travelers.

Dr. Ron Langevin described a case of a 19-year-old frotteur from the point of view of the victim. The young man was a "loner" (a common media description of someone whom psychologists would portray as having poor social skills). He progressed from the passivity of the frotteur to the greater risk taking of toucheurism. His victim's account is as follows:

I was just sitting on the train with my girlfriend talking when this guy (the accused) came on the train and sat down beside us. We ignored him but he started to talk about sex. I told him to shut up but he kept on talking. He reached over and touched my breast. I hit him in the face with my fist and he just sat there then. We got off the train at the next stop and he followed us. He came up beside me and touched my breast again. I grabbed him by the hair and

kicked him and took him to the ticket taker at the station who called
the police.

This man's increasing boldness, aggression, and poor judgment
landed him in jail. He also definitely chose the wrong woman to touch,
given her own appropriately aggressive responses to events both on and
off the train. This case illustrates the progressive and compulsive qualities of his frotteurism and toucheurism, so pronounced that the man
was charged with a crime.

Dr. Langevin summarized another case of a toucheur who imperson-
ated a physician, a role that permitted him to fondle the bare breasts of
female patients. This schizophrenic man had married eight times (not
necessarily a diagnostic sign of schizophrenia), but he never had con-
summated any of the marriages. He could achieve orgasm only by fondling, kissing, and sucking female breasts.

THEORIES OF FROTTAGE

Dr. Kurt Freund and his colleagues at the Clarke Institute have proposed a model of "courtship disorders." In the normal sequence of
courtship behaviors (translation for younger readers: "How to Find a
Sexual Partner"), the individual begins by searching for a prospective
partner, and once she is found, interacts with the person without touching; at the next stage, direct and obvious touching occurs during fore-
play, leading to the final stage of sexual intercourse. Novelty is one of
the attractions, and so the disorders of courtship hardly ever involve
someone with whom the man is already acquainted.

It remains theoretically controversial whether there is any meaningful
correlation with frottage or other courtship disorders such as voyeurism
or rape. Thus far, the evidence seems to be that in some cases frotteurism
may lead to toucheurism, which in turn may lead to attempts at rape,
but that in other cases this progression does not occur. Some men show
all of the disorders; some show just one or two. Dr. Langevin stresses
that it is rare that frottage and toucheurism ever occur as a "fixed erotic
preference" in their own right.

Toucheurism particularly is a form of sexually aggressive behavior and results from poor impulse control. Failure to control socially inappropriate urges to touch has occasionally occurred in psychotic and mentally retarded persons. More commonly, these urges arise in otherwise normal men who are under the influence of alcohol, drugs, or a sex drive so strong that any of many human or animal targets would satisfy them. Freud called these latter individuals "polymorphous perverse." TV talk show experts now call them "sex addicts."

One 26-year-old mentally retarded man had normal sexual desires but little awareness of social norms and even less restraint over his impulses. While at the shopping mall, he would see an attractive woman, smile, and say "hello" to her. If she smiled and said "hello" back, he considered her to be his girlfriend and promptly grabbed her breasts. Most of us learn that, regardless of temptation, this kind of interaction must be delayed.

In frottage, Drs. Freund, Langevin, and others believe that there is an abnormally rapid buildup of arousal in the early stages of courtship—partner appraisal and pretouching. Touching women in the breast and genital areas and making crude sexual invitations before one has been formally introduced is too much, too soon, by all contemporary social standards. The only exception would be in the business of prostitution, and even then the implicit rules require that you pay before you play.

Dr. Magnus Hirschfeld, an sexologist infamous because of his own transvestism and bisexuality, in addition to his genuine expertise, relied on a distortion of the sense of touch in his explanation of frottage. He believed that frotteurs possess a "pathological oversensitiveness" (hyperesthesia) in their genitals. Any ever-so-slight contact by rubbing would bring about a "pollution," Hirschfeld's colorful term for ejaculation. Since the slightest friction could readily occur in the natural jostling within crowded public places, these sexually anomalous, physically sensitive men were called "frictionists." This view suggests that the acts of frottage are certainly not intentional. Just as "pollutions" can occur during "wet dreams" or result from a full bladder, so may they be caused by the impaired and "irritable" nervous system of a frotteur. Hirschfeld also notes that the next day these men tend to feel fatigue or depression and display "an impaired working capacity." It seems unfortunate that the frotteurs do not have a chance to fall asleep immediately after the act so that they could function well the next day.

Dr. John Money theorizes that frotteurism results from a distortion that occurred in the man's "developmental lovemap." The lovemap arises from the experiences of sexual rehearsal play in childhood. Abuses can happen because of too much punishment, prohibition, and prevention. Prudish parents might be horrified by children's sex play or masturbation and become punitive, thereby affecting the developing child's lovemap. Consequently, our lovemaps can become defaced, distorted, or redesigned with detours. "A lovemap carries the program of a person's erotic fantasies and their corresponding practices. Distortions, therefore, get carried over into fantasies and practices." The experiences encountered by the individual early in life, in reality or in fantasy, determine the specific type of paraphilia that such a person will exhibit at puberty or in adulthood.

Despite his belief in the role of faulty learning in the paraphilic's developmental lovemap, Money suggests that the best treatment would be a combination of counseling and medication. Specifically, he recommends an antiandrogen hormone (medroxyprogesterone acetate, known by the trade name of Depo-Provera). This drug is intended to "diminish the subjective experience of sex drive and, in addition, may have a direct erotically tranquilizing action on erotosexual pathways in the brain. Its effects are reversible."

THERAPIES FOR FROTTAGE

Since so few case reports of frotteurs have appeared in the literature, there are also scanty accounts of therapeutic efforts devoted to this problem. As mentioned, Money suggested a combination of counseling and Depo-Provera. Dr. Roger Perilstein of the Duke University Medical Center and his colleagues Steven Lipper and Leonard Friedman reported an "apparently successful treatment" of a case of voyeurism-frotteurism with the controversial drug Prozac. Their patient complained that his urges to take photographs of "pretty young women" and to rub against women were causing him marital conflict. After 7 to 10 days of drug therapy, his interest in these activities diminished markedly, even during masturbation. His doctors attributed this improvement to the drug, which somehow affected the neurons that govern sexual activity, especially compulsive activity. Sexual activity with his wife was unaffected by the treatment.

Psychiatrist Wayne Myers accounted for his case of Mr. A (discussed earlier) from the perspective of classic psychodynamic theory:

> Mr. A noted that not only the women he rubbed up against, but the other passengers as well, were all passive participants in the scenarios he was enacting or imposing upon them. The sexual acts with the women had a "dreamlike" quality, which once more recalled the primal-scene experiences of his childhood. The female victims of his sexual aggression were seen as being especially passive and helpless, as he had felt himself in the early bedroom scenes.
>
> In addition, when he came to recognize the hostility inherent in his acts of frottage, he realized that the trance or dreamlike nature of these episodes also served to protect the women from the consequences of his rage. Even though he could "kill people or have sex with them in dreams, no one really gets hurt. After all, they're only dreams." The layers of clothing interspersed between the patient and his victim also served to protect the woman from the instrument of his rage, the "dangerous" phallus.

From the perspective of behavior therapy, very scant attention has been given to the problem of frottage. California psychiatrist Michael Serber developed an innovative, behavior-oriented treatment for long-standing paraphilic behaviors called "shame aversion therapy." If the patient is not psychotic and is able to experience shame when engaging in the problem behavior, Serber suggested that his new therapy could be applied.

The treatment consists of having the paraphiliac engage in the inappropriate behavior under the controlled conditions of the therapy consulting room, with volunteers playing the "victims." Three observers watch the enforced display soberly and without comment. Most patients experience extreme discomfort and anxiety during this therapy. Dr. Serber reported excellent success with transvesites, pedophiliacs, and exhibitionists. Unfortunately, the 33-year-old frotteur treated in his case study obtained no change in his two sessions of shame aversion therapy.

As appealing as this type of therapy may sound, it appears to be ineffective for frottage.

CROSS-CULTURAL FROTTAGE

A report on sex life in Brazil, by participant-observer Eugene Ressencourt, appeared more than four decades ago. Perhaps, since then, the standards and mores of that country have changed.

As compared with contemporary American guidelines, Brazil has traditionally followed very conservative, religiously based guidelines for dating and social contacts between young men and women. The public image of Brazil's sexual mores is contradictory, given the inhibitory influence of the church within the context of ritualized free expressionism each year during the Carnival festival.

Young Brazilian women in the 1950s did not date, in the sense of going out alone with a man after dark, or even dance cheek-to-cheek. Of course, premarital sexual contacts were out of the question. Yet the society permitted a curious substitute—"bowlining" (*bolinagem*), from the verb *bolinar* meaning "to rub up against a person."

Ressencourt described this custom in Brazilian dating, which we would understand simply as "socially acceptable frottage" (a term that most American psychiatrists would consider to be an oxymoron). He even admits, "from meticulous firsthand observation," that some girls and women achieve orgasm on the dance floor through *bolinagem.* He suspects that some Brazilian males may also seek orgasm in this way. Since dances for young people are closely chaperoned, it takes a special skill to hide these exciting rubbing movements during the dancing.

> *Bolinagem,* in Brazilian social lore, is a surreptitious manner of caressing engaged in by and between men and women under a great variety of possible circumstances: on crowded buses and street cars and elevators, at public gatherings, in fact, wherever convenient. This surreptitious rubbing is done in such a clever way as to appear accidental; no words are spoken, no change of facial expression takes place, and no outward familiarity is evidenced in any manner. It is a game that is usually played by two, but either person may be

active or passive as wish and opportunity afford. Many girls and women play this game with strange men, for there seems no harm in it whatever.

There are many possible variations in the game; rubbing elbows, arms, shoulders, limbs, feet, buttocks, etc.—the most popular being when a man presses himself close against a woman's buttocks from directly behind, especially on a moving bus. If in any way repulsed or called to account, a man can always say, with a look of hurt surprise, "Why, I beg your pardon, madam, for pushing. The bus is *so* crowded!"

A favorite spot for one particular use of this game is the cinema matinee. Many teen-age girls are permitted by their elders to attend the neighborhood movies in the afternoon if there are two or more to go together in force. Well, teen-age boys make a practice of looking for attractive girls to sit next to at these matinees; and they play this game of *bolinagem* by rubbing elbows and legs—with the hope that it may go much further than that. Sometimes furtive friendships are formed in this way, and a girl and a boy will make a kind of "date" to meet again another day at a certain section of the audience; and in time, intimacies may develop to the point at which the pair masturbate each other with a cloak draped across their laps and a ready handkerchief for the boy. It is not too difficult for some teen-agers to have "dates" in this fashion; the girl usually gets the boy's phone number and manages to sneak calls to him when her family is out of earshot.

But the game of *bolinagem* is really most exhilarating on the dance floor, particularly when applied to Brazil's own national ballroom dance—the *samba*—which always takes precedent over the imported waltz, tango, fox trot, rumba, etc. The *samba* is an African dance pattern adapted for ballroom use to the off-beat rhythm, fast or slow, or what in Brazil is called *samba* music—which has there developed into a kind of blue, satirical folk-type song orchestrated for syncopation with modern jazz instruments plus a symphony of African-style tom-toms. . . . This unique and original dance is a hip-to-shoulder-jerk action with relatively little foot movement, and it is particularly adaptable to mutual abdominal and pubic massage when opportunity is afforded to apply the principles of *bolinagem*.

And we think our *lambada* is sexy and wild!

We don't recommend touching unconsenting others for your own sexual gratification. It is unfair and usually illegal. Further, it is socially inappropriate and intrusive. We do believe, however, that it is bizarre to consider frottage to be a mental disorder. Touching and the good feelings that follow are critical learning events for the developing healthy child. Let us always remember that rubbing and touching can be sexually exciting for everyone—males and females, homosexuals and heterosexuals.

Suggested Further Readings

Fogel, G. I., & Myers, W. A. (Eds.) (1991). *Perversions and Near-Perversions in Clinical Practice.* New Haven: Yale University Press.

Langevin, R. (1983). *Sexual Strands.* Hillsdale, NJ: Lawrence Erlbaum Associates.

Langevin, R. (Ed.) (1985). *Erotic Preference, Gender Identity, and Aggression in Men.* Hillsdale, NJ: Lawrence Erlbaum Associates.

Money, J. (1986). *Venuses Penuses.* Buffalo: Prometheus Books.

Wilson, G. (Ed.) (1986). *Variant Sexuality; New Theories and Research.* London: Croom-Helm, Ltd.

CHAPTER 4

Vampirism
The Ungrateful Dead

In spite of space travel, fax machines, and personal computers, our modern fascination with the bizarre and the occult shows no sign of decreasing. It may be that those of us in industrialized societies have grown increasingly dissatisfied with the cold facts of science that have given us a sterile, demystified technocracy. However, the supernatural that we are urged to ignore contains powerful positive virtues, which most certainly contribute to its appeal.

Consider the case of two powerful icons, the vampire and the werewolf. The attractions of these symbols turn out to be many and varied. For example, in the case of the vampire we have the irresistible appeal of ageless, eternal youth, immortality, enormous sexual magnetism, unlimited exercise of power over others through terror, and freedom to indulge forbidden impulses. Of course, there has to be a down side. Vampiring *is* night work, the basic black wardrobe can get monotonous, the liquid diet must become boring, sleeping arrangements are untidy, and less fortunate people are frequently hostile and vengeful. The occupational hazards of werewolfery must certainly include the possibility of flea and tick miseries, rabies, mange, and, inevitably, the serious nutritional consequences of an exclusive raw meat diet.

In addition to the escapism and power fantasies so evident in vampire and werewolf mythology, the vampire myth addresses the virtually universal human ignorance and fear of death by holding out the hope of some sort of life thereafter in the hereafter. Psychoanalysts tell us that another sort of denial may also be operating here, the unwillingness to acknowledge the ravening beast that skulks not far below the surface in each of us. Thus, when we are confronted with a dismembered and half-eaten child's body, we are compelled to attribute it to something non-human, surely a monstrous beast, since such gruesome behavior is far removed from any semblance of human comportment.

The vampire image we have presented thus far is the product of romantic fiction, glamorized by eighteenth- and nineteenth-century Gothic novelists and twentieth-century filmmakers and soap operas. The word *vampire,* or *vampyre,* comes from the Magyar *vampir,* a word of Slavonic origin. The modern-day version of the vampire is peculiar to the Slavonic peoples of the Balkans and Eastern Europe. The first written use of the word in English occurs in *The Travels of Three English Gentlemen,* ca. 1734. While they were staying at a German castle, one of the three diarists noted that their host, Baron Valvasor, was worried about some frightening local creature called a "vampyre." According to the diarist: "These vampyres are supposed to be the Bodies of deceased Persons, animated by evil Spirits, which come out of the Graves, in the Night-time, suck the Blood of many of the Living, and thereby destroy them."

Today the romantic vampire image is enjoying unprecedented and spectacular popularity. When Martin Riccardo published his exhaustive 1983 English language bibliography, *Vampires Unearthed,* there were 33 anthologies, more than 300 novels and short stories, 200 movies, 43 newsletters and journals, poetry, cook books, joke books (*Die Laughing*), songs and recordings, ("Dracula's Greatest Hits"), even children's literature on the subject. For example, the "Bunnicula" rabbit vampire books have sold over 3 million copies, and take-offs on familiar classics such as *The Hardy Boys and Nancy Drew Meet Dracula* and *A Child's Garden of Vampires* are also successful. Today, an astonishing number of Americans belong to nearly 20 vampire-inspired organizations in the United States. The Count Dracula Fan Club in New York claims more than 2,500 members who pay annual dues of $50 each, entitling them to a monthly newsletter. Los Angeles has its own counterpart, the Count Dracula Society. The Camarilla is an international vampire fan association with more than 2,000 members. Then there are the Vampire Pen

Pal Network and the Vampire Information Exchange, as well as the genre fanzines *Dead of Night* and *The Vampire Journal.* In 1991 a set of lobby cards from Bela Lugosi's *Dracula* movie sold for $55,000 at a Christie's auction. In 1992 alone, there were six new vampire films. Anne Rice's latest Vampire Lestat novel is always assured of a long stay on the *New York Times* best-selling fiction list. The movie version of her Vampire Lestat character, played by Tom Cruise, opened to rave reviews in Fall 1994, and a sequel is planned. However, on the dark side, there are rumors of ugly vampire-bashing incidents in large cities. As a result, some self-identified vampires are going to great lengths to stay in the closet, concealing their origins by referring to themselves as "Carpathians" rather than disclose their Transylvanian birthplace.

The cinematic vampire image portrayed by Bela Lugosi and his successors is usually that of a tall, pale, classy, somewhat threadbare aristocrat, graceful, courtly but sexy, with a slight middle-European accent. He often has an air of resignation about him, a certain world-weariness that sometimes evokes pity along with a sexual thrill and fear. He has seen and done it all. He is partial to black capes, could use some good dental work on his rather obtrusive canines, and often confounds enemies by changing into a bat and flying off. A similar description is provided by Dr. Stephen Kaplan, director of the Vampire Research Center in Elmhurst, New York, an organization that issues deadly serious annual reports about everything vampirical. According to Dr. Katherine Ramsland, writing in the Nov. 1989 *Psychology Today,* Kaplan attributes our fascination with vampires to a combination of their perceived immortality, sexuality, dominance, and charisma. Every year Dr. Kaplan sends a 99-item questionnaire to everyone who had contacted the Center claiming to be a vampire or to know one personally. On the basis of his questionnaire he recently concluded that worldwide there are more than 725 real vampires, and more than 500 real and possible vampires and vampire claimants in the United States. Somehow we are not surprised to learn that California leads the nation with 33 vampires, while New York trails with a mere 30. The results of one recent census yielded the following vampire description:

He—Looks to be 26 years old, has dark brown eyes and black hair, is 5′10″ tall, and weighs in at a trim 170 lbs.

She—Looks to be 23 years old, also has brown eyes and black hair, and has a well-distributed 120 lbs. on her 5′6″ body.

Not at all distinctive, this person could be the boy or girl next door. The vampires described by ancient folklore and legend were much less glamorous and tidy. Their ranks were filled with homeless strangers who lurked around tombs and village graveyards seeking shelter from the elements. Other vampire candidates were locals who had died suddenly under suspicious circumstances, such as being struck by lightning. However, folkloric vampires were never described as batlike, nor did their unique dentition attract attention. Not all folk legend vampires killed their victims by sucking out the victims' blood. Those that did, however, generally went right for the heart rather than rely on the stereotypical nibble on the neck. Instead of being depicted as tall, thin, and aristocratic, their unearthed corpses were consistently described by locals as swollen, of ruddy and florid complexion, with stubby arms and legs. The body showed no signs of rigor mortis, no decomposition whatsoever, and was "full to bursting of fresh blood."

Dr. Paul Barber, the foremost anthropological vampire scholar, in his authoritative book, *Vampires, Burial, and Death,* presents convincing evidence that similarities in the vampire's appearance and behavior across so many different cultures is due to the simple fact that this is the characteristic appearance of a dead and decaying body following the natural process of decomposition. Frightening phenomena, such as the body groaning and writhing, the fresh blood around the corpse's lips and mouth, and the profuse expulsion of gobs of blood when the trunk is punctured with a stake, are attributable to the same cause. Dr. Barber believes that what vampire legends attributed to supernatural agency is typical of a dead human body after a month or so in a shallow grave, often wrapped only in a shroud. The natural decay process would have been retarded by burial, especially in the cold of winter. Nevertheless, the accumulation of internal gases forces blood to the periphery, causing the corpse's characteristically ruddy complexion, as well as the gross distension of the abdominal organs and blood vessels. Often there are frightful gurgling sounds, which the superstitious peasant naturally interpreted as vampiric growls. When the internal organs burst, there is an eruption of blood from the nose and mouth. The swelling of the face has exposed and exaggerated the size of the teeth, and the lips often split and bleed. The outer layers of skin have peeled away, revealing fresh pink skin beneath. In similar fashion, the fingernails and toenails have also fallen off, exposing the underlying nail bed. When the chest cavity is violently punctured by staking, gobs of blood erupt, often accompanied by blood-curdling groaning sounds and flailing movements of the body produced mechanically by the deflation process. Not a pretty picture!

Many detailed aspects of the legendary vampire's appearance and habits reflected local customs. For example, vampires generally did not travel well but were doomed to sneak around the cemeteries where they had been buried and unburied. The exception was the Gypsy vampire who traveled far and wide as befitted his ethnic heritage. European vampires are almost always male. The closest female counterpart is the succubus, an evil female spirit. She visited sleeping men and used her insatiable sexual appetite either to suck the soul out of her victim directly or to cause such debility that he perished, wasting away from fatigue or disease. We really seem to have lost something today with our reliance on technical medical explanations such as chronic fatigue syndrome.

Can we unearth a basis in reality for the legends? For ancient peoples the vampire legends helped to explain the death of innocent infants and seemingly healthy persons, as well as bestial acts of monstrous "inhuman" violence such as cannibalism. The doers of such terrible deeds no longer seemed human. If nonhuman, then he or she must be a wild animal, or a hellish demon, or a wild animal inhabited by an evil spirit. In later centuries the Christian belief in Satan supported the superstition that the sinister vampire, the undead, was the personification of evil. It was called a "revenant," meaning one who returns, neither alive nor dead, a creature who had flunked the entrance exam for heaven and so was doomed to work its evil will on the rest of us.

THE MAKING OF A VAMPIRE

Some vampires are born, some are made. In olden days it was pretty easy to join the ranks of the undead. The anthropologist J. DuBulay in his study of death symbolism in the Greek vampire, listed the nine most common circumstances that medieval people believed could result in vampirism, represented by the following:

1. People who met with sudden or violent death, such as suicide, or those who were struck by lightning or killed in a vendetta but still unavenged.
2. Stillborn infants.
3. Those who did not receive the full and due rites of burial.
4. Those who died after having been excommunicated from the church.
5. Perjurers who took God's name in vain or who died under a curse.
6. Those who died unbaptized or apostate.
7. Those who led a life of evil, and those who dealt in black magic.
8. Those who had eaten the meat of a sheep that had been killed by a wolf. (Given the yen for mutton in the Middle Ages and the sizeable wolf population, this last category must have included a pretty large group.)
9. Those over whose dead bodies a cat or other animal had passed. This is a wild card. During a funeral, evidently, an errant stray dog could nullify a lifetime of piety and goodness.

Local custom contributed other colorful characteristics that were also vampiristic risk factors. For example, Russian peasants as late as 1889 considered alcoholism to endanger the soul. At the slightest sign of local problems such as crop failure, they would dig up the offending corpse and throw it into the nearest river. Bulgarians were suspicious of the dead bodies of robbers, arsonists, prostitutes, and dishonest barmaids. Sometimes potential vampires could be identified quite early in life. In many countries throughout medieval Europe those at risk of future vampirism included infants born with a red caul (amniotic membrane) or a red birthmark. The Russians believed that children with a cleft lower lip were vampire raw material, while in Poland infants born with teeth needed watching. In Rumania potential vampires included the seventh-born child in a family, infants with an extra nipple, and infants with red hair and blue eyes. Redheads were particularly dangerous, alive or dead, because of the folk belief that Judas Iscariot, the betrayer of Jesus, had red hair. In Serbia, Bulgaria, and Rumania a particularly vicious pack of red-haired vampires was called "Children of Judas." They killed their victims with one tremendous bite, which drained all the victim's blood instantaneously. To add insult to injury, the victim's flesh was imprinted with the Devil's stigmata in the shape of three scars, XXX, symbolizing Judas' reward of thirty pieces of silver for betraying Jesus.

LYCANTHROPY

Lycanthropy is usually defined as the delusional belief that one has been transformed into a wolf, or the display of animalistic behavior indicative of such a belief. The more general term *therianthropy,* or shape-shifting, refers to changing into any sort of animal. However, while there certainly are cases of people who believed themselves to be transformed into animals such as birds, gerbils, rabbits, and pussy cats, there are no reports of injury or death inflicted by vicious thumping or pecking. On the other hand, individuals convinced that they have metamorphosed into wolves have for centuries committed the most gruesome acts of murder, mutilation, and cannibalism.

The belief that such metamorphoses are possible is quite ancient and part of the folklore of many different cultures. For example, Maylaysians believed that the ghosts of dead wizards entered the bodies of tigers. New Zealand natives believed that the souls of the neglected dead would enter the bodies of lizards to seek revenge. In the biblical Book of Daniel, for example, the Babylonian king Nebuchadnezzar (605–562 B.C.) was:

> ... banished from the society of men and ate grass like oxen; his body was drenched by the dew of heaven until his hair grew long like goat's hair and his nails like eagle's talons.

Eventually God took pity on him and restored him to human form.

In medieval Europe the wolf was the most hated and feared natural enemy, a cunning adversary and the perfect partner for the Devil or his demons. It is no wonder, then, that the wolf became the embodiment of the people's worst fears. Ancient physicians and theologians debated the possibility of a person's actually changing physically into an animal such as a wolf. Since there were numerous historical accounts of such shape-changing, could it be that onlookers were somehow enchanted, deceived, or hypnotized? At first many Christian theologians claimed that outside diabolical spirits could physically transform a person, or that a person could self-induce such changes by means of black magic. However, this view was rejected by no less an authority than St. Augustine (354–430 A.D.) who wrote:

> The Devil creates no new nature, but that he is able to make something appear to be that which it is not.

In other words, the Devil could make one person behave like a wolf, believe himself to be one, and fool onlookers into thinking it was so, but the actual physical body would not change. This view was reinforced in the infamous book *Witches Hammer,* the definitive fifteenth-century diagnostic manual for interrogating (read "torturing") suspected witches and warlocks. The monks who wrote the book reiterated that the physical body cannot be transformed. However, they claimed that evil charms and spells may create a subjective delusion so that a person appears to himself and others to be a wolf. This illusion was called "sight-shifting," as distinct from "shape-shifting," the actual physical transformation of a person into an animal shape.

With advances in medical knowledge, the religious explanation of demonic enchantment was at first combined with the medical view and then replaced by it. Soon enlightened physicians proclaimed that lycanthropy was a form of mental illness, a form of mania or melancholy, induced by herbs or ointments or, more likely, by the powerful conviction that these ointments could induce lycanthropy.

In modern psychiatry, lycanthropes are regarded as relatively harmless mental cases, but the historical versions were exceptionally bloodthirsty. In late sixteenth- and early seventeenth-century France, the werewolf, called the *loup garrou,* was a major source of terror. In one particularly gruesome case the mutilated bodies of four children, two boys and two girls, were discovered scattered around the outskirts of a small village. The nude remains had been partially eaten, with large chunks having been torn from their arms and thighs. One boy's chewed leg had been ripped from the torso and carried off. Suspicion fell on an elderly hermit, Giles Garnier. When he was arrested, more than 50 villagers testified that they had seen him, in the shape of a wolf, eating meat that they later found out was human flesh. Garnier "freely confessed" under torture that he had killed and eaten the children while transformed into a wolf. During his trial the Roman Catholic court expressed particular outrage, because Garnier admitted that if he had not been caught he would have eaten some of the flesh on meatless Friday. He was quickly condemned and burned to death. Such widespread werewolf panics ultimately led to the deaths of hundreds of innocent people, since those suspected of being werewolves were ripped to pieces in the search for the wolf fur that supposedly grew on the *inside* of the skin. Authorities estimate that between 1520 and 1630 A.D. more than 30,000 werewolf cases were recorded.

Werewolves were similar to vampires primarily in terms of their murderous potential. Although vampires were evil spirits neither alive nor dead but ghostlike, werewolves were living beings who took on the characteristics of wild beasts. In much of the folklore of medieval Europe, the werewolf after death turned into a vampire, even if it was killed properly by the familiar silver bullet cast from a sanctified silver chalice.

The association between carnivorous animals and the buried human corpse was no doubt the product of the earthy logic characteristic of medieval thinking. People observed that dogs and wolves tended to skulk around cemeteries at night, especially during wars, plagues, and famines. The need to dispose of large numbers of corpses often required mass burial in shallow graves scratched out of the earth. Dogs and wolves driven by starvation would undoubtedly have been attracted by the odors and noises of decomposition. Thus, there is no great mystery as to why they would be found so frequently sniffing and digging at grave sites.

This interpretation also affords a naturalistic explanation for the superstitious belief that the dead, in the guise of some beast, could rise from the grave. The sight of disturbed earth and signs of digging, and the beastly paw prints around the grave, would surely be interpreted as evidence that some hideous Thing had risen from the dead. The wolf in the graveyard could easily be seen as having *emerged* from the disturbed grave rather than as trying to dig its way in for dinner.

So far we have examined the factors that may have given rise to vampire and werewolf legends. Now we present contemporary case reports of vicious homicides and assaults committed by individuals proudly claiming to be actual vampires or werewolves. Case histories of lycanthropy and vampirism reflect the wide range of symptoms seen in these conditions. Whenever possible we concentrate on the most well-documented cases of the twentieth century, because reports from earlier times are of questionable accuracy. Police science was very primitive then, objective reporting rare, and the populace very superstitious, increasing the possibility of distortion and exaggeration.

Although both lycanthropy and vampirism involve the adoption of an animal identity, studies by the psychiatrist Dr. Paul Keck and his colleagues at Harvard University in their article, "Lycanthropy: Alive and well in the twentieth century" indicate that vampirism is not only more common than lycanthropy, but can result from any number of psychological problems, ranging from frank insanity to youth cult adulation and imitation. On the other hand, lycanthropes are clustered at the severely psychotic end of the continuum. Dr. Keck and his associates have presented the largest number of modern lycanthropy (i. e., therianthropy) cases in the literature. They did this by collecting all such cases admitted to their 250-bed hospital over the past 12 years. Among the 5,000 patients admitted, they discovered only 12 clear examples. In 11 cases the patient was diagnosed as psychotic, severely mentally ill, but no particular diagnosis predominated. One such case is described as follows:

Mr. Carlson is a 24-year-old single man who was admitted with a history of alcoholism, severe depression, and the unshakeable belief that he was a cat trapped in a human's body. He had known he was a cat for 13 years, ever since the secret was disclosed to him by the family cat, who also taught him cat language. He spent all his spare time in the company of felines, hunted with them, had sex with them, and frequented what he termed cat night spots, better places to prowl than their human counterparts. He also confided that a major source of his depression was his unrequited love for a tigress at the local zoo. His delusion remained unchanged despite treatment with the full range of anti-psychotic drugs, as well as 6 years of psychoanalytic psychotherapy. We could properly call this condition "species identity disorder."

Of the remaining patients in Dr. Keck's menagerie, there were two other cats, six wolves, a bird, and a gerbil (this patient had raised gerbils as a hobby). Following the expert Dr. Keck in this matter, we must conclude with him and his fellow investigators that lycanthropy, while exceedingly rare, is alive and well, or at least undead, in the twentieth century.

CLINICAL VAMPIRISM

South African forensic psychiatrists Hemphill and Zabow have argued for the autonomy of "clinical vampirism" as an independent psychological disorder, with the practitioners termed "vampirists," rather than regarding it as one of several injury-pain-death disorders. They reject the term *vampire* as referring either to a bat or to a mythical, supernatural, nonliving creature given to murderous bloodsucking. On the other hand, they define a *vampirist* psychologically as a person demonstrating three characteristics: a morbid fascination with death, no sense of identity, and, most important, a sexualized periodic craving for blood. They argue that the vampirism triad is unique and not a primary symptom of any other psychiatric disorder. It is most likely to be discovered during psychotherapy or in the treatment of self-injuries. Various authorities have referred to the thirst for blood by many names, such as hematophilia, hematomania, hematodipsia, hemosexuality, and hemothymea.

Hemphill and Zabow in the 1983 *South African Medical Journal* present three vampirist patients from their practice, all of whom demonstrate the vampirism triad. All three were white males from stable middle-class homes with no family pathology. All were physically and mentally healthy except for their self-mutilations, with IQ scores between 110 and 120. They all rejected Dracula movies as garbage and were totally uninterested in the occult.

Alex had been expelled from five schools before he was 13. He had spent virtually his entire adolescence and young adulthood in custody. He was a violent burglar, drug user and dealer, and had been declared a habitual criminal. As a young child he had tantrums, and was prone to violence and cruelty to his pets, being fascinated by blood, pain, and torture. In prison he relieved frustrations by tearing rats apart and drinking their blood. From age 4 he sucked his own blood and when older opened his veins for that purpose, claiming that it warmed and relaxed him. A homosexual and masochist, he would often bite the neck of a sex partner to suck his blood. In the prison hospital he was preoccupied with blood and death, and made numerous sadistic red-ink drawings. During severe bouts of depersonalization he became unsure of his real identity and in fact seemed to have three different personalities.

Bernard was a 19-year-old man who had bummed around South Africa for two years, living by crime and indulging heavily in alcohol and other drugs. As a child he showed the familiar pattern of violence, cruelty to animals, and aggressive hostility toward others. From age 16 on he would stab strangers on impulse and enjoyed burning stores and smashing windows. Fascinated by blood ever since childhood, he used to lick his own scratches. He also bit the heads off birds and a pet guinea pig to suck their blood. He frequently cut himself deliberately to drink blood, claiming that it soothed him. He too was unsure of his true identity and even joined a criminal gang in order to gain one. In prison he cut himself whenever he was unobserved, and once became violent when restrained from smashing glass to cut himself further. While still in custody several years later, he died during surgery, from loss of blood, perhaps?

Carl was a 22-year-old man who had been hospitalized with broken bones from car accidents when he was 5 and 8 years old. He greatly enjoyed the hospital experience and began sucking blood from his skin graft during the second hospitalization. During adolescence he sucked his own blood so frequently and vigorously that he required numerous blood transfusions. In contrast to the previous two cases, he was a mild and pleasant child who hated cruelty, violence, and suffering. He said he had always been fascinated by the taste of blood and frequently craved it. When in the hospital he enjoyed watching blood transfusions, and frequently visited the emergency room to see the sick, injured, and dying. He also complained of severe depersonalization, having no solid idea of who he really was or what he was capable of doing, and said he only felt real in the hospital. Upon release he would always manage to injure himself, sometimes severely, and then was usually rehospitalized. That behavior pattern suggests that we may be describing a case of Munchausen's syndrome [see Chapter 2] rather than a true vampirist.

The twentieth century has produced a number of vicious blood-drinking murderers who also are best classified as clinical vampirists. No serious discussion of real life vampirism would be complete without them.

The Monster of Dusseldorf

Peter Kurten (1883–1931) was a vicious child murderer whose hideous crimes earned him the name "Monster of Dusseldorf." He grew up in an abusive family and frequently saw his drunken father beating and raping the mother he adored. Kurten wasted no time embarking on his murderous career. At age 9 he was suspected of drowning a playmate by pushing him off a raft. As an adolescent he discovered that the joy of sex with sheep, goats, and pigs was magnified by stabbing them during the episode. In and out of prison as an adult, in his twenties he confessed to poisoning several inmates in the prison hospital. At age 30 he broke into a house and strangled a 13-year-old girl, also slitting her throat and drinking her blood.

He was married at age 38, to an older woman who had herself been imprisoned for murdering her husband. Kurten's foolproof romantic courtship method consisted of repeatedly threatening to kill her until she agreed to marry him. Throughout the marriage she was unaware of the 29 murders attributed to him. When he confessed to her, she promptly turned him in.

Kurten began his murder spree in earnest in 1925. He killed men, women, and children with clubs, knives, and his bare hands, often drinking the victim's blood. Greatly annoyed at the slow pace of his decimation of the Dusseldorf population, he developed grandiose plans to blow up the city or set it afire. He actually did burn down numerous barns and other buildings with people inside.

At his trial he shouted angrily that no one could understand him, that he needed blood like an alcoholic needed liquor. At least one journalist took him seriously and reported that Kurten suffered from "hematodipsia," a sexual thirst for blood. Kurten also told the examining psychiatrist that he hoped he would be able to hear the sound of his own blood running into the basket as the executioner cut off his head. He was convicted of nine murders, sentenced to death, and promptly beheaded in 1931.

The Hanover Vampire

Fritz Haarman (1879–1925), the notorious "Hanover Vampire," was beheaded "with a heavy sword" in 1925 for biting to death 27 known victims. The corpses of some of the victims were used to ensure the success of Haarman's butcher shop. It was quite fitting that the method of execution was beheading, one of the most common traditional means of destroying a vampire.

Brutalized at home by a drunken father, young Fritz began his education at a church school. Because of his low intelligence, he was soon transferred to a military school for noncommissioned officers. Although he was regarded as a good soldier, unspecified illness led to his discharge and return home. Within a short time he was accused of molesting children and sent to an insane asylum. However, he escaped, fled to Switzerland, and then returned to live with his father in Hanover once more. He reenlisted and apparently was a crack soldier in an elite army brigade. However, illness again forced his discharge and a return to the hostile paternal home. Soon he sank to the level of a homeless derelict and petty thief, repeatedly jailed for minor offenses.

After Germany's disastrous World War I defeat, he opened a small restaurant-butcher shop in the slums with money earned as a police informant. His little shop prospered, mainly because he seemed always able to procure large amounts of fresh meat at low prices in a time of great hunger and scarcity. Nearby was the Great Railway Station, frequented by fugitives, homeless drifters, deserters, and young runaways. The police used Haarman to keep an eye on the station and its more unsavory inhabitants. He became a familiar figure, wandering about the cavernous structure in the dead of night, occasionally waking a young runaway to check his papers. Every so often the kindly Haarman would invite a youth to his apartment attached to the butcher shop for a mattress and a meal.

In 1919 Haarman met Hans Gans, his future partner in mass murder. Gans was homosexual, a member of a minority group which in that time and place was widely regarded as depraved and perverted. Gans instigated most of the murders, and for trivial reasons, such as coveting one youth's shirt. He also acted as a decoy and frequently selected the victims. The prey were lured to the apartment, where they were fed a big meal and then suddenly assaulted with tooth and knife. The rear of the structure faced the river, where some of the bones were dumped. Haarman and Gans were finally discovered after Haarman got involved in a loud argument with a young man he had made advances to at the train station. The police searched Haarman's rooms and found numerous body parts hidden in a cabinet.

At his trial Haarman remained silent and impassive as his crimes were recounted in horrifying detail. Most of the victims were between 12 and 18 years old. Many of the bodies were made into sausage meat, which Haarman sometimes cooked and served to his favorite customers. Estimates of the number of victims varied from 24 to as high as 50. The newspapers reported that more than 600 people had disappeared in Hanover, many between ages 14 and 18, quite possibly at the bloody hands of Haarman and Gans. Haarman himself calmly testified for days in great and revolting detail about some of the murders and disposition of the corpses. Although he vigorously denied that he was insane, he insisted that he carried out the murders in a trance, unaware of what he was doing. The judge quickly rejected this argument, pointing out that Haarman himself admitted that the victims had to be restrained by hand in a particularly intricate way so that he could inflict the fatal bite on their throats. That maneuver required definite deliberation and conscious purpose. Loudly blaming each other, Haarman and Gans were swiftly sentenced to death and life imprisonment, respectively, leaving behind a populace revolted by the gory confrontation with clinical vampirism in modern dress.

The Case of the Sacramento Vampire

One of the most gruesome cases occurred in the mid-twentieth-century United States, in broad daylight, and was solved by the new FBI *Behavioral Sciences Unit,* made famous in the movie thriller

Silence of the Lambs. For the first time the FBI was able to use its brand-new sexual homicide profile, as developed by FBI Special Agent Robert Ressler and his associates. The logic behind the profile has remarkable parallels to the criminal detection methods of the internationally renowned fictional detective Sherlock Holmes, so we call this incident "The Case of the Sacramento Vampire."

In January 1978, Russ Vorpagel of the FBI Behavioral Sciences Unit received a frantic call from the police of a small town north of Sacramento, California, asking assistance in a particularly gory homicide. A truck driver returned home to find his 23-year-old pregnant wife dead of stab wounds, her abdomen ripped open. The major knife wound was a slash from chest to umbilicus. The intestines were protruding, several internal organs had been cut out, and others were missing. There were stab wounds in the left breast and animal feces had been stuffed into the woman's mouth. Finally, there was distinct evidence that her blood had been collected and drunk.

The intense violence and sexual nature of the murder was an ominous signal that the murderer would strike again soon. The prospect of additional murders made it especially urgent that the killer be stopped immediately. Special Agent Ressler's use of the homicide profile, then, was a desperate attempt to prevent more deaths. In the Holmes tradition, the profile is a combination of known characteristics of previous murderers, the physical evidence at the crime scene, and logical inferences. It is based on the observation that serial sexual murderers are overwhelmingly white males in their mid-twenties and their crimes are committed in white neighborhoods. Based on the bizarre nature of the murderer's behavior, he was classified as a "Disorganized" killer. This means that he probably suffered from a severe mental disorder.

The profile goes on to describe the slasher as a thin, unkempt white male in his mid-twenties, likely with blood on his clothes. "Souvenirs" from the crime scene would be found in his filthy home or car, which would be within a mile or two of the murder. He was probably a high school or college drop-out with a history of severe and increasing mental illness, probably paranoid in nature. He would not have served in the military, would most likely be unemployed, living alone, and possibly receiving some sort of disability income.

The prediction that the killer would be emaciated and unkempt was based on research showing a high correlation between temperament and body type. Schizophrenics are often very thin, exemplifying the so-called ectomorphic body type, because of poor eating habits or delusions that food is poisoned, and they are notoriously neglectful of personal hygiene. Such a smelly and disheveled person would offend any roommate or employer and would certainly be rejected by the military. At his extreme level of disorganization, he would surely have been unable to function in high school or college. With an irregular work history at best and severe mental disability, he would be qualified for some form of public financial assistance. He has probably taken 8 to 10 years to arrive at his current severe mental illness. Paranoid psychosis has a slow developmental pattern of that sort, often beginning in adolescence, so the man is probably in his mid-twenties now. If any older, he would probably already have committed numerous bizarre crimes, including homicide. Since nothing of that kind had occurred nearby, this was likely his first homicide. The killer may also have been released from psychiatric custody within the past year, but no longer, because he could not have controlled himself that long.

In addition to the more objective observations, Ressler guessed that if the murderer had a car it would be filthy and trash laden. However, he would probably be too psychotic to drive to a murder scene, do the deed, and then get in his car to drive home or conceal his movements.

Four days later four more murders were discovered nearby, indicating a rapidly escalating level of violence. The victims were a 36-year-old housewife, her 6-year-old son, and a 52-year-old family friend. The woman's 22-month-old nephew was missing from his blood-stained crib and presumed dead. All had been shot to death, the woman slashed obscenely as in the prior murder, and her blood drunk. Again, nothing was missing; there was no logical motive for the crime. The family station wagon was found, doors ajar and key in the ignition, several blocks from the home.

The second murders provided valuable new information, and the profile was revised accordingly. The revised profile reiterated that the murderer was a loner living one-half to one mile from the abandoned station wagon, which may even have been abandoned very close to his home. With the new information, 65 police officers combed the immediate area house to house, and discovered that a dog had been disemboweled close to where the station wagon had been abandoned. Then a young woman reported a frightening encounter at a shopping mall with a former high school classmate. She described him as cadaverously thin, with sunken eyes, a yellow crust around his mouth, wearing a bloody sweatshirt, and ranting about UFOs and Nazi plots. He followed her and tried to force his way into her car, but she broke away. The man was Richard Trenton Chase, and a police task force immediately surrounded his apartment, which was less than one block from the abandoned station wagon.

Chase proved to be an incredibly close fit to the FBI profile. His truck and apartment were a shambles. Police found a bloody knife and boots in the truck. In the apartment they discovered three food blenders containing blood, a refrigerator overflowing with body parts and brain tissue, and numerous collars from pet dogs and cats Chase had killed. Subsequent inquiry revealed that his mental state had declined rapidly since high school. He had no friends, had become defiant, and began heavy drug use. He managed to graduate and was employed briefly in a succession of dead-end jobs. As his mental condition deteriorated, he was arrested for drunkenness, possessing an illegal gun, and minor drug offenses. Two years prior to the murders he had been sent to a nursing home after he tried to inject rabbit blood into his veins. At the nursing home he was known as "Dracula." He earned the nickname after he terrified the nurses by biting the heads off birds he had snared, and several times he was found with blood on his mouth and clothing. Defending his actions, he said he was being poisoned, his own blood was turning to powder and he had to replenish the supply. Discharged from the home in 1977, Chase subsisted on a small disability check that was supplemented by his parents. His level of violence accelerated, at first confined to torturing and killing dogs and cats he adopted via newspaper ads and from the Humane Society. Later, he bought a gun and began randomly shooting at people from ambush, then graduated to the mutilation murders and blood drinking that led directly to his arrest. His lawyers' attempts to plead insanity were rejected by the jury. He was found guilty of six counts of first-degree murder and was sentenced to death in the San Quentin gas chamber. However, just after Christmas in 1980 he committed suicide with an overdose of antidepressant pills.

THEORETICAL VIEWS

Explanations of the causes and meaning of vampirism and lycanthropy vary from the colorful, but highly speculative, interpretations of psychoanalysis to the potential causal role of an uncommon inherited blood disorder.

Psychoanalytic View

Curiously enough, modern psychoanalytic theory resembles the medieval theological explanations that attributed lycanthropy and vampirism to evil forces within the person. Psychoanalysts agree with Freud's biographer and confidant, Dr. Ernest Jones, that these disorders represent regression to a primitive, animalistic level of personality functioning. Failure of repression results in the inability to inhibit powerful oral-sadistic needs, which threaten to explode into destructive action and produce hideous crimes of violence.

In this view, such oral-sadistic rage is caused by maternal rejection. However, the individual refrains from attacking the depriving mother for fear that this would result in his own annihilation. Therefore, these sadistic impulses are disowned, banished to a split-off portion of the ego. The destructive weapons are those of the late oral stage, the teeth and mouth. The vampiristic attack consists of three acts: (1) a life is taken by oral means, a sadistic biting attack, (2) the love object is restrained and controlled while the vampire is feeding, and (3) after feeding, the victim also becomes a vampire, so there is a merger between victim and feeder.

The vampire is a creature suspended between two worlds, one of the living dead, neither of this world nor of the inner world of the unconscious. This failure to be completely in either world is exemplified by fear of not having a mirror reflection, a very weak sense of self. Psychoanalysts attribute the enduring popularity of the vampire myth to a safe projection of our own repressed oral-sadistic impulses to bite and kill. The vampire's dilemma also arouses our sympathy. We can identify with the vampire's wish to be loved, but, overwhelmed by such unfulfilled oral needs, it becomes destructive and thereby unlovable.

Biological View

Imaginative investigators have suggested an ingenious medical explanation to account for the legendary vampire's appearance and behavior.

There is a rare genetic blood disease called iron-deficiency porphyria, which prevents the person's body from metabolizing iron. This leads to anemia and a buildup of iron-free red-pigmented porphyrin cells in the skin. The patient's symptoms include emaciation, extreme and painful sensitivity of the skin to light, together with bloodshot eyes and reddened teeth resulting from porphyrin deposits. The dry, parched skin of the face shrinks and splits and draws the lips apart, causing the reddened teeth to appear elongated and bloody. As if this isn't bad enough, the disease is accompanied by severe psychological problems ranging from manic-depression to delerium. Taking a giant step in speculation, these theorists ask: In the Middle Ages when medical knowledge was primitive, what better way to remedy one's anemia and other symptoms of the disease than by ingesting the iron-rich blood of another person? Porphyria theory, then, rejects the supernatural and portrays our fanged nocturnal blood drinker as the victim of a rare blood disease. All well and good, except that our best historical descriptions of exhumed vampires either mention their plump, robust appearance or describe them as unchanged. There are no hints of a disfiguring disease. Furthermore, not one of our modern vampires has porphyria. For these reasons there are very few current supporters of the porphyria theory.

Sociobehavioral View

From the perspective of behavior theory, a passion for blood drinking would be acquired in the same manner as any other behavior, through some sort of reward or reinforcement; definitely an acquired taste. As with other paraphilias, careful inquiry will often turn up some accidental pairing of sexual arousal and the deviant behavior; that is, blood drinking or fantasies about it. To illustrate, Dr. Richard von Krafft-Ebing, the pioneering sexologist, reported the following unusual case:

> Mr. Miller, a young male patient whose sexual activity had been limited to masturbation, consulted the good doctor because of his overpowering lust for blood. It began quite accidentally when a maid who was washing windows broke the glass and cut her hand badly. Miller impulsively grabbed her hand and began sucking the wound to stop the bleeding. During this contact he suddenly discovered that

he had a powerful erection, immediately followed by an orgasm. From then on he was driven to taste the fresh blood of young women. At first he was able to bribe another housemaid to let him prick her finger and watch it bleed as he experienced orgasm. When his mother caught him at it, she promptly fired the maid. Then Miller turned to prostitutes who, for an exorbitant price, would let him inflict a small cut or scratch. Occasionally this would enable him to have sexual intercourse. He tried many kinds of therapies, but despite temporary gains he was never able to overcome his blood addiction. From the behavioral view, then, vampirism is seen as the result of the accidental coupling of compelling erotic arousal and the sight and taste of blood.

BUT ARE VAMPIRES REALLY REAL?

We have described real people who love to suck blood, their own or that of other people. They are the clinical vampirists. For some of them, drinking blood becomes a super sexual turn-on. Still others must drink the blood of those they have first killed in order to enjoy full sexual gratification. Some blood drinkers suffer from schizophrenia, a severe psychological disorder characterized by bizarre fantasies and distortions of reality. They may believe that they can change into bats or wolves, or that they have returned from the dead. However, there are no genuine vampires. There is no credible evidence for supernatural beings who reside in coffins during the day, emerging at night for blood cocktails siphoned from virginal victims, immortal demons vulnerable only to silver bullets and oak stakes pounded into the ancient ticker. These features appear only in fictional vampires.

The fictional vampire has been studied painstakingly by scholarly anthropologists such as Dr. Paul Barber. As previously noted, his investigations explain the origin of the vampire phenomenon as the creation of an ignorant and fearful medieval European peasantry in times of great stress and loss of life, such as famine, plague, and war. In plague epidemics, for example, there were too many bodies to be buried deeply in individual graves, and corpse handlers fearful of infection tended not to examine carefully all those presumed dead. These hurried undertakings resulted in some people being buried alive and then trying desperately to claw themselves out. Such shallow graves would also have tempted starving dogs and wolves, who may have mistakenly been seen as frightful creatures *emerging from* the disturbed graves. The sacred ground of graveyards and tombs was one of the few places where vagrants, deserters, and the homeless of the day could find shelter, and perhaps a scrap of food from a kindly deacon. These tattered, unkempt, and odiferous outsiders might well have been mistaken for menacing corpses. Finally, the peasantry's ignorance of the natural appearance of a decaying dead body after days or weeks in the earth gave rise to superstitious explanations for natural phenomena, such as the corpse's bloody lips or the noise made by a gas-filled body when its abdomen is punctured.

In the context of our two universal and enduring human mysteries, the origin of life and the inevitability of death, it is likely that such simple observations by simple people not only gave rise to vampire legends, but also provided the specific characteristics of the vampire itself. Today we continue to promote these legends primarily because it amuses us to do so, and because for some it can be quite profitable.

Suggested Further Readings

Barber, P. (1988) *Vampires, burial, and death.* New York: Yale University Press.

Keck, P., Pope, H., Hurdon, J., McElroy, S., & Kulick, A. (1988). Lycanthropy: Alive and well in the twentieth century. *Psychological Medicine, 18,* 113–120

Masters, A. (1972). *The natural history of the vampire.* New York: G. P. Putnam's Sons.

Prins, H. (1990). *Bizarre behaviours.* London and New York: Tavistock/Routledge.

Ressler, R., & Shachter, T. (1992) *Whoever fights monsters.* New York: St. Martin's Press.

CHAPTER 5

Sex Slavery and the Stockholm Syndrome

From Terror to Love

Patty Hearst, the hostages held in Iran and Lebanon, coerced prostitutes such as the Korean "comfort girls" who served as sex slaves for Japanese troops in World War II, battered women, kidnap victims, and Nazi concentration camp inmates share an extraordinary experience—they all have undergone unusual stresses and brutality. Of those who survive such traumatic events, some have displayed paradoxical, even bizarre, reactions to their experiences. Incredibly, some have felt sympathy for and emotional attraction to their captors. This pattern is so unusual that it is now recognized as a predictable, even desirable, sequence of emotions and behaviors, called the "Stockholm syndrome."

The term *Stockholm syndrome* has been credited to FBI Special Agent Supervisor Conrad Hassel. The name derives from a 1973 attempted bank robbery in Stockholm, Sweden, in which four employees were held hostage by the primary robber and his accomplice over a period of 131 hours. Despite their terror and unwilling confinement for nearly six days, the incident ended with the three women kissing their captors and the male hostage shaking hands with them. The ordeal received extraordinary media attention at the time, and these positive reactions of the "victims" completely mystified the world's observers.

In this chapter we discuss cases of hostage taking and sex slavery in which individuals were kidnapped and held for very long periods of time either for political purposes or for pure sexual exploitation. These terrible experiences have generated examples of the Stockholm syndrome in some victims, but, interestingly, not in all of them. We also review the major psychological explanations for the appearance of the Stockholm syndrome.

DEFINING THE STOCKHOLM SYNDROME

Psychologists and law-enforcement hostage negotiators have referred to the Stockholm syndrome variously as an "unholy alliance," "pathologic transference," "spontaneous identification under stress," and an "automatic, probably unconscious, emotional response to the trauma of becoming a victim."

Psychiatrist Frank Ochberg of the National Institute of Mental Health and George Washington University Medical School is a consultant to the FBI and a prominent expert on the experience of being a victim of terrorism. Dr. Ochberg considers the syndrome to be due to a reawakening of the fears and pleasures of infancy in the adult victim, who is terrorized and yet thankful to and dependent on his or her captors. The appearance of any or all of the three following conditions defines the Stockholm syndrome, according to Ochberg:

1. The victim has positive feelings toward his captor.
2. He has negative feelings towards the authorities responsible for his rescue.
3. The hostage's positive feelings towards the hostage taker are reciprocated by the hostage taker.

The syndrome is promoted by several factors: the intensity and duration of the experience, the degree of dependence on the captor for survival, and the psychological distance of the hostage from government authorities. For example, if the incident lasts just an hour or so, the syndrome may not develop to a noticeable degree. Almost always the victim feels, and actually is, dependent on the hostage taker for continued life. In fact, the police become perceived threats to life as the rescue effort is made. Ordinary citizens who just happened to be present at a scene where hostages were taken, as in the Stockholm bank, are more likely to display the Stockholm syndrome than individuals formally associated with government, such as ambassadors and military officers.

Development of this syndrome actually increases a victim's chances of surviving. Sensitive and clinically aware law enforcement negotiators will do what they can in a hostage situation to foster some positive emotional ties between the hostage and the hostage taker. To the extent that the hostage taker, in turn, develops a concern for the hostage as just a regular person with responsibilities and concerned family members, the hostage's chances for being released unharmed significantly improve. This development meets Ochberg's third criterion for the syndrome.

Although well-informed police will encourage development of such feelings because they benefit the hostage, the syndrome actually works against the police in resolving the situation and at any criminal trial later. For example, because of a professed caring for the hostage takers, and possibly some real sympathy for their political or religious cause, a hostage may not follow police orders during an assault, may actually warn the hostage takers in order to save them from being killed or captured, and may even falsify information in contacts with negotiators. At trial, former hostages often end up as hostile witnesses to the prosecution's case.

The original incident in the Swedish bank, which gave the syndrome its name, offers a number of examples of how the hostage takers and their victims bonded emotionally during their time together. Most of the time the four hostages and two hostage takers were confined in the bank's vault for safety deposit boxes. The vault was 47 feet long by 11 feet wide by 7½ feet high. Although ventilated, it retained a close, oppressive quality for its six inhabitants. Hostage Elisabeth Oldgren complained of feeling claustrophobic in the vault. When the robber Jan-Erik Olsson placed a rope around her neck, in effect a leash, to let her out to walk a few feet, she reported later how free she felt and how "very kind" Olsson had been to her.

At another point Elisabeth was unleashed and permitted to go to the bathroom with another hostage, Birgitta Lundblad, completely unsupervised. They passed policemen in the bank and were just a few steps from safety. Yet they did not avail themselves of the opportunity and returned to their imprisonment. In response to a whispered question during their trip to the bathroom, Elisabeth did signal to the police the number of hostages that were being held. For that small act she "felt like a traitor."

Other indicants of a reciprocal relationship between hostages and hostage takers began to appear. Olsson allowed the women hostages to call their worried relatives, certainly an act of kindness and concern. During the first night in the vault Elisabeth awoke shivering from the cold, and Olsson protectively placed his wool jacket around her shoulders. At another point his attentiveness included wiping away Elisabeth's tears and giving Kristin a bullet from his submachine gun as a keepsake. He magnanimously permitted the nervous Birgitta to smoke, even though it was against the bank's rules to smoke in the vault.

The captors permitted the police commissioner to enter the vault to "inspect the hostages" to assure their well-being. When he did so, he detected the hostages' hostility toward him and a "peculiar amity" between them and Olsson's accomplice, Clark Olofsson. (In a strange twist to the story, Olofsson was involved in the incident only because the police, at his friend Olsson's request, brought him to the bank *from* prison *after* the actual hostage taking had been completed by Olsson.) During his "inspection," the hostages pleaded with the commissioner that he permit all six of them to leave the bank together undisturbed.

In a phone call arranged with the Swedish prime minister, Olof Palme, hostage Kristin Ehnmark angrily begged to be permitted to leave with Olsson and Olofsson. She made it very clear that she trusted them, not the police or any other government officials.

After some delay hostage Birgitta Lundblad reached her mother by phone to inquire about her own children. Following the conversation, she concluded that it was the police who were keeping her from seeing her children. She believed that Olsson, who had two children of his own, would never have taken her hostage if he had known at the time that she was a mother.

The only male hostage, Sven Safstrom, had been offered a deal by Olsson, who wanted to make a dramatic gesture to convince the police of his seriousness. Olsson told Sven that he planned to shoot him. However, rather than kill him as he intended originally, he agreed merely to shoot him in the leg. A signal was to be given, and Sven was to position himself in a place where the police could see him fall. But Olsson never gave the signal. Sven remained grateful as he recalled his feelings later: "All that comes back to me is how kind I thought he was for saying it was just my leg he would shoot." At various points Sven spoke of Olsson as "our protector" and "an emergency God." After his rescue Sven tried to hate his captors and their criminal acts, but could never quite do so.

Another example of the hostage takers' concern was their insistence that the police provide sanitary supplies for one of the hostages who had begun to menstruate. The strength of their demand indicated to the police that a genuine bond of friendship was developing.

Several days into the hostage crisis, Kristin awoke screaming from a nightmare. It was her captor Clark who comforted her.

The public and the press speculated about possible rape or other sexual contact between the women and the hostage takers. Kristin admitted that she had held hands with Clark and that he had given her "tenderness." "But there was no sex," she said. "It made me feel enormously secure. It was what I needed."

Police lab technicians found traces of semen on the vault's carpet during their examination after the incident. On the second evening of the siege, one of the women reported that Olsson approached her and asked if he could lie next to her. She consented. When he asked if he could caress her, she replied, "Yes, you may."

In her testimony to the police later, she defended her behavior as a calculated plan. "I thought that if I could get on an intimate footing with him, I might be able to persuade him to give up his whole enterprise, or maybe if some of the anxieties he surely had pent up within himself were relieved, he would not want to go on with this whole thing. We had our clothes on, but he was allowed to touch my breasts and hips. He became rather excited and wanted to know if he could continue. He wanted to have intercourse." She says that she refused. It was important to her not to give Olsson control. She implied that the semen stains came from his coming via masturbation.

The crisis ended after the police had laboriously drilled a series of holes in the roof of the vault and then pumped in 15 flasks of tear gas. Everyone in the vault was in great distress—choking, vomiting, eyes burning, gasping for air. The police were yelling for the captors to throw out their weapons and to send out the hostages first. Even then, the hostages refused and rejected rescue, fearing that the police would shoot Olsson and Olofsson. After embracing and kissing their captors, the hostages exited simultaneously and safely with the hostage takers.

Journalist Daniel Lang interviewed Olsson in prison. Olsson's comments confirm that the Stockholm syndrome had indeed developed in him, the captor, as well. His humane treatment of his hostages was due to a developing emotional relationship with them.

Olsson complained, "It was the hostages' fault. They did everything I told them to do. If they hadn't, I might not be here now. Why didn't any of them attack me? They made it hard to kill. They made us go on living together day after day, like goats, in that filth. There was nothing to do but get to know each other." Kristin had been aware of this principle when she explained why the hostages tried to please their captors: "If someone likes you, he won't kill you." Of course, this axiom is not *always* true in life (see Chapter 12 on necrophilia).

It should be clear that the psychological effects of this experience were not all positive for the hostages. Each of them was forever changed. The more common and expected aftereffects of living through a trauma also appeared in these individuals—sleep disturbances, nightmares, fears, startle reactions, flashbacks, and depression. Sven strangely could not muster the negative emotions against his captors that he thought he should feel. Elisabeth, too, could not understand why she did not hate them. More accurately, she was displaying an emotional numbness, which is quite characteristic of trauma victims.

One final curiosity to the Stockholm case was that nearly a year later, Birgitta yielded to an impulse to visit Clark Olofsson in prison. The urge came upon her as she and her husband were driving by the institution. She refused to provide details of her visit, except that

Clark did not apologize for anything. Her view was still tolerant: "He needn't have."

Perhaps the most bizarre aspect of hostage and kidnap victims' behavior occurs when they have a safe and sure opportunity to escape, yet do not do so. This opportunity occurred early in the Stockholm bank siege. Battered wives are often accused of foolishly staying with their batterers even when they have many unsupervised opportunities to escape or call for help. Psychologists and feminists are well aware of why it is extremely difficult for these women simply to walk away from the situation.

The following cases are examples of captivity, much more brutal and lengthy than the Stockholm bank incident, in which escape could have happened but did not. In addition to prolonging the horrible experience, failure to attempt to flee caused serious consequences later at trials, when the lay citizens on the jury just could not understand. The cases of Colleen Stan and Patricia Hearst both illustrate this interesting and puzzling aspect of the Stockholm syndrome.

SEX SLAVE COLLEEN STAN

The case of Colleen Stan is one of the most shocking and cruel kidnappings ever to occur in America. Colleen was a 20-year-old college student in Eugene, Oregon, seeking a ride to visit friends in Westwood, California, a small town in the northern part of the state. She was picked up hitchhiking on May 19, 1977, by Cameron and Janice Hooker and their baby daughter in their family car. It all seemed totally innocuous. But once she was inside that blue Dodge Colt, that day began a seven-year sentence in hell for Colleen. Cameron produced a knife at Colleen's throat, then handcuffed, bound, and gagged her. She had been taken without a struggle, not even a scream. Over the following years she was imprisoned in extremely tight quarters, starved, beaten, tortured, hung from rafters, raped, and forced to work for her "master." She became a sex slave.

Colleen's slavery was eventually made "legal" by her signing a formal slave contract. Cameron reproduced the following contract which he had found in a pornographic bondage and discipline (B & D) magazine:

THIS INDENTURE, made the 25th day of January in the year of Our Lord One Thousand Nine Hundred and Seventy-Eight, BE-TWEEN Colleen Stan, hereafter known as Slave; AND Michael Powers [sic], hereafter known as Master; WITNESSETH:

That Slave, for and in consideration and in humble appreciation of such care and attention as Master may choose to afford her, has given, granted, aliened, enfeoffed and conveyed, and by these Presents does give, grant, enfeoff and convey unto Master:

ALL of Slave's body, and each and every part thereof without reservation, every bit of her will as to all matters and things, and the entirety of her Soul,

TOGETHER with, all and singular, every privilege, advantage and appurtenance to the same belonging or in anywise appertaining;

ALSO all the estate, right, title, property, claims, ego and id of Slave in, of and to the same and in, of and to every part and parcel thereof;

TO HAVE AND TO HOLD, all and singular, the above-described body, will, Soul and premises, with all appurtenances thereof, unto Master and any of His assigns forever.

AND the said Slave does covenant, promise and agree:

1. She shall immediately, diligently and enthusiastically comply with and submit her full being to any and all directions or desires of Master or His assigns which He or They may express by word, signal, action or any other means.

2. She shall at all times afford Master absolute respect, shall address Him only as "Sir" or "Master," shall station herself in a physical position subordinate to His whenever possible, and shall speak to or otherwise distract Him only when granted His permission.

3. She shall constantly maintain her female body parts in such circumstances as will demonstrate and ensure that they are fully open to Him. In particular, she shall never cross her legs in His presence, shall wear no undergarments at any time, and shall cover no part of her body with apparel or material of any description except when the act of doing so and design of the item are expressly approved by Him.

4. She shall preserve her female body parts for the exclusive use of Him and His assigns, which use shall be the sole source of her pleasures, and she shall engage in no self-gratification nor any physical contact with any others.

AND Slave does hereby irrevocably declare and acknowledge her everlasting unconditional dedication to serving Master to His full satisfaction; AND she ashamedly confesses that prior indulgence of her untempered conduct by others may have permitted her to become afflicted with inferior habits that may prove unsatisfactory to Master, from which imperfections she implores Master to free her by retraining with corporal punishment or any other means which He, in His unquestionable wisdom, deems effective toward directing her to her sole ambition and life-destiny of perfectly fulfilling His every desire of her.

IN WITNESS WHEREOF, Slave has hereunto set her hand, and Master has designed to Seal these Presents by permanently affixing his Collar about her neck, on the date first above written.

After a feeble protest that he could never have her soul, the trembling Colleen Stan signed her name on a line marked "Forever Slave." In addition to the collar, Cameron ensured Colleen's captivity symbolically by piercing her right labium and inserting a gold ring.

What purpose did this paper contract serve for Cameron Hooker? After all, he already had total access to Colleen. He could do anything he wished to her. Several advantages did accrue for Cameron. With its legalistic language the contract gave credibility to his story that a large and powerful organization of slave traders, "the Company," was behind Colleen's abduction and was monitoring everything. The contract also played into Cameron's sexual fantasies of dominance and control over women. Finally and importantly, this document (and changing her name to merely an initial—"K") contributed to the dehumanization of Colleen, perhaps in both her eyes and those of her captor, something which would aid in continuing her captivity and degradation.

The nonexistent Company was the threat that helped keep the slave in her place. Hooker made it clear that if she attempted to leave or to contact her family, not only would the Company arrange to have her crucified over five days, but any family member contacted would also be killed.

Cameron Hooker, a skilled carpenter, built a variety of devices to fulfill his fantasies. One was a rack on which Colleen was chained and stretched. Another was a beam from which he regularly hung her (and occasionally his wife, Janice) by the wrists. Sometimes she was hung upside down. The hanging itself was excruciatingly painful, but it usually was preparatory to sexual abuse, whipping, and, at times, electrical shocks and burns on her breasts.

Perhaps worst of all was "the Box," in which Colleen was confined nearly every hour during the first three years. She would be allowed out only for sessions of rape and abuse and a rare bath. This wooden coffinlike box was double walled with a lid on top. It measured about 3 feet high and 6½ feet long. Colleen was kept in this box naked, blindfolded, with wax earplugs, and chained from her neck to her ankles. The lid was closed and padlocked. Air could enter through several ventilation holes drilled for that purpose. Incredibly, the Box was kept *under* the Hookers' marital bed.

Given the horrors of Colleen's experiences, several aspects of the case made it difficult for many people, including potential jurors later, to comprehend:

1. In March of 1981 Cameron drove Colleen to Riverside, California, to visit her family. He met them as her "boyfriend," and she returned with him to northern California and captivity.
2. Sometimes Colleen was permitted to jog alone (although Cameron carefully timed her absences).
3. She cared for the Hookers' children unsupervised.
4. Eventually, she obtained a chambermaid's job in a local motel while still under Hooker's control. Why did she never attempt to escape?
5. Why did she write special poems and speak of her "love" for Cameron?

Janice Hooker was the key to breaking the case, probably because of her own emotions of jealousy and guilt. She sought counseling from her pastor Frank Dabney in Red Bluff, California, to whom she revealed some of the sordid details of the kidnapping and sexual abuse. With her permission, the pastor notified the Tehama County sheriff. Cameron Hooker was arrested on November 18, 1984. Colleen Stan was now free, at least physically.

Three documents that Colleen "voluntarily" wrote during her captivity proved troublesome to explain during Hooker's trial. The first was a card written on the third anniversary of her kidnapping:

Sometimes I feel that being your slave has made me more of a woman. But then there are other times when I feel it has made me less of a woman. You know how to make me feel good about myself. And I love you so much for it. I only wish that my dreams could be fulfilled with you. Because I feel a strong love and need to be with you. I'll always serve you with singleness of heart.

K

This is my Christmas letter to express and give my love to my Master. You ask me to tell you how much I love you but I haven't ever been able to tell you because I don't know the right words to describe how much I love you but I seem to be falling deeper and deeper into love with you with each passing day. I find love hard for me to express with words. But you bring the passion out in me and it's a way of expressing my love for you. You've also spiritually inspired me and I can't tell you how much I love you for it. More than any words I know could ever tell. It's not easy being a slave but your love makes it worth being your slave. I hope that your [sic] right about how things will change for the better and that I'll have your child some day. I promise you I'll give you a son. I know you'll be proud of him and I hope you'll love him as much as you love me. I know that you know that I have great faith in God, I read this in St. Luke: For with God nothing shall be impossible. And I think you know how important it is to me to do everything with God in my heart, I need and want his guidance and strength. I can't explain how happy it made me feel inside when you told me that if I ever have your child that you would take me as your spiritual wife. I pray it will be someday. That God will recognize our love and commitment and that he'll join us to be one and that even though I'll be your bondmaid (slave) and second wife that no one or anything will ever separate us. I wish you a Merry Merry Christmas and the best of New Years. I pray that God will always hear your prayers and always answer them. And that the Holy Ghost will always be with you to guide you and to give you insight and understanding so that you will always do that which will make your soul feel good.

I love you more than words could ever say.

K

Love is not a single act, but a climate in which we live, a lifetime venture in which we are always learning, discovering, growing. It is not destroyed by a single failure, nor won by a single caress. You cannot learn to love by loving one person only, for love is a climate of the heart. My love for you is growing with every changing day. You fill my life with happiness and love. And I pray that that happiness and love will never end.

Love,

K

Do these messages sound like those from a kidnap or rape victim? Could Colleen's confinement be a fake? Could she really have changed into a willing participant-lover? The conditions to which Colleen had been subjected were extreme. Is her subsequent behavior an example of the Stockholm syndrome in its extreme?

Answers to these questions can be gleaned from the testimony of clinical psychologist Dr. Chris Hatcher, one of the foremost authorities on the psychological effects of being held hostage. He testified as an expert witness at Cameron Hooker's trial. Christine McGuire, the prosecuting district attorney, summarized his opinions in her book on the Stan case, *Perfect Victim*.

Dr. Hatcher described 16 techniques of coercion which can be used to alter radically a person's behavior, attitudes, and value systems. Colleen's "love letters" easily were accountable as her efforts to please Cameron by echoing her captor's beliefs.

D. A. McGuire's exact account of Hatcher's testimony follows:

The first step, he said, is a sudden, unexpected abduction, followed by isolation as soon as possible. "Refuse to answer questions, place them in a cell-like environment, remove their clothes, and begin humiliation and degradation." . . . A cell-like environment stimulates a feeling that one's worst fears are being realized, raising the level of fear and anxiety. Removal of clothes magnifies the feeling of vulnerability.

The second step in breaking someone, the doctor continued, is to physically or sexually abuse the person, to expose the captive's vulnerability and shock her or him. "In other words, not only has the victim been stripped of their clothes and placed in a physically vulnerable position, but you are going to whip or abuse in some other way, specifically with sexual manipulation, to illustrate just how exposed and vulnerable they really are" . . .

"The third step is extremely important," he said, "and that's to remove normal daylight patterns. All of us, both biologically and psychologically, are used to a certain day and night kind of sequence, and this has been well-documented in various types of scientific literature. Removing this, either by placing someone in a constantly lit or constantly dark environment, is very disorienting, and is a rather standard part of the techniques employed . . ."

The fourth step, Dr. Hatcher explained, is "to control urination, defecation, menstruation, and to be present when these activities are performed. Basically, what you want to do here is destroy a person's sense of privacy."

He also pointed out that "if a person soils himself, and isn't able to clean that up, the sense of shame in sitting or lying in their own waste product is really quite extraordinary, and individuals become very motivated to do what they can to get permission to clean themselves up. Most people have not had the experience since being a small infant, of sitting or lying in their waste product over a period of time. It takes you back to a period of vulnerability."

The fifth step is to control and reduce food and water. Hatcher stated the obvious: "If you don't get that food and water, you are going to die. So, on the one hand, they may be torturing you and preventing you from leaving, but on the other hand, they are bringing food and water." This helps make the captive dependent upon the captor.

The sixth step is to punish for no apparent rhyme or reason. Initially, the captive tries to figure out some rationale to the intermittent beatings but, finding none, eventually has to simply accept that punishment will occur with no reason.

The seventh step is to "require the victim to constantly ask permission for anything or any behavior." This would involve asking permission to take a tray of food. It is a type of training procedure.

The eighth step is to establish a pattern of sexual and physical abuse. This "indicates to the person that this is what their new life is now going to be like." It's a way of "getting the person to realize things have changed in a permanent sense."

The ninth step is to "continue to isolate the person. The captor has now become the source of food, water, human contact, as well. That's important—information, as well as pain. All of us are information-hungry people. If you put us in a restricted environment without newspapers or magazines or television, that's real nice for a while, but if it happens that you are totally cut off and weeks pass, all of us get a little hungry to find out what's going on.

"Cut that off and tie it to one person. Being a source of information is extremely important. As well as human contact—the captor has a tremendous amount of power because he's the human being that you see, he is that only point of contact . . ."

The tenth technique, he said, is to "present a goal or a model of future behavior, a model of how to please the captor."

The eleventh is to threaten family and relatives with a similar fate.

The twelfth is to threaten to sell the captive to an even worse master.

The thirteenth is to continue to beat and torture the captive at irregular intervals.

The fourteenth, called "irrelevant leniency," is to allow small privileges for no reason, making the captive more confused and more pliant.

The fifteenth is to obtain further confessions and signed documents, having the captive give over more and more control in writing.

And the sixteenth and final technique is to incorporate new behavior goals. Dr. Hatcher pointed out: "It's enormously time-consuming to carry out a successful coercion. It takes a lot of time, a lot of thought, a lot of energy, and people have difficulty doing that over a period of time. They have to attend to other processes of life, and I'm speaking of the captor. So, you need to establish some type of pattern where you won't have to be constantly physically monitoring this person." Some ways to do that are to allow the captive to tend to personal hygiene, allow clothes, some privacy. And, Hatcher explained, it's important to permit the captive some degree of freedom, without the captor's constant presence, and then suddenly appear, giving the captive a feeling the captor is omnipresent.

Dr. Hatcher added, "There are many historical examples where slaves not only outnumbered their masters in terms of manpower but also had the opportunity to attempt an escape, and yet that's done in only a very small percentage of cases."

Further, the psychologist said, it's common that captives once free, express the idea "that they want to let God or someone else take charge of retribution or punishment. . . ." Additionally, Hatcher said, victims are often reluctant to press charges because criminal proceedings would force them to relive the experience.

Cameron Hooker utilized all 16 of these techniques in his enslavement of Colleen Stan. He was well-educated in coercion by a variety of articles in S & M (sadism and masochism) and B & D literature. Colleen's experience was extraordinarily traumatic. Her extreme fear for the safety of her family, as much as for her own welfare, and her genuine belief of the outlandish stories about the Company accounted for Colleen's willingness to stay with the Hookers despite the opportunities for escape that later arose. She had been totally dependent on Cameron for her very existence. Her guiding principle was that if she could please him, perhaps she could survive.

PATRICIA HEARST

The general public is not very familiar with the case of Colleen Stan or the Stockholm bank siege. However, the name Patricia Hearst is quite widely known. Her experience remains both controversial and still difficult for many to understand.

Patricia is the daughter of wealthy newspaper publisher and media magnate W. Randolph Hearst, Jr. She was living with her boyfriend Steven Weed in Berkeley, California, when she was kidnapped at gunpoint from their apartment on February 4, 1974, by two men and a woman. Her life was to be forever changed. Like Colleen, Patricia eventually received a new name—Tania.

The kidnapping was the work of a very small revolutionary group, the Symbionese Liberation Army (SLA). The SLA had declared war on the United States. Their victim was not chosen at random. She symbolized the oppressive, fascistic corporate enemies of the people. Patricia Hearst was a "prisoner of war." Her three captors took her to an apartment in nearby Daly City and kept her in a padded closet about 6 feet long and 2 feet wide. Other than using the bathroom, she spent the first two weeks of her captivity in that small space. She was subjected to continuous loud soul music, verbal abuse, and, eventually, sexual abuse and rape. The SLA retained physical control over Patricia Hearst until *she* was arrested in late 1975.

The SLA, let by General Field Marshal Cinque Mtume (originally Donald DeFreeze), practiced coercive persuasion (brainwashing) with uncommon expertise. Ms. Hearst, in her definitive book on her experiences, described the operating factors of her captivity:

> Cinque's interrogations, the threats, the metallic clicking of the rifles when I thought they were going to kill me, the sex forced upon me in the closet, the offer to join them or die, the bank robbery, the criticism/self-criticism meetings, the weapons, the combat drills, the political indoctrination, my fears, my desire not to anger them, and my subsequent inability to escape or even to telephone anyone for help.

During her political retraining, Patricia Hearst was christened with the new name "Tania," after the revolutionary Tania Burke who had fought and died alongside Che Guevara in the Bolivian jungle. "Tania" was given weapons training and indoctrinated with radical ideology and a hatred of the police ("pigs"). The new "freedom fighter" issued communiqués to the media announcing that she had joined the SLA.

Cinque planned a bank robbery and Tania was included. On April 15, 1974, the Hibernia Bank branch in the Sunset District of San Francisco was robbed and one man was shot. More than 400 photographs of the robbery were eventually available. Tania/Patricia was easily identifiable. She was armed, but the carbine she carried was not operable.

On May 16, 1974, Tania participated in a second crime, the robbery of a sporting goods store in Los Angeles. She served as a backup and, as instructed, fired her submachine gun in the air to provide cover for the others' escape.

It was a year and a half before Tania/Patricia was arrested by the FBI for the Hibernia Bank robbery. Patricia Hearst was no longer held by the SLA. She now became a prisoner of the government, just as Cinque had predicted. He also had advised her, if arrested, to refuse to sign anything. Indeed, when the police asked her to sign a "Waiver of Rights" form, she refused. When being booked into the jail in San Mateo, the clerk routinely asked for the prisoner's occupation. Patricia's reply was "urban guerrilla."

Obviously, the law enforcement authorities were not there to rescue Patricia Hearst. They had been vigorously trying to find her, but only to arrest her. These events were happening just as Tania had been taught by her captors. She fully expected to be tortured and perhaps killed by the police. Her identification with her captors was complete. She was displaying the Stockholm syndrome in the extreme, before it was very clearly understood or anticipated by law enforcers.

In her book, Patricia reflected:

> My sisters and I had been brought up to believe that we were responsible for what we did and could not blame our transgressions on something being wrong inside our heads. I had joined the SLA because if I didn't they would have killed me. And I remained with them because I truly believed that the FBI would kill me if they could, and if not, the SLA would. In my mind now, I was a "bad girl" for doing all that and now would have to be punished.

The wealthy Hearst family was able to retain the most expensive counsel (F. Lee Bailey and his legal team) and the best psychiatric consultants, including Dr. Louis J. West, Chairman of the Department of Psychiatry at UCLA. Dr. West likened Patricia's experiences to those of prisoners of war. He diagnosed her with "traumatic neurosis with dissociative features," noting that she had been "subjected to powerfully effective coercive manipulation by her captors."

Another distinguished consultant, Dr. Martin Orne of the University of Pennsylvania, interviewed and evaluated Patricia. Orne concluded:

> Miss Hearst, you really shouldn't feel embarrassed. Stronger men than you have cracked and cooperated with the enemy under less torturous conditions. The only thing surprising about all this is that you are here with us today. You suffered severe sensory deprivation being tied up and blindfolded in that closet for so long. Other people subjected to such sensory deprivation would have given up the will to live. They just curl up and die, deprived of their senses for so long. You survived and that is remarkable in itself. You are a survivor.

Despite her famous and flamboyant lawyer and the prestigious psychiatric testimony, Patricia Hearst (Tania) was convicted on March 11, 1976.

OTHER EXAMPLES OF THE STOCKHOLM SYNDROME

On September 10, 1976, TWA flight 355 from New York to Tucson was hijacked and eventually landed in Paris. The entire episode lasted for 25 hours before the hostage takers surrendered. One of the victims' later description reveals the very clear presence of the Stockholm syndrome:

> After it was over and we were safe I recognized that they had put me through hell and had caused my parents and fiance a great deal of trauma. Yet, I was alive. I was alive because they had let me live. You know only a few people, if any, who hold your life in their hands and then give it back to you. After it was over, and we were safe and they were in handcuffs, I walked over to them and kissed each one and said, "Thank you for giving me my life back." I know how foolish it sounds, but that is how I felt.

A train from Groningen to Amsterdam was boarded and hijacked by seven gunmen on December 2, 1975, near the town of Beilen, Holland. The terrorists, members of the Free South Moluccan Youth Movement, sought publicity for policy changes regarding Moluccan independence and the release of certain political prisoners from Dutch and Indonesian jails. Originally 72 passengers were taken hostage, but over time the number was reduced to 23. The train engineer had been shot, and two hostages eventually were executed. The incident dragged on for 13 days.

One of the hostages who had been chosen for execution, newspaper editor Gerard Vaders, was spared at the last minute. Interestingly, at that time his final requests to pass messages to his family and arrange for their future care allowed the terrorists to see him as a unique and special human being, which led directly to his life being saved by those who were ready to murder him.

Mr. Vaders's later recollections illustrate two prominent features of the Stockholm syndrome, his anger at the establishment authorities and his sympathy with the criminals:

> There was a growing sense that the authorities were mishandling the situation. They sent us food, but no utensils. The mayor of Beilen made a stupid announcement. And you had to fight a certain feeling

of compassion for the Moluccans. I know this is not natural, but in some way they come over human. They gave us cigarettes. They gave us blankets. But we also realized that they were killers. You try to suppress that in your consciousness. And I knew I was suppressing that. I also knew that they were victims, too. In the long run they would be as much victims as we. Even more. You saw their morale crumbling. You experienced the disintegration of their personalities. The growing of despair. Things dripping through their fingers. You couldn't help but feel a certain pity.

David Jacobsen was kidnapped in Beirut, Lebanon, on May 28, 1985, and held for 532 days. He described the actions of Wadgid Duomoni, a Syrian-born Lebanese resident who also had been captured. When Duomoni was released after one month and driven home, he invited his captors in for tea, and they accepted. This scenario "boggled the minds" of Jacobsen and fellow hostage Terry Anderson.

WHEN THE STOCKHOLM SYNDROME DID NOT DEVELOP

David Jacobsen is adamant that he and his colleagues did not feel sympathy for their captors in Lebanon. The subtitle of his book is *My Nightmare in Beirut*. He writes:

> Unequivocally, I can say that none of the people taken in Beirut, whom I know, ever suffered the Stockholm syndrome. I loathe those who took me prisoner. For all the gentle words from the Hajj and the kindly gestures of the guards, we knew they were the enemy, ready to kill us without hesitation if it suited their purposes. I would be delighted to throw away the keys to their cells if they were ever convicted of the crimes against us. . . . I refuse to dignify them as "political extremists" or "religious zealots." I regard them as a gang of thugs who have committed a series of brutal crimes.

Yet Jacobsen's own account suggests that at least one aspect of the Stockholm syndrome did occur—the hostage takers developed positive concerns for their hostages. Upon release they kissed him on his cheeks in traditional Arab fashion. "They begged my forgiveness for what they had done," Jacobsen wrote. "They assured me the kidnapping and my long captivity was not aimed at me personally. It was only a job and they always sought to be kind and protective."

Fellow hostage Terry Anderson also claims to have felt no trace of the Stockholm syndrome. Anderson was the hostage held longest in Beirut (from March 16, 1985, until December 4, 1991). Despite his very long captivity, though, Anderson describes himself now as "not bitter or angry." He says, mildly, that he "did not particularly like" his captors and that "they were not necessarily evil men, but they certainly were doing evil things." We might have expected a somewhat stronger condemnation.

The phenomenon of the Stockholm syndrome is so strong that it even appeared among FBI agents who were merely *simulating* being held hostage, according to Robert Ressler, who was in charge of the FBI's hostage negotiation training. Again, it developed in some, but not all, of the men during the exercises.

PSYCHOANALYTIC THEORY

The psychoanalytic explanation for the Stockholm syndrome involves three major components:

1. The survival value of "identification with the aggressor," which serves to protect the ego (self). That is, the hostage identifies with the captor much like a child identifies with the same-sexed parent. During the Oedipal period there is a rivalry for the love of the opposite-sexed parent, and the same-sexed parent presents an aggressive threat. The child's identification with the powerful parent produces safety and security. The threat in a hostage situation presumably resembles the fears of castration in the Oedipal dilemma.
2. The reinstatement of the extreme dependency of childhood, that is, a kind of psychological infantilism.
3. The roles of the defense mechanisms of rationalization, guilt reduction, and "identification in reverse."

Having been nice to their captors in an effort to survive, psychologically the hostages must give a reason for their own behavior. So they rationalize that the captors are not so bad and may just be misunderstood. Having cooperated and sympathized with their takers and possibly lied to the police, the hostages tend to feel great guilt. These two mechanisms allow the captive to identify with the captor. The third allows the captors to develop fondness for the captives, perhaps out of gratitude for the hostages' cooperation and support. Hostage takers are thought to have an unconscious craving to be loved and respected.

As an FBI authority on the syndrome, Thomas Strentz suggests that it does not even require positive acts by the captors toward the hostages. The mere absence of negative experiences can be enough to promote it. Even if injured, some victims can readily rationalize the injuries as accidental, or somehow necessary, or even the result of some failure of their own.

Psychologists Dee Graham, Edna Rawlings, and Nelly Rimini have pointed out six similarities between hostages and battered women within the context of the Stockholm syndrome. For example: (1) the victimizers in both cases are usually male; (2) the strategies used by the victimizers are parallel: isolating the victims both physically and psychologically, creating feelings of helplessness and total dependency, reinforcing their control with threats of and actual violence, and dominating via sexual abuse; (3) women and hostages are symbolic targets of their entire group, for instance, all women or all members of a particular political or religious group; (4) it is necessary to adopt submissive strategies in order to please the dominant power, and to use defense mechanisms such as denial, rationalization, and self-blaming to help their own survival; (5) both battered women and hostages develop counterproductive responses, such as denial of their own terror and anger, seeing the victimizers as all-powerful, and exhibiting high anxiety and physical stress reactions; and (6) in both instances a successful outcome is defined simply as survival. They conclude that the abusive context of many marriages contributes to the development of the Stockholm Syndrome in many battered women.

BEHAVIORAL THEORY

From a behavioral perspective, it is clear that hostage takers control the most powerful reinforcers for the hostages: food, air, drink, and their continued survival. These are biological reinforcers and are, therefore, of primary importance. Hostages will engage in any behaviors that will bring forth these reinforcers. Typically, such behaviors include cooperation, subservience, praise, sympathy, and other forms of compliance with what is perceived to be the wishes of the captors.

The behavioral perspective also concurs with the theory that once certain behaviors are practiced and become established (for example, positive actions toward the hostage takers), the corresponding positive attitudes and emotions will follow. Learning by association is a major avenue for new, and perhaps otherwise unpredictable, views to be acquired.

Why would hostages seem to feel affection for the criminals or batterers holding them captive? The behavioral view does not rely on the concept of the "unconscious" to explain the phenomenon. Rather, it is because their captors hold and control the reinforcers. Those reinforcers are the keys to survival, a very powerful reward indeed.

Long before the 1973 siege in Stockholm, Machiavelli was apparently aware of the psychological factors at play in such a situation, when he noted in 1513: "Men, when they receive good from whence they expect evil, feel the more indebted to their benefactor."

Suggested Further Readings

Echols, M. (1991). *I Know My First Name Is Steven.* New York: Windsor Publishing.

Hearst, P. C., & Moscow, A. (1982) *Every Secret Thing.* Garden City, NY: Doubleday & Company.

Jacobsen, D., & Astor, G. (1991). *Hostage: My Nightmare in Beirut.* New York: Donald I. Fine, Inc.

Barry, K. (1979). *Female Sexual Slavery.* Englewood Cliffs, NJ: Prentice-Hall.

McGuire, C., & Norton, C. (1988). *Perfect Victim.* New York: Dell Publishing.

CHAPTER 6

Autoerotic Asphyxia
Breathless Sex

Masturbation *can* kill! We, as an enlightened society, are finally getting away from the old horror stories about the dangers of masturbation: blindness, acne, insanity, nervousness, depraved criminality, and palmar hair. Modern and liberal mental health authorities now assure us that masturbation not only won't hurt us, but in some cases of sex therapy might even be therapeutic. Well, not so fast . . .

One form of autoeroticism is indeed so dangerous that an estimated 1,000 or more people die from it each year in the United States alone. Sexual asphyxia is the practice of self-induced oxygen deprivation for purposes of heightening the experience of orgasm.

Although such deaths have been recorded in individuals as young as 9 and as old as 77 years, more than one-third of such cases involve male teenagers. The well-known character actor Albert Dekker, who played Dr. Cyclops in horror movies, died this way, according to Dr. Thomas Noguchi, Hollywood's "coroner to the stars."

The "in" people within the sexual underground use various terms to describe the practice: "huffing," "scarfing," "fantasy," "ecstasy," "flying to the moon," and "headrushing."

Sexual asphyxia is becoming more widely known in general society as well. P. D. James's novel *An Unsuitable Job for a Woman* involved a *faked* case of autoerotic asphyxia in an effort to disguise a murder. Miami medical examiners R. K. Wright and Joseph Davis reported a real case, in which a murder by hanging was disguised as an accidental sexual asphyxia.

The medical and psychological authorities have their own technical vocabulary to refer to the same phenomenon: autoerotic asphyxia, asphyxiophilia, autoasphyxiphilia, hypoxophilia, cordophilia, ligottism, autostrangulation, masochistic asphyxia, occlusion bondage, eroticized repetitive hanging, passive sexual algolagnia, and Kotzwaraism. All of these terms refer to the same practice of deliberately arranging for oxygen restriction at the moment of orgasm to maximize the sexual pleasure. It is indeed risky, because accidents do happen and people die, because they almost always are alone.

One exception was the unfortunate Franz Kotzwara, reputed to be the best double bass player in Europe in the late 1700s. Kotzwara died from autoerotic asphyxia in the company of a London prostitute by the name of Susannah Hill. He left his own name as a legacy, more associated with a bizarre sexual appetite than as the talented composer of the sonata "Battle of Prague."

On September 2, 1791, Kotzwara visited Ms. Hill, showed her his scars from past sessions of abuse for pleasure, and respectfully requested that she cut off his penis for a guinea. She declined. No doubt she was concerned about violating the law by practicing surgery without a license. He then gave her money to go off to buy some food, liquor, and a rope. Upon her return he formed a noose with the rope and proceeded to hang himself, after instructing Ms. Hill to cut him down in precisely five minutes. From all accounts, she did as ordered. Unfortunately, despite the best efforts of the local physician, who was promptly summoned and who in the medical wisdom of the time, bled the patient, Kotzwara could not be revived. Five minutes is really too long to be hanged, even for sexual pleasure. That five minutes can stretch into eternity.

Susannah Hill was tried for murder and acquitted. Because of the "danger to public morality," all the official court records were ordered by the judge to be destroyed. Nevertheless, the practice of deliberate asphyxia by a variety of means for the purpose of the ultimate sexual pleasure continues to this day.

Historians have suggested that Kotzwara probably was following the advice in the pamphlet *Modern Propensities,* written by one Martin Van-butchell, an eccentric medical quack of the period. Interestingly, the year of Kotzwara's death (1791) was also the year that the Marquis de Sade published *Justine,* in which Therese helps Roland to achieve ecstatic and indescribable pleasure by hanging him briefly.

Erotic hangings have appeared in a number of literary works including *Ulysses, Naked Lunch,* and *Cities of the Red Night.* Motion pictures, too, have depicted erotic hangings, such as in *The Ruling Class* and the Japanese film *In the Realm of the Senses.* Victorian London even featured a social interest group known as the Hanged Men's Club. Then and now certain houses of prostitution and free-agent call girls specialize in assisting clients in practices of asphyxiation. Anthropologists point out that the joys of temporary strangling can be traced to ancient Mayan tribes, the old Celts, the Shoshone-Bannock Indians, and Eskimo children's games. Clearly, the association between sexual excitement and the cessation of breathing has a long, and perhaps checkered, history.

Nevertheless, the practice is a secretive one. Families and friends of victims are usually shocked to learn that the deceased engaged in such activities. Their shock typically turns to embarrassment, and they may begin efforts to cover up critical evidence before the authorities arrive. Consequently, many autoerotic deaths are wrongly reported as suicides rather than accidental deaths.

If a child's sex education class and parent's brief review of the "birds and the bees" do not mention autoerotic asphyxia, how does one learn of it and how to do it? Several other sources exist. Popular films and literature, as mentioned earlier, constitute one source, at least for the more intellectual person. Of course, it is described in the technical medical and forensic literature as well. Occasionally the subject may appear in newspapers and magazines and on TV talk shows, which raises an interesting ethical and legal dilemma.

How do responsible media, including this book, present accurate information about a dangerous practice without subtly encouraging someone to try that adventurous but risky behavior? On May 11, 1988, the "Oprah Winfrey Show" was devoted to the topic of autoerotic asphyxia. The host gave several clear warnings that the program was not suitable for children. One of Oprah's guests, Diane Herceg, had lost her teenage son, Troy, to the practice. Mrs. Herceg had sued *Hustler* magazine, which had published an article called "Orgasm of Death." The article also included warnings about the dangers. However, 14-year-old Troy died with that magazine article lying at his feet. Was the magazine legally responsible? After an appeal to the Supreme Court, the final ruling just said no.

Yet what about Oprah's program itself? Dr. Park Dietz, a widely recognized expert on autoerotic asphyxia, had vigorous discussions with the program's producers prior to that taping and refused to appear on the show because of the risk of enticing one or more viewers to try it. Even with warnings, and perhaps because of such warnings, impressionable people of all ages might be inspired to imitate this novel approach to sexual excitement. Sure enough, at least two deaths were documented by Dr. Dietz as a direct result of Oprah's program, those of an 11-year-old boy and a 38-year-old man.

In the latter case the assistant and chief medical examiners of Ventura County, California, Drs. Ronald O'Halloran and Warren Lovell interviewed the victim's father, who had found his son and had begun resuscitation, albeit unsuccessfully. The son had indicated he was going to watch the "Oprah" program that day, the television was still playing on that same channel, and he was found shortly after the end of the broadcast.

Thus, at least two autoerotic deaths are known to have immediately followed that "Oprah" broadcast, as educationally well-intentioned as it may have been. What we do not know, though, is how many lives may have been *saved* by that very same show, which repeatedly warned of the dangers of a variety of autoerotic practices.

Even the "Playboy Advisor" (Sept. 1976), in response to a query, once advised, "There are better ways to go—or come. . . . This form of self-abuse has been around for years, which is more than we can say for some of the people who have tried it."

Most people probably learn of autoeroticism by word of mouth. Peers pass on methods of "secret delights," such as the sexual pleasures of interrupted breathing or the action of chemical enhancers such as amyl nitrite ("poppers"). Adolescents may accidentally come to associate pleasure with short-term asphyxia, such as feeling giddy from inhaling model airplane glue or the gas from the whipped cream can.

Folklore about the effects of execution by hanging have contributed to the public's beliefs about the erotic potential of strangulation. One example is that when a man is hanged, he obtains an erection. It then becomes easy to make the connection that there is indeed some sexual pleasure at the time. Even though an *apparent* erection sometimes may occur, there are medical explanations other than sexual arousal. For example, the tumescence may be due to generalized settling of the blood, gravitation, or possibly even sudden rigor mortis. An early twentieth-century sexologist, Iwan Bloch, added to the misconception by describing the "voluptuous sensations" associated with hanging. Thus, the hedonists' delusion evolved: if one could survive a hanging by providing for an escape or quick termination, imagine how much pleasure one would feel. (Kotzwara, of course, miscalculated.)

The French are noted for their sexual sophistication and liberal attitudes. It is relevant that the French phrase for orgasm, *le petit mort,* translates literally as "the little death." With every male orgasmic emission, he dies a little. This concept is not far removed from the bizarre semen-loss syndromes discussed in Chapter 9.

AUTOEROTICISM INJURIES

Death is, of course, the most extreme by-product of autoerotic activities. In addition, many serious injuries have resulted from sexual self-stimulation.

Sex educators Drs. Joan Atwood and John Gagnon in 1987 described the masturbatory behavior of 1,177 college students. Their data showed that 93% of the men and 48% of the women had masturbated to orgasm at some point in their lives. Given that these numbers are a little dated and represent self-reports, they probably are underestimates. The gender difference may be a more reliable finding.

Men and women have gone to extraordinary lengths in pursuit of more and more pleasure. Often they will insert a variety of products and foods into their bodies, which eventually come to the attention of surgeons for removal. Contrary to their original intent, the stimulation may not be pleasurable but often excruciatingly painful. For some men the injury, the delay in obtaining medical attention, and the subsequent surgery, have resulted in the partial or even total loss of the penis.

In one case a man inserted dry spaghetti into his penis, producing what the urologists refer to as "endourethral stimulation." When the spaghetti broke and was retained, serious physical effects occurred. A surprising number of penis injuries occur as a result of establishing too close a relationship with vacuum cleaners and electric brooms. The penis itself can also be strangled by hair, rubber bands, string, or encircling metal rings. In time, gangrene can develop and the tissue will drop off permanently. Not a pretty sight!

Both men and women have inserted items into their rectums, and women into their vaginas, which must be retrieved later by the surgeon. The most common surgical finds have been light bulbs, bottles, hairbrush handles, electric vibrators, cucumbers, carrots, bananas, and sausages.

B. R. Burg, writing in the very serious medical publication *Journal of the Royal Society of Health,* (Vol. 107, p. 60–61) in 1987, warned, "The trapped vibrators present particular hazards. After they have been inserted past the point of recovery, they usually cannot be shut off. It is often hours before the injured summon sufficient will to go to the hospital, and in that time the constant vibration can cause considerable discomfort or pain, particularly if the vibrator has been equipped with long-lasting alkaline power cells rather than ordinary batteries." They just keep going and going. Rarely do we hear such a good argument for buying the less expensive product.

Of course, the greatest risk to a person is when masturbation is accompanied by some form of oxygen deprivation, as in short-term hanging. The number of possible *negative* consequences is staggering, and these are usually irreversible: brain damage, memory loss, disorientation, epileptic seizures, dementia, delirium, motoric restlessness, sexual hyperexcitability, muscle spasms, loss of reflexes, learning deficits, difficulty in swallowing, abnormal vocal utterances, "open eye coma," and death itself. *We do not recommend asphyxia for pleasure.*

METHODS OF AUTOEROTIC ASPHYXIA

Hanging is far and away the most popular method of seeking extra sexual excitement via oxygen deprivation. Other techniques that alert medical examiners have uncovered include suffocation through the use of large plastic bags, gas masks, or rubber suits, chest compression, strangulation, wrapping in multiple blankets, sniffing gases in plastic bags, excess of nitrous oxide gas (formerly a common dental anesthesia), abdominal ropes, electrocution, and drowning.

These deaths are nearly always accidents. There are very few cases of autoerotic suicide in which it is clear that the deceased did intend to die in the throes of autoerotic asphyxial ecstasy. Suicidal intentions can be inferred from a note left behind or by the obvious absence of an escape mechanism by a person known to be knowledgeable in safety practices.

Accidents happen when, somehow, the apparatus fails or the person miscalculates how long consciousness will remain. For example, sometimes the key to a lock is dropped or a pulley jams, or an electrical short is the immediate cause. Most commonly, loss of consciousness occurs sooner than expected, and the slumping over produces the fatal asphyxia by compression of the neck. Obviously, an unconscious person cannot carry out any escape plan.

An unusual case worthy of special mention was described by Medical Examiner Joseph Rupp of Corpus Christi, Texas, as "The Love Bug." A 40-year-old airline pilot on his day off was fatally strangled by his automobile (a Volkswagen Bug) during an autoerotic episode. He had removed his clothes and put on a harness of link chain. The chain was wrapped around his neck and waist, much like a parachute harness. One end was attached to the car's rear bumper. He had put the car in low gear (automatic transmission) with the steering wheel fixed in a counterclockwise position. He then jogged or was dragged alongside the slowly moving car. It appeared that when he attempted to stop the car, he forgot to detach himself from the chain. The car ran over the chain, and it accidentally wound around the rear axle, pinning him fatally to the rear left fender. Death was by asphyxiation due to pilot error.

Sometimes asphyxia is part of having sex with another person, male or female. The presence of someone else can be an added safety feature during "rough sex." Medical Examiner Russell Henry of Richmond, Virginia, reminds us, in what may reveal his own cultural stereotyping, "It is alleged that it is frequent practice among some Orientals for the sexual partners to mutually grasp each other's throat in a strangling gesture, and it is said that fatalities not infrequently result from this practice." Even with a cooperative friend available, there can be no

100% guarantee of safety. Recall the case of the late Franz Kotzwara, whose instructions were apparently quite carefully followed by Susannah Hill.

WHO ARE THE AUTOEROTIC FATALITIES?

The most common victim of autoerotic practices is an adolescent or young adult male. The experts estimate that only 5% to 7% of such deaths occur in females. The characteristics of the scene in female cases (secrecy, protective padding to the neck, some malfunction of the asphyxial apparatus, and obvious signs of masturbatory activities) are all similar to those in male cases. FBI Special Agent F. A. Sass speculates about "masochistic overtones" in one case because the woman, before dying, had attached clothespins to her nipples.

Exact statistics are difficult to obtain, because until very recently many coroners and medical examiners erroneously classified these deaths as suicides. Families would also pressure the authorities to suppress the true circumstances of such deaths because of their own embarrassment and shame.

Clearly, the problem is substantial. The FBI's estimates suggest that 1,000 to 2,000 such deaths occur annually in the United States. The Metropolitan Life Insurance Company loses 250 policyholders each year to autoeroticism. Psychiatrists William Sheehan and Barry Garfinkel studied medical examiners' reports of adolescent suicides in two Minnesota counties over a 10-year period. They concluded that 31% of all adolescent hanging deaths resulted from autoerotic asphyxia.

Autoerotic victims are predominantly heterosexual, well educated, and appear strikingly "normal" to friends and family. Their autoerotic masturbatory activities were previously unknown to others and, almost by definition, occurred in secret behind locked doors or in remote locations. Some investigators suspect that older practitioners less often die in the process because their maturity helps ensure a greater caution and attention to safety devices. Despite the predominantly heterosexual orientation of the victims, one feature of the death scene suggests some psychological disturbance, or at least deviant preferences, in the deceased. For example, in one-quarter to one-third of cases there is evidence of partial or complete cross-dressing.

THE AUTOEROTIC DEATH SCENE

Certain characteristic features can be observed at the scene where the autoerotic victim is found. (We use the masculine pronoun unless otherwise indicated, because so many of the victims are male.) These descriptors allow for the determination that the death was due to accident, not suicide. Of course, not all features are present in all cases, but the following are the most common elements.

The scene itself is either a very remote area, such as outdoors in the woods, or a place where privacy can be ensured. Typically, the indoor scene is a hotel room or locked bedroom, bathroom, basement, or attic. Ironically, it is the secrecy that enhances the risk. A partner, if present, can react to emergencies.

Generally, there is no suicide note, which is no surprise, since the victim dies trying to extend his pleasures, not end them. He is either totally or partially naked, in contrast to most suicides, who remain clothed. Usually, his genitals are exposed, which indicates masturbation. Evidence of ejaculation, such as semen stains, is often present. Sometimes a condom or a handkerchief is available to collect semen. If there are any clothes on the body, they frequently are distinctive women's items such as bras, panties, girdles, pantyhose, and high heels.

The evidence of bondage can be extensive, but is sometimes limited to the rope or belt used for the hanging. The structure and operation of the asphyxial apparatus is crucial for understanding the victim's intent and what may have gone wrong. Police investigators must distinguish the autoerotic death from suicide and homicide. When the victim's hands are bound behind his back, observing the exact formation of the knot is vital to understand whether he indeed could have tied it himself.

A critical sign is the use of a towel or scarf, which may be wrapped around the rope to protect the victim from telltale burns or damage to the neck that could reveal the practice to others. Clearly, the protective padding suggests that he had planned to live and did not want to provoke questions or concern by friends.

In some cases the scene yields evidence that hanging episodes have been carried out a number of times previously. There may even be grooves worn on a door or a rafter. The apparatus may have been permanently installed there. Psychiatrist Harvey Resnik refers to the syndrome as "erotized repetitive hangings." For many novices, though, the erotized hanging does not get repeated.

The eroticism theme is obvious, because frequently soft- or hard-core pornography is present and in view for purposes of sexual stimulation. As noted previously, in some cases the visible magazine article is on the topic of autoeroticism. The photos, women's wigs and underwear, rectal inserts, and bondage items are all known as "fantasy props" to facilitate masturbation.

Surprisingly, it is rare for the body to be found fully suspended. The victim is usually resting at least partly on the floor or ground. The accident may have been due to some slippage, producing errors in judgment and an early loss of consciousness, which then became permanent.

Finally, it is common for the body to be displayed in front of mirrors, positioned so that the individual could easily view his genitalia and the cross-dressing garments. One victim, a university professor, took a series of Polaroid photos that documented the stages of his cross-dressing, masturbation, and, ultimately, fatal hanging, which happened accidentally. In another case the entire episode, including the man's death, was recorded on videotape.

THE AUTOEROTIC PRACTITIONER'S PERSPECTIVE

Most of what we know about autoerotic asphyxia has been deduced from postmortem physical examinations of the bodies and the settings where death occurred. Very few reports exist describing the views and motives of living practitioners of the various forms of autoerotic stimulation.

One exception is the case of a 15½-year-old male seen by San Diego pediatrician Myron Faber. The patient had been instructed in the technique of self-hanging during masturbation by a cousin who demonstrated the practice. They then hanged together. The patient had been regularly hanging himself for one-half to two minutes for 3 years before coming to the clinic. At first he hanged himself every other week, but the frequency had built up to two to four times a week.

An even greater shock is that both parents seemed to be aware of their son's behavior but did nothing to intervene, nor did they discuss it. We might refer to these parents as "terminally permissive." The mother even listened at her son's door and would dutifully launder any female clothing that he soiled during the act. The father actually had repaired a broken clothes bar, which his son had been using for hanging, without inquiring how the break occurred.

Dr. Faber, as the therapist, did inquire why his patient practiced self-hanging and reported his reasons: "(1) He wants to get his mother angry; (2) it relieves his depression, at least for a short while; (3) it makes him feel good; and (4) he wants to get his family 'riled up' so that he can do more with his dad and get the family working together on things."

Based on letters and diaries left behind, it seems that many practitioners of autoerotic asphyxia are indeed aware of the dangers of their activities. The need for elaborate escape mechanisms is itself a tribute to the risks involved. Those who have died in this manner include doctors and nurses and even a police officer who had previously attended one of the FBI's seminars on the topic.

Drs. Cassie Wesselius and Ralph Bally describe a 24-year-old U.S. Marine who had been practicing autoerotic hanging for 10 years. He sought professional help because he feared that he had caused himself permanent damage, which was affecting his ability to walk. The precipitating event was a period of six sessions of cutting off his oxygen with a T-shirt while masturbating in bed. After ejaculation, he felt very weak and his legs were shaky. He was a frequent and vigorous masturbator. While in the Marines, the frequency of his self-asphyxiation had declined from two to three times a day, because he no longer had as much privacy or access to female clothing.

Perhaps the most detailed case of an autoerotic asphyxial practitioner ever described was presented by the renowned sexologist Dr. John Money and his colleagues at Johns Hopkins University in their 1991 book *The Breathless Orgasm*. Their very verbal patient, Nelson Cooper, describes his fantasies, his behavior, his difficulty in obtaining help, and his view that this syndrome is an "addiction":

I am an asphyxiophiliac. I started to strangle myself when I was sixteen. I didn't hang myself, however; I choked! I strangled myself in front of an angled mirror, using a nylon pantyhose. I wore a tight pair of men's 100-percent-nylon, see-through bikini underwear and pretended the whole time that a homosexual killer was throttling me. I struggled like mad in front of a mirror which was aimed at my buttocks and legs. After I choked to the point where my dizziness got too much for me, I broke off the pantyhose, fell to the floor as if I were dead, and immediately masturbated until I climaxed in a super, great orgasm. Then, and only then, was I relieved and the curse or spell was lifted for the time being. I always promised to myself that I would never do it again. But when it struck, there was no stopping it.

I could tell when I was losing control: I felt butterflies in my stomach; I smelled something burning far away; there was a pressure on my temples; and a feeling of sexual excitement began to build. These feelings got stronger and stronger until my hands began to shake, I broke out in a cold sweat, and my head was spinning. Finally, I'd lose control and would dress up and plan my own death. The excitement that I felt in my brain was similar to the feeling of speeding downhill on a roller coaster.

This addiction was impossible to fight. I fought it for seven years. At times I thought I'd won. But somehow I lost the battle every time. I was not rational when doing this sexual act. I could think of nothing but the struggle and the strangling. Of course, I knew it was not normal from the very beginning. I would be the first to admit that it was both abnormal and dangerous. I gave signals to my high school counselors, even telling one that I masturbated as much as twelve times a day. She just said that it was okay to unwind.

By the time I was twenty, I was in counseling therapy. But there was no therapy for my condition. I told the counselor with great fear that I was having terrible fantasies of stranglings and drownings when I masturbated. He just sat back and calmly said that as long as they remained fantasies, they were normal. I thought to myself, 'That's rotten advice,' but I was afraid to tell him this because I knew I needed help and I didn't know where else to get it. Well, I didn't believe my fantasies were normal, but I couldn't stop. When I told him that I was strangling myself for a sexual thrill of some kind, he didn't believe me. He thought I was doing it for attention.

At twenty-one, the next stage, I was getting worse and worse. I got the same attacks every month and they would last for several days in a row before I could not do it any more—until the next month. My neck had so many burns it looked like I had a ring around it. I tried throwing all of my ritual materials away—the bikinis and the pantyhose. But when I got another attack, I would find myself roaming the underwear sections of department stores to buy new pantyhose and bikinis. Then I would do it again in front of the mirror.

I called hotlines for mental health but was accused of abusing the lines by teasing and harassing the nurses with weird, bizarre stories about what I was doing.

Mr. Cooper is very much interested in educating mental health professionals about his bizarre autoerotic practices and fantasies. In order to help others, he wrote an extraordinary letter to a professional association of sex therapists and educators. His own words provide the best testimony of the subjective experience of one who risks death in exchange for sexual pleasure. This excerpt from his letter also reveals the torment he feels because of the loss of control of his private fantasies and behavior:

Dear Members of the Association,

To be at the mercy of a paraphilia is like being a slave to lust and ecstasy. It commands me. I have no will of my own when my paraphilia takes over. It usually takes over without warning, and once it starts, it must finish all the way to the end of its course. Like a virus taking its course. Like a tornado storm taking its course. Swift like the tornado, destructive in accuracy like the zig zag of the funnel cloud. My temples pound like the thunder putting pressure on them. Then when the oxygen to my brain is cut off, I hear a mass of head noises intensifying like hail falling from the sky and smashing onto a Fiberglas [sic] roof. Tingling sensations of incredible ecstasy tickle through my sex organ. It starts to swell in beautiful hardness through my nylon bikini underwear while the nylon leotard of a beautiful woman tightens, tighter and tighter around my neck, until I cannot make any more of my marvelous choking sounds.

My windpipe is totally closed, and I cannot breathe or scream, but I try because it adds to the fantastic excitement to see my stomach suck in and out with no air coming in. And it's marvelous to see my lungs go up and down trying to suck in air, but nothing comes in. My saliva or the spit in my mouth is building like mad, and I try to swallow it, and it's fascinating to swallow, but the spit doesn't go anywhere. It just bounces back into my mouth, and then I try to force it down, but it still won't go down. Then more spit builds up in my mouth, and the whole time I'm watching my body's reaction to all of this in front of the mirror, while at the same time I'm struggling and strangling and fighting my attacker, who is also homosexual like me, but in the paraphilic fantasy attack only. Then when I cannot take it any more I release the women's leotard and my windpipe opens once again.

Then I fall to the floor, and I masturbate with my fingers on my genitals, and have in mind a beautiful girl getting strangled or drowned to death. Her last choke is at the great point of orgasm, and then the milky white stuff squirts out, and I get great relief, as if a ton of rocks was just lifted off my back. The sticky stuff is all over my chest and some on my one arm. I don't wipe it off. I let it stay there and get hard when it dries. Then I'm exhausted and tired and weak, and I want to sleep, but I don't sleep because then I'm terrified. I say to myself, "Why did I do this? I told myself I would never do it again." I keep telling myself this. I have been telling myself this for the past two years, even though I started over six years ago, but it was not this severe. It grew as time went on, and it gets worse as I get older. I've been saying to myself all this time that I won't do it. I won't do it. But I did anyway.

Lots of times I smell something burning before I go out of control. Then I have some head noises starting, and my fingers tremble a little. Then I start to breathe quicker, and I get butterflies in my stomach. Then the great rush begins. Oh, I was recognizing the warning signs in time, but I had no one to go to. Anyone I did go to, numerous psychiatrists and psychologists, lectured me not to call up the hotlines for mental health, freaking out the nurses and nurses' aides answering the phones. They didn't believe me. . . .

So there you have it, absurd, bizarre, weird, perverted, whatever it's being called by people who don't understand my problem of being at the mercy of a paraphilia. My mind never rests even in my sleep. I dream of women drowning by somebody pulling them under, or I dream of jumping in front of the mirror to strangle myself for my superb pleasure of lust and ecstasy, which runs and is practically ruining my life.

Sincerely,

The Asphyxiophiliac Still Living

No one could have said it better.

PSYCHODYNAMIC THEORIES

Psychoanalytic explanations for autoerotic asphyxial practices rely heavily on concepts such as fear of castration and a desire to punish oneself because of guilt over sexual behavior, particularly masturbation. Child psychiatrist John Edmondson, for example, holds that these self-punishing dynamics are much more relevant than simply the desire to enhance sexual pleasure.

Psychiatrists Willard Shankel and Arthur Carr presented the case of Donald, a 17-year-old transvestite patient, who had been hanging himself, while cross-dressed, since the age of 10 or 11. Their explanation of this behavior was also based on Freudian psychoanalytic concepts: "The transvestite dons women's clothing, hangs himself, terminates the act short of harm, and masturbates. He seems symbolically to be declaiming that a woman has a penis, that he is a woman with a penis, and that the threat of castration is not real and can always be cast off."

Sex educator Edward Saunders of the University of Iowa School of Social Work suggests that the threat of death "may be the principal cause of the behavior." Young adult males often pursue high-risk activities in many areas of their lives. Sexual acting out with others and via masturbation would be consistent with this risk-taking life-style and an assumed aura of invincibility.

BEHAVIORAL THEORIES

Drs. Wesselius and Bally, discussing their Marine patient who had been engaging in autoerotic asphyxia for 10 years, initially proposed a psychodynamic formulation of his case. However, they then concluded with a classic behavioral explanation:

> This behavior . . . could develop in the same manner in which masturbatory activity is learned through discovery, which then becomes strongly reinforced through intense pleasure. Once accomplished, it quickly becomes an habituated behavior. During the time of [the patient's] adolescence his only apparent source of sexual material was a magazine which usually contained subject matter that paired sex and violence. His fantasy reflects the type of material which he read. . . . Once accomplished, the behavior became self-reinforcing. Thus, when feeling anxious, he sought a sexual release which for him included asphyxiation combined with masturbation. In spite of guilt and fear, the pleasure of the activity bids him to repeat it, as sex is one of the strongest reinforcers.

Indeed it is.

The case of the adolescent Donald described earlier by Drs. Shankel and Carr can be understood from a behavioral perspective as well. The development of the young man's attraction for women's clothes was strengthened by his history of masturbating and ejaculating while wearing stolen panties. Ejaculation is a biologically reinforcing event, which was often paired with the cross-dressing. According to behavior theory, the association of two events is a classic method to learn a new behavior.

We know that the presence of one paraphilia (an abnormal sexual interest) in a person, such as practicing autoerotic asphyxia, will increase the probability that the person may exhibit other paraphilias as well. For example, forensic pathologist Lauren Boglioli and colleagues described a multicomponent case of self-asphyxiation in a 27-year-old man as learned from the "psychological autopsy" that augmented their traditional physical autopsy.

Their behavioral reconstruction of his life indicated that he exhibited at least *nine* different paraphilias in addition to transsexualism: *asphyxiophilia* (he was found nude hanging by a leather belt wrapped over a wooden beam; semen was dripping from his penis); *klismaphilia* (he had given himself a champagne enema during the episode); *masochism* (wrist scars indicated previous self-mutilation, and cigarette burns appeared on his nipples); *sadism* (frequent physical abuse of his girlfriend, including kicking her in the abdomen when she announced her pregnancy); *pictophilia* (use of pornographic magazines depicting lesbian activity and female bondage; his wife posed for pictures wearing garter belts and other clothes similar to those he had seen in the magazines); *telephone scatophilia* (phone sex with women who advertised this service); *kleptophilia* (breaking into a neighbor's house to steal women's clothing); *biastophilia* or *rapism* (arrested for randomly assaulting a woman while he was wearing female clothing); *transvestophilia* (as in the previous example; in addition, his body was found hanging while wearing only a wig and high-heeled shoes). He had taken the champagne enema while looking at himself in a mirror and reading an article about sexual homicide. The champagne was considered to be a contributing factor to his death, because alcohol is absorbed into the bloodstream very rapidly via the rectal mucosa. His intoxication clouded his judgment and his ability to avoid the fatal asphyxia. Champagne can still go to your head, even if it enters the body elsewhere.

THERAPIES FOR AUTOEROTIC ASPHYXIA

Therapy for practitioners of autoerotic asphyxia is not an especially well-developed art, because there have been so few customers. Those who survive the practice tend to continue it because of the overall pleasure, while those who by error or accident do not survive are, of course, not candidates for therapy. A few individuals, such as Nelson Cooper, feel that their desires for self-asphyxia are out of control and do seek assistance. Occasionally, a well-informed parent may become aware of a son's interests and masturbatory activities and will encourage him to obtain help. In the case of the pilot who was strangled by his VW, his wife knew of his custom-made chain harness but never inquired about its purpose.

Psychotherapy

Most psychoanalytically oriented therapists would concur that depth therapy can allow the individual to achieve insight into the unconscious conflicts that are being expressed in this bizarre, self-destructive behavior pattern. Presumably, insights achieved in therapy would then translate into more socially acceptable and ego-gratifying expressions of sexuality. Some therapists have used psychoactive medications, such as lithium carbonate or Depo-provera, as adjuncts to their psychotherapy.

Behavior Therapy

The most extensive behavior therapy approach for this problem was the treatment of a 35-year-old married man who had been trying to suffocate himself for sexual pleasure three times a week, as reported by forensic psychiatrist Peter Haydn-Smith and his colleagues at the Bethlem Royal and Maudsley Hospital in London.

Two specific behavior therapy techniques were employed in this case of "masochistic asphyxiation": covert sensitization and the teaching of coping strategies. In covert sensitization the undesired behavior, the deviant fantasy, was linked by instructions from the therapist with one or more unpleasant fantasies, such as being discovered while engaged in the practice or being attacked by wasps. Repeated imagining of this pairing was designed to reduce the deviant fantasy.

The doctors provided the patient with several methods designed to reduce the deviant fantasies. To eliminate his customary opportunity to masturbate, which included acts of bondage and suffocation, after his wife retired to bed, the patient was instructed to retire at the same time as his wife. Second, someone from the nursing staff of the hospital would always be available and prepared to talk with him. Third, he was given a cassette tape to play, on which the doctors and nurses urged him to resist the deviant urges and to phone the staff as needed for more encouragement. Finally, the couple was given sexual skills training and educational sex videotapes as a means to improve their sexual functioning. An impressive follow-up after $2\frac{1}{2}$ years indicated that the fantasies were infrequent and well controlled.

CONCLUSION

How pleasurable can an orgasm be? Is autoerotic asphyxia worth the risk? Most of us would like to live on to experience still more orgasms.

This life-threatening and bizarre behavior is difficult for most of us to understand. A clue comes from journalist Michael Grumley in his description of the delights of bondage: "Danger acts as an aphrodisiac, anonymity as a lubricant."

Suggested Further Readings

Bluglass, R., & Bowden, P. (Eds.). (1990). *Principles and Practice of Forensic Psychiatry.* New York: Churchill Livingstone.

Dietz, P. E., & Hazelwood, R. R. (1982). Atypical autoerotic fatalities. *Medicine and Law, 1,* 307–319.

Hazelwood, R. R., Dietz, P. E., & Burgess, A. W. (1983). *Autoerotic Fatalities.* Lexington, MA: Lexington Books.

Money, J., Wainwright, G., & Hingsburger, D. (1991). *The Breathless Orgasm: A Lovemap Biography of Asphyxiophilia.* Buffalo, NY: Prometheus Books.

Schlesinger, L. & Revitch, E. (Eds.). (1983). *Sexual Dynamics of Antisocial Behavior.* Springfield, IL: Charles C. Thomas.

CHAPTER 7

Capgras and Other Misidentification Delusions
Replaced by an Impostor

Everything is beginning to look strange to me, sort of artificial. Sometimes I get the feeling that everything around me is unreal, like a stage set, and everyone is acting a role. Who can I really trust? I finally got up enough nerve to mention it to my wife and she gave me a really strange look and told me I should see a doctor. It's not really like her. In fact, it's crazy but I'm beginning to wonder more and more if I really know that woman at all. She's been really irritable and nervous lately, not at all like her old self. In fact, I really can't put my finger on it, but there are these little differences that sometimes makes me think she isn't my wife at all. When I compared old pictures from when we were first married with ones we took last year, you could actually see some of these changes. I wonder if comparing fingerprints would prove anything.

The mental process portrayed here describes the typical onset of the Capgras delusion, a rare and colorful psychological condition first reported in detail by the French psychiatrists Capgras and Reboul-Lachaux in 1923. They described a woman tormented by the conviction that imposters or exact doubles had replaced first her husband and then her daughter, in order to steal her inheritance and property. This fixed belief was all the more interesting because it appeared without any other evident mental disorientation or psychological disturbance.

Sir Henry Head, the famed and aptly named British neurologist, described a patient who had sustained a penetrating head wound to the frontal brain during World War I. The patient believed that there were two Boulognes in France, first the city he went through on his way to the battlefield and then the exact replica Boulogne, the one he passed through on his return to England. Sir Henry added that his patient was rational in all other respects, except that he wrote letters to his mother even though he knew she had been dead for many years. Apparently, Head chalked up the letter writing to mere garden variety British eccentricity.

Fascination with the idea of having a double has a long history. The concept appears in many early human societies as the belief that everyone is accompanied through life by two extensions of the personality, a good person and an evil spirit double. The ancient Egyptians called the person's spirit double the *ka*. After a person's death elaborate copies or doubles of furniture, weapons, foodstuffs, and similar goods were placed in and about the burial chamber so that the person would be well supplied in the afterlife. This custom was sometimes carried to extremes, as when favorite pets, chariot horses, and even servants were killed so that their *ka* could accompany the person. An individual's mirror image and shadow were thought to embody the spirit double, and special customs evolved to prevent evil forces from seizing them. An ancient Hebrew burial custom requires that for the obligatory seven days of mourning following a death, all mirrors in the home must be covered, lest the grieving spirit of the living depart. Traditionally, vampires as soulless creatures were believed to have no reflection in a mirror.

As late as the sixteenth century, people believed that the spirit double or soul could leave the body. This explains the common primitive belief that it was dangerous to wake a sleeper. The sleeper's soul, wandering in dreamland, might be unable to return to the body, thus causing illness or death. When witch hysteria reached its peak in the fifteenth and sixteenth centuries, many people believed that witches' doubles floated about poisoning wells, destroying crops, and generally causing great harm. Even when eyewitnesses presented strong evidence that the suspect was elsewhere when some evil deed occurred, the misfortune was still attributed to the suspect's double. Many innocent people were executed on the basis of such bizarre beliefs. Even today, Haitian folklore assumes that the soul can be extracted from the body by witchcraft and used to enslave the owner, who becomes a "zombie."

To be confronted by one's own double was particularly ominous, a sure sign of impending death. The ancient Greek philosopher Aristotle was the first to describe the double in an objective way. He reported that a man he knew was terrified because he could not go out for a walk without encountering his double walking toward him. Queen Elizabeth I of England immediately before her death was terrified to see a pale and shriveled vision of herself stretched out on her death bed. Goethe and the poet Shelley also claimed to have seen their own death images. Empress Catherine the Great of Russia adopted an activist stance. Upon seeing her double floating toward her, she ordered her bodyguards to commence firing immediately. Apparently this did the trick, as she lived on for a number of years.

The evil twin, or sinister double, theme was prominent in nineteenth-century romantic fiction, such as in Oscar Wilde's *Portrait of Dorian Gray* and Robert Louis Stevenson's *Dr. Jekyll and Mr. Hyde.* The poet Heinrich Heine wrote a poem about one Peter Schlemyl who, having sold his shadow to the Devil, was tormented by the suspicion that he had actually sold his soul. The hapless and reflectionless Peter also appears in Offenbach's *Tales of Hoffman.* Maupassant and Dostoevsky not only wrote fictionalized accounts of the double experience, but also admitted to personally experiencing it, as did the great master himself, Sigmund Freud. In Dostoevsky's novel, *The Possessed,* the mad woman, Marya Timofeyevna, has been secretly married to Stravrogin, but in their hometown at a social function he fails to acknowledge her as his wife. When he comes to visit her some days later, she, in turn, fails to recognize him and laughs in his face, saying, "You're like him, very like, perhaps you're a relation, only mine is a bright falcon and a prince, and you're an owl, a shopman." She goes on to accuse Stavrogin of murdering her prince, calls him an imposter, and demands to know whether he required a big bribe to commit such a terrible crime.

In current books and movies, such as *The Invasion of the Body Snatchers,* hostile aliens aim to take over the world by breeding identical copies of people, with the evil clones doing the dirty work for their horrible masters. In *The Stepford Wives* uppity wives who will not conform to traditional submissive female roles are replaced by duplicate androids, who are servile and obedient.

Stimulated by the romantic nineteenth-century literary fascination with doubles, curious psychiatric investigators began to study the phenomenon. They soon identified five distinct types of identity distortion. Most of these delusions appeared in the context of very severe psychological disturbance or brain damage. In addition to the underlying mental or brain disorder, virtually all of these patients experience *depersonalization*. That is, they are extremely disturbed by feelings of unreality in which everything appears to be strange and unfamiliar, including their own identities.

Although these disorders used to be called "Capgras syndrome," modern psychiatric usage recognizes that there are important differences among them. These false beliefs are now classified as "delusional misidentification disorders."

THE DELUSIONAL MISIDENTIFICATION DISORDERS

The *Capgras delusion* describes individuals who are disturbed by the firm belief that family, friends, and/or items of personal significance have been replaced by copies or impersonating doubles. *Autoscopic delusion* refers to a person's belief that one or more doubles of him- or herself exists. It is a more general form of the *delusion of subjective doubles*. The major distinction between these two delusions is that normal people as well as psychologically disturbed people report autoscopic experiences. The *Frégoli delusion* refers to a state in which an individual claims to recognize the same persecutor masquerading as many different people, although acknowledging that the similarity is psychological rather than physical. Finally, the rare *intermetamorphosis delusion* is defined by a person's belief that people have the capacity to transform themselves into other people, interchanging their identities both psychologically and physically.

Capgras Delusion

The following case study reported by Canadian psychiatrist Dr. Robert Bankier aptly illustrates the Capgras delusion.

Mr. Acton, a 29-year-old married man, finally got up enough courage to approach an attorney with an astonishing tale of his long-term intimidation and victimization by blackmailers. Six years before, while drinking at a hotel bar, he picked up an attractive young woman named Joan and took her home in his car. Shortly after this, he said, Joan began calling him on the telephone demanding money. She threatened to make things rough for him unless he paid her off for keeping quiet about their liaison. When he refused to pay, he said Joan began tape-recording his conversations. She also convinced him that she had photographs of him having sex with other women. Despite the fact that he had never actually heard the tapes or seen the incriminating photos, he believed in their existence and in Joan's remarkable power over other people. For these reasons he had been too terrified to seek legal assistance earlier. However, this all had changed about a year prior to the consultation. At that time Joan had joined forces with a woman doctor named Browning. The doctor must also have had extraordinary powers, since Mr. Acton reported that she had operated on his wife, using exceptionally long surgical instruments via the oral and rectal routes so that no telltale scars were visible. His Capgras delusion evidently began at that time.

Dr. Browning, Mr. Acton said, called him to relate that, unfortunately, his wife was suffering from leukemia and required an exchange blood transfusion. This precluded her returning home any time soon, so Dr. Browning thoughtfully arranged for a double to be sent home to Mr. Acton in her place. Acton claimed that this double was created through a miracle of plastic surgery. In appearance, behavior, mannerisms, tone of voice, habits, and so forth, it so closely resembled his wife that he was completely unable to tell the difference. Fortunately, the double confessed to him that she was an imposter named Rhoda. Further phone calls from Joan instructed him to live with Rhoda and take no action or suffer drastic consequences. However, Rhoda left something to be desired as a wife surrogate, since she would neither sleep with him nor have sex.

After several months of this arrangement Dr. Browning was replaced by two other women doctors. One, known as Dr. Switzer, performed additional surgery on his real, pre-Rhoda wife. The other revealed herself as Dr. Taylor, a psychiatrist. Although he has never seen either of these doctors, Mr. Acton reported that Dr. Taylor recognized him in a restaurant and, to his face, fully confirmed his beliefs about his wife's illness and subsequent replacement by wife-clone Rhoda.

About 10 months before Mr. Acton's present mental hospitalization, he said he received a phone call from Joan telling him to leave Rhoda, so he packed a bag and left, moving in with his older brother. However, the phone calls and threats continued unabated until he could stand it no longer and confided all to his brother. The brother was exceptionally understanding and fully confirmed all Mr. Acton's suspicions (folie à deux, see Chapter 8). This state of affairs ended when Mr. Acton received a letter from his real-life wife's attorney notifying him that she was filing for a legal separation on the grounds of desertion, nonsupport, and cruelty. This confused Mr. Acton, since he had been convinced that his wife was dying of leukemia. He finally decided to seek legal advice and thus revealed his elaborate and imaginative delusional system.

Mr. Acton was in good physical health and had no family history of mental illness or prior psychological disturbance. He was treated initially as an outpatient and given antipsychotic medication and psychotherapy. Unfortunately, these treatment efforts were unsuccessful, and he was transferred to a mental hospital.

Dr. D.N. Anderson of Sefton General Hospital, Liverpool, reported the following unusual case of 74-year-old Mr. Davis. In this case, the delusional misidentification was restricted to emotionally significant personal items and material objects.

Mr. Davis had always been a private, compulsive, dogmatic person with few friends. Hard-working and practical, he prided himself on his superior craftsmanship in repairing clocks and mending things around the home. He presented a highly unusual delusional system involving his belief that his wife and her nephew, a successful accountant, were conspiring to deprive him of his most cherished possessions. He said that he has been aware of the plot for 10 years, although it may well have been going on even longer. Over the years Mr. Davis kept a meticulous typewritten list of more than 300 items that he believes were stolen. These included household items such as screws, nails, paintbrushes, screwdrivers, and personal belongings such as underpants, shirts, boots, and his electric razor. To add insult to injury, he maintained, many of the items were replaced by identical but vastly inferior copies. He claimed that only he could detect the minute differences between the genuine objects and their doubles, as they were essentially identical in size, shape, color, and manufacturer's name. For example, the counterfeit clock had loose hands, the replacement paintbrushes had fewer bristles, the replacement boots were more worn, the bathing suit did not fit as well, and the replacement toaster oven had different shelves.

Mr. Davis was convinced that his wife and nephew were selling the original items to make money, and believed that even a handful of nails was valuable enough to make this profitable. He was also convinced that the nephew had introduced rats into his apartment to persecute him, and claimed to have been bitten by them. As a result, he emptied the apartment of all stuffed furniture that could shelter the rats, such as chairs, mattresses, and couches. Mr. Davis believed that the nephew had secretly gotten his wife hooked on heroin in order to ensure her collusion in the plot. He was sure his wife had placed sedatives in his food so she could slip out and continue to plot with her nephew while he was asleep. Firmly convinced that he was under attack, Mr. Davis refused antipsychotic medications and failed to keep outpatient psychiatric appointments.

Misidentifications may also extend to the animal kingdom. One 17-year-old high school student, who was convinced that he was the victim of a sinister conspiracy, even began to suspect that his faithful pet dog had been replaced by a double. During a telephone conversation with his mother he asked her to make the dog bark into the phone and then refused to accept it as his real dog. Upon actually seeing the dog several days later, he claimed as further proof that the imposter dog's fur was a different color.

Autoscopic Delusions

Autoscopy (literally, "seeing one's self") refers to an uncanny experience in which an individual sees a double or illusory image of him- or herself. It differs from other misidentification delusions in that it is not as frequently associated with severe mental illness or nervous system pathology. It is a terrifying perceptual experience in which a person is suddenly confronted by his or her own image, similar to an out-of-body experience. When this experience occurs in the context of severe mental disorder or brain damage, it is called the delusion of subjective doubles.

Dr. N. Lukianowicz of Barrow Hospital, Bristol, published the following picturesque cases:

> Ms. Burns is a 56-year-old retired schoolteacher who has experienced intense autoscopic hallucinations since her late husband's funeral. She is the only child of a high-court judge. Since childhood she has been a worrier, with a rigid personality and predisposition to deep depressions. When she was 26 she married a 41-year-old lawyer. Their marriage was apparently quite happy, even though childless. She retired from her job at age 48 because of pervasive depression.
>
> As she returned home from the cemetery following her husband's funeral, she opened the door to her bedroom and immediately became aware of somebody else in the room. In the late afternoon twilight she noticed a woman in front of her. Ms. Burns immediately reached out her right hand to turn on the light, and the strange woman made the same movement with her left hand so that their hands touched. She felt icy cold in her right hand and a feeling as if all the blood had drained out of her hand. With the light on she noticed that the stranger wore an exact replica of her own coat, hat, and veil. In spite of this unusual experience Ms. Burns was neither surprised nor frightened. Instead she felt deprived of any feeling. Without bothering any more about the intruder, she began to undress and removed her hat, her veil, and her coat. The woman in black silently imitated her every move. Only then, looking into the stranger's face, did she become aware that it was she herself staring at herself, as if in a mirror, and mimicking her own movements and gestures. It then occurred to her that it was her double, her second self looking at her. At that moment she felt that her other self was more alive and warm and vital than she was. Suddenly feeling extremely tired and weary, she lay down on her bed. Just as soon as she closed her eyes she lost sight of the apparition. Almost at once she felt stronger, "as if the life of this astral body" were coming back into her own body. Soon she was fit to get up, to change her dress, and to prepare her supper.
>
> Since that evening she was visited almost daily by the double, mostly at dusk when she was alone. She would see it only when she looked straight ahead, and would lose sight of it as soon as she turned her gaze sideways or up and down. She could also make the double disappear by closing her eyes, but it would reappear after

she opened them. Then, with her own eyes closed she could "see" the double before her *with its eyes closed.* The image was life-sized. The most distinct parts of it were the face, torso, and hands. The lower part of the trunk and the legs were less sharply visible; they were rather "misty, as if they were transparent." Yet she knew and felt the exact position in space of the phantom's limbs at any given moment. Soon she noticed that whenever she experienced her autoscopic hallucination, she "felt mildly amazed and bewildered" and had "a perplexing feeling of unreality." Although she knows it is only an hallucination, nevertheless, she can see it, feel it with all her senses. It has a distinct emotional existence for her. Emotionally, she feels it as a living, integral part of herself; in her words, "It is me, split and divided."

Not all reports of autoscopic phenomena have quite the spiritual quality of Ms. Burn's experience of her double, as illustrated by the following:

Mr. Franz, a 32-year-old engineer, was positively abusive toward his other self. He reported seeing the image of his own face suspended before him, as if looking in a mirror. This phantom face would imitate all his facial expressions, and Mr. Franz would frequently tease it by forcing it to copy his grimaces. At times Mr. Franz's behavior toward his double bordered on the sadistic, despite his regarding the apparition as a part of himself. For example, he enjoyed striking the phantom on its head, and the helpless specter was unable to avoid the blows. It had to remain in front of him, always just within the reach of his right jab. Presumably, Mr. Franz was willing to endure a few bumps and facial bruises in order to keep the provocative double in line.

Frégoli Delusion

Another group of individuals are certain that numerous others are imposters, that people in their environment are individually replaced from time to time by the same one or two persecutors. The persecutor is said to change faces, and may adopt the guise of the mailman on one occasion, then a nurse, or perhaps a neighbor next. One is never sure whether that really is the paper boy or another incarnation of the enemy. This form of misidentification is called the Frégoli delusion, after the famous turn-of-the-century Italian actor Leopoldo Frégoli, a master of disguise and a genius at impersonating others during stage performances. Frégoli's name earned psychiatric immortality when an uneducated woman with delusions of grandeur became convinced that all her persecutors were actually Frégoli in disguise. She complained that they would take the form of one and then another of the familiar persons in her environment. As distinct from the Capgras delusion, in the Frégoli delusion there is false recognition without another actual physical identity or "doubling." This is illustrated in the following case reported by psychiatrist Karel de Pauw of Northern General Hospital, Sheffield, England.

Ms. Cameron is a 66-year-old woman who had received successful outpatient psychotherapy for anxiety and depression on four occasions in the 20 years prior to her current difficulty. She had no family history of psychological disorder. However, her medical background revealed that she had a hysterectomy at age 55 and suffered a blood clot in the left frontal brain following a fall 5 years before the current crisis. This brain injury resulted in headache, dizziness, hypertension, slurred speech, disorientation, memory defects, and other similar evidence of brain damage. Although these problems responded well to treatment, she had a recurrence one month before the current hospitalization with Frégoli delusions. A CAT scan showed a moderate amount of deterioration of brain tissue, and her brain wave recordings were clearly abnormal. Psychological tests showed that while intellectual performance was intact, there were some memory and orientation defects, such as incorrectly remembering her age and inability to remember faces.

Ms. Cameron almost missed her appointment because she said she had to make a complicated detour around town to outwit her pursuers. Her current symptoms began when she became convinced that her married male cousin and a lady friend had moved into her neighborhood and were following her in various disguises. They did this because they believed that she was a threat to them due to her knowledge of their love affair and criminal activities, such as dealing in stolen cars and other goods. She described in vivid detail the intricacies of their makeup, the wigs, the dark glasses, the false beards, and the different clothing. The woman always wore chic, expensive outfits, which the patient had never been able to afford for herself. They changed cars frequently, or else had the car spray painted in order to follow her undetected. Sometimes they even used two cars so that they could head her off. She knew that a local car dealer was helping them.

On a number of occasions Ms. Cameron confronted strangers on the street and demanded that they remove their disguises and reveal their true identities as her cousin and his lover. She reported their activities to the local police and took complicated routes to throw them off her trail. During the day she kept her curtains drawn, but opened them at night so that she could spy on them outside the house. She claimed that she could easily recognize the cousin and the lover, who sometimes dressed as a man, by their gait, their voices, and characteristic postures.

To understand the real significance of these bizarre delusions it is important to note that Ms. Cameron, as a divorced 35-year-old, had had a love affair that produced her only child, a daughter who was raised by the patient's sister. The love affair continued secretly for more than 20 years, despite her lover's marrying someone else. The affair had finally ended 10 years prior to Ms. Cameron's current mental breakdown. The secret lover and father of her child was none other than her cousin, the persecuting villain in her current Frégoli delusional system.

Delusion of Intermetamorphosis

The fifth type of identity disturbance is called the delusion of interme-tamorphosis. According to patients experiencing this disorder, individuals in their environment participate in a veritable round-robin of continually changing identities. For example, one patient was convinced that sinister forces had switched the identities of young people with old people, that her brand-new coat was replaced by an old, shabby imitation, that her two prized young hens had been switched with old ones, and that her husband was really her neighbor—and then her doctor. In a reverse twist, another patient was sure that female patients, or any unknown women, were not really women, but were all actually her husband. The following case is also illustrative.

Ms. Lori Roberts, a shy and introverted 19-year-old woman, is the eldest of two daughters born to a quiet farmer and his irritable wife.

Lori seemed to enjoy a normal and uneventful childhood. However, at the age of 18 she began showing the first of the many peculiar behaviors so characteristic of early schizophrenic psychosis. Her school work deteriorated as she developed insomnia, concentration problems, depersonalization, auditory hallucinations, and false memories of familiarity. She proclaimed that she was endowed with godlike abilities and prophetic powers. Later, intermetamorphosis delusions became prominent and began dominating the clinical picture. She became firmly convinced that Mr. R, her theology teacher, was madly in love with her. She reciprocated with rich, secret erotic fantasies, which continued long after he moved away. She claimed that Mr. R was able to alter his appearance psychophysically so as to be physically and psychologically identical to various people, such as a taxi driver, a salesman, a pedestrian, and a priest. After three months of inpatient treatment with high doses of major tranquilizers she gradually improved enough to be released, symptom-free and with insight into the imaginal nature of most of her previous beliefs.

In describing behavior disorders we often find that people do not always fit into our neat categories. This is certainly the case in studies of misidentification disorders. Consider the following examples reported by psychiatrists Siomopoulos and Goldsmith in a letter to the American Journal of Psychiatry:

Mr. Ernst was arrested in an assault case, but objected to being addressed by his recorded name. He insisted that he was not Mr. Ernst but actually Mr. Kaplan, and that he had adopted the identity of Ernst, a writer whose works he admired. He excused the arresting officers by saying that he did indeed bear a certain resemblance to Mr. Ernst and was carrying Mr. Ernst's credit cards. In fact, except for a minor difference in the shape of his nose, he resembled Mr. Ernst so closely that even Mr. Ernst's parents didn't know he was Mr. Kaplan when he assumed Mr. Ernst's identity a year ago. When he was asked about the background of Mr. Kaplan, he was unable to furnish any information, but he did give relevant information about Ernst's place of birth, family, friends, and interests.

In a similar case, Mrs. Loring, a 43-year-old wife and mother, was admitted to a mental hospital after she became reclusive and suspicious and neglected to look after herself and her small children.

When addressed by name, she denied that she was Mrs. Loring, or that her husband and children were hers. She insisted that her husband was an imposter, while she herself was a part of an American secret political organization. This group had altered her features to look like the real Mrs. Loring by means of enforced plastic surgery. She was actually 15 years younger, but otherwise looked very similar. She had been placed in Mr. Loring's home merely to replace his real wife, who had eloped some years before and was awaiting a space ship to take her back to her home planet, Uranus.

THEORETICAL VIEWS

There are many speculative ideas as to the causes of delusional misidentification, but three general viewpoints are prominent. The Freudian psychoanalytic viewpoint emphasizes the causal role of childhood emotional trauma and unconscious conflicts experienced while the person is in the grip of the Oedipus complex. According to Freud, the Oedipus complex consists of the little boy's developing an incestuous lust for his mother and consequent rivalry, jealousy, and hostility toward his father. Conversely, the little girl develops a crush on her father, and hostility and resentment are directed toward the mother. These intense emotions are so distressing as to require a severe distortion of reality in order to defend against the intense psychological pain. The biological view, on the other hand, stresses the causal role of biological factors in delusional misidentifications, particularly damage to the brain and nervous system. The third view is the behavioral perspective, which assumes that misidentification delusions are learned patterns of behavior.

Psychoanalytic View

Capgras and Reboul-Lachaux's early psychoanalytic theory was based on their initial observation that doubling or imposter delusions were confined to women. They speculated that the girl child's unresolved Oedipus complex generates strong incestuous sexual desires for her father and corresponding resentment of the formerly beloved mother as a feared and hated rival. The consequent anxiety and mixed emotions produce a psychotic resolution; that is, the individual must distort reality in order to deny the incestuous nature of the unacceptable unconscious sexual longings. Thus, the delusion that the real father has been replaced by an imposter, a different and unrelated person, eliminates the concern about the incestual need. The loving and nurturant mother has been replaced by a double, a hateful stranger, who can then be an acceptable target for the girl's hostility. Unfortunately, this rather neat formulation required substantial revision upon the discovery that there were numerous instances of male Capgras patients, as well as cases in which the accused imposter or substituted object had no emotional relevance for the patient at all.

Dr. Robert Berson of Sarah Lawrence College has contributed the most comprehensive modern version of the psychoanalytic theory of delusional misidentifications, with an extensive review and commentary on 133 cases. According to Dr. Berson, explanations of delusional misidentification that assign a causal role to brain damage or other physical disease are incorrect. He cites the fact that the disorder does not involve marked deterioration of mental functioning. There is no evidence of the clouding of consciousness, the disorientation, or the memory disturbance typical of brain disorders that cause significant psychological impairment.

Dr. Berson holds that delusional misidentifications represent a psychotic resolution of the anxiety generated by ambivalence toward the parents held since childhood. Early childhood emotional trauma during the Oedipal phase arouses in the child unacceptable incestuous and murderous impulses. These feelings are directed toward the parents, but because these same parents have also been nurturant and loving, they are simultaneously loved and hated. This ambivalence generates intense anxiety, resulting in a splitting of the parents into "good/bad Mommy" and "good/bad Daddy." In Capgras delusions, before the break with reality, the "good" parent is consciously cherished, while the "bad" one is repressed and expelled from consciousness. To resolve the two fundamentally opposed views of the same person, that is, the ambivalence of a simultaneously loved and hated significant other, the hated other is transformed into an imposter who has replaced the beloved other. The patient responds to the now-conscious repressed feelings as follows:

"Mother never aroused such feelings in me before; therefore, this must not be Mother but an imposter, someone who is out to do me harm."

Dr. Berson's formulation receives partial support from the observation that in Capgras disorders there is a high incidence of paranoid ideas of persecution, which sometimes lead to violent attacks on others. For example, a 32-year-old man had problems at work and moved back home to live with his parents. They nagged him about returning to work and criticized his fiancée. This convinced him that these people were not his real parents, but strangers who had kidnapped him. He came to believe that the bogus parents were actually machinelike beings who had been suppressing him all his life. His parents were unsuccessful in placing him in a mental hospital, because the patient thought the purpose of the placement was to turn him into a homosexual. Upon returning home from the psychiatric interview, he attacked his parents with a meat cleaver, seriously injuring his mother.

A Japanese woman expanded her Capgras delusion to include duplicates of her relatives, neighbors, the village, and even Japan itself. Finally, reasoning that she would need the help of the police to find her true family, she shot and killed a complete stranger in order to get their attention. In another incident, a young man who had a strong suspicion that his stepfather had been replaced by a robot decapitated him in order to look for the batteries and microfilm in the man's head.

Biological View

Despite the attractive complexities of psychoanalytic theories, biological formulations have continued to appear in the professional literature. Scientists have now reported on more than 400 cases worldwide. A large number of bodily disturbances have been implicated in Capgras delusions, including cortical atrophy, traumatic head injury, malnutrition, alcoholism, diabetes, lack of oxygen to the brain, migraine, epilepsy, and pituitary gland tumor. Emotional ambivalence, the central concept in the psychoanalytic theory, has been undermined by the finding that in numerous cases large numbers of different and unrelated people are doubled, such as the mailman, shopkeepers, and store clerks. Obviously, the patient cannot harbor deep emotional attachments to all these peripheral people. It also strains belief that an intense emotional ambivalence could extend to a Siamese cat, letters, paintbrushes, a wristwatch, and assorted items of clothing and hardware, all of which various patients have proclaimed to be clever replacements or doubles.

Current scientific research has accumulated convincing evidence of the importance of neurological damage in causing at least some delusional misidentifications. Ultrasensitive modern brain-imaging methods for studying the microscopic inner workings of brain cells and fibers have replaced crude old-fashioned neurological tests. Neuroscientists using these new and sophisticated methods have detected subtle brain defects in more than one-third of the cases reported in the scientific literature. These results have forced us to revise our theories as to the basic mechanisms underlying misidentification delusions.

Some researchers believe that both neurological damage and psychological stressors, acting together, are the predisposing conditions for these disorders. Delusional misidentification is thus viewed as the result of the severe distortion of higher mental processes caused by both biological and psychological stress in vulnerable individuals. The particular form or type of delusion is thought to be the product of the patient's unique psychological history and his or her current situation, within the limits set by the person's biological handicap. In other words, many different organic injuries could release a delusional process in those people with emotionally distressed backgrounds and few psychological strengths to enable them to cope with and adapt to such injury.

Recently, Dr. D. N. Anderson, a British psychiatrist in the Department of Psychogeriatrics of Sefton General Hospital in Liverpool, proposed a specific model to illustrate just how the biological and psychological interaction could produce certain types of Capgras delusions. He assumes that brain lesions damage the brain's visual recognition pathways. This occurs at a stage where visual images are provided with emotional meaning and familiarity. In this way, familiar persons, places, or possessions would now look strange and evoke unfamiliar and incongruous feelings. The patient can recognize another person as familiar, but is unable to attach meaning or feelings to the image of the person. The puzzled patient resolves this disturbing inconsistency by concluding that the person (or object) cannot possibly be that which it physically resembles. Therefore, it must be a double or an imposter. If this process occurs in a person who has psychological problems and is already mentally unstable, then the necessary elements are all present for delusional misidentifications.

Sociobehavioral View

None of the theoretical explanations of misidentification delusions we have described so far consider the possibility that they represent a learned pattern of behavior. From this perspective, the belief in a non-existent double could have been learned because such a belief would have reward value (reinforcement) for the individual. For example, the conviction that there is an exact double of one's self might be rewarding because it could serve to reduce guilt over some real or imagined sin ("The double did it, my evil twin, not me"). Or perhaps an individual who has long repressed hostility toward a spouse or parent could express it by claiming that the victim was not the real husband or mother, but a wicked counterfeit who deserved assaulting. In a small child, the imaginary double might serve to reduce loneliness or to take the blame for breaking an expensive vase. Research on many different behavior disorders has demonstrated that bizarre behavior such as proclaiming loudly that one is surrounded by enemies masquerading as doctors, is frequently rewarded by special attention. In some instances one may even gain immortality in a published case history. Behavior modification theory explains Capgras delusions and other disorders by employing elementary learning principles, such as reinforcement, as illustrated in our hypothetical examples.

TREATMENT

Authorities are virtually unanimous in agreeing that misidentifications rarely occur as a primary clinical problem in an otherwise healthy person. Instead, they develop secondarily against the background of some profound mental disorder such as schizophrenia, or some serious physical problem such as traumatic head injury. Professionals also agree unanimously that the primary problem must be treated first, or in conjunction with treatment of the misidentification symptoms. In the case of a primary mental disorder such as schizophrenia, a wide variety of antipsychotic drugs have been used, but generally with only modest temporary success. Patients diagnosed as severely depressed are often given mood-elevating or antidepressant medications. Some psychiatrists have administered electroconvulsive shock therapy (ECT), but this procedure is cited just as often as worsening the symptoms as helping them.

Counseling and psychotherapy are not recommended as the major forms of treatment, since they have also proven to be unsuccessful. Instead, they are generally employed as adjunct treatments and are used in a supportive manner to help the person better distinguish reality from delusion.

All forms of misidentification disorder involve tremendous stress for the patient. Imagine a bill collector hiding behind the innocent facade of the little neighbor girl come to sell you Girl Scout cookies—or strolling down the street and suddenly encountering yourself approaching from the opposite direction! And whom could you tell about these terrifying experiences, when your best friend, or the family doctor, or your minister, has probably been replaced by sinister imposters? For our unfortunate delusional misidentification patients, surrounded by danger in so many disguises, loneliness must seem like a blessed state.

Suggested Further Readings

Anderson, D. (1988) The delusion of inanimate doubles. *British Journal of Psychiatry, 153,* 694–699.

Berson, R. (1983) Capgras syndrome. *American Journal of Psychiatry, 140,* 969–978.

Enoch, M. (1963) The Capgras syndrome. *Acta Psychiatrica Scandinavia, 39,* 437–462.

Rudnick, F. (1982). The paranoid-erotic syndromes. In Friedmann, C., Faguet, R. (Eds.). *Extraordinary disorders of human behavior.* Ch. 7, 99–120 New York: Plenum Press.

Todd, J., Dewhurst, K., & Wallis, G. (1981) The syndrome of Capgras. *British Journal of Psychiatry, 139,* 319–327.

CHAPTER 8

Folie à Deux
Shared Insanity

No condition illustrates more dramatically our human need for support from our fellow human beings than the group of severe personality disorders called *folie à deux* (dual madness), formerly called "contagious insanity," and today known officially as induced psychotic disorder. It involves the transference of delusional ideas from a psychotic individual to an intimate associate who has been under his or her influence for an extended period of time. The official diagnostic manual of the American Psychiatric Association (DSM IV), a comprehensive account of the symptoms of all known psychological disorders, describes *folie à deux* as a delusional system that is induced in a second person, the secondary partner, as a result of a close relationship with another person, the primary partner. The primary partner already has a psychotic disorder accompanied by prominent delusions, particularly paranoid suspicions. Folie à deux has been expanded to include transmission of psychosis to three, four, or many other people (folie à trois, folie à quatre, folie à plusières).

This disorder provides us with the most compelling evidence of the destructive mental and emotional devastation caused by isolation, loneliness, and abandonment. The secondary, or submissive, partner is gradually worn down by the primary, dominant partner and eventually surrenders, preferring to adopt crazy ideas rather than threaten his or her only human social relationship.

It is no accident that one of the worst punishments our early ancestors could administer was the expelling of an offender from the tribe, an almost certain death sentence. During the Middle Ages religious excommunication excluded the offender from divine grace and eternal salvation. In more recent times criminals and prisoners guilty of especially wicked offenses have been consigned to solitary confinement. Isolation, often used as a form of torture, can force changes in its victim's attitudes and values.

Folie à deux is also of intense professional interest because it may shed some light on the question of whether one person can drive another person mad and, if so, the mechanisms for producing such induced mental contagion. Learning how insanity is created would go a long way toward telling us how to reverse the process and might allow us then to avoid the risk factors responsible for producing the condition. In addition, folie à deux is also of great theoretical interest, because it presents a natural laboratory for studying the role of hereditary and biological factors in mental disorders. For example, if unrelated persons were just as likely as biological relatives to develop psychosis through prolonged close association, this would support an environmental interpretation of some mental disorders.

The French psychiatrists Lasègue and Falret stimulated modern interest in folie à deux with their 1873 paper describing and classifying patients they had treated. At first they did not consider it to be a psychiatric disorder at all, but merely a case of extreme "absurd credulity" or excessive gullibility on the part of the submissive partner. They also pointed out that heredity could not afford a complete explanation, since the process frequently involved unrelated partners, such as spouses.

While folie à deux and its variations are uncommon, they are by no means rare. The professional literature describes more than 200 case reports. The actual incidence of the disorder is probably underestimated, however, because usually only the most disturbed member of the pair comes to the attention of the mental health system. We also know that delusional individuals are often clever enough to conceal their bizarre ideas from doctors.

Reports of socially induced bizarre group behavior go back at least as far as the fifteenth century, when a nun in a German convent suddenly began biting the other nuns. Victims of the nipping nun bit back, and soon this dental diversion spread from convent to convent throughout Germany, Holland, and Italy. Group outbreaks of hysterical dancing, called "Saint Vitus' dance," reached epidemic proportions. In Italy these manic outbursts were called "tarantism," because victims showing the characteristic hyperactivity and convulsions were thought to have been poisoned by a tarantula bite. As the poor wretches danced and gyrated wildly in the roads, susceptible onlookers would be drawn into the mass frenzy as others dropped out, exhausted. A remnant of this colorful era survives in the Italian folk melodies and dances called "tarantellas."

In the seventeenth century the great British physician William Harvey wrote an account of two sisters, both of whom were experiencing false pregnancies. In eighteenth-century Colonial America, groups of Swiss and German Lutheran immigrants produced a number of mass-delusional religious cults. In one typical group, a charismatic leader claimed to be God the Father, another the Son, and a third the Holy Ghost. After a power struggle, God exposed the Son as Satan in disguise. The unfortunate Son was chained in a pit in the forest, where he was covered with pillows and stomped on until he suffocated. The Holy Ghost suffered a similar fate, strangled in his bed. After committing many other crimes, the ringleaders were brought to trial and hanged.

In the early nineteenth century a nun in a large French convent suddenly began meowing like a cat. Soon other nuns began to imitate "the meowing nun" until finally all the nuns met together regularly every day and meowed for several hours. Early in this century there was a flurry of interest in the legal implications of Svengali-like madmen forcing a submissive partner to attack or even murder some third party, usually another family member. Such an incident occurred frequently enough to be called "le crime à deux." Group or mass suicides ("suicides à deux ou à plusieres") were known to be induced or instigated; the Jonestown massacre is a shocking modern example. As illustrated by the Jonestown massacre case, there is also a definite tendency for such violent crimes to spread beyond the immediate family.

A leading expert on such crimes, Dr. H. Phillip Greenberg of Guy's Hospital, London, cites the example of a turn-of-the-century Russian sect, the Old Believers, who came under the evil influence of a psychotic young woman. She convinced the members of the sect that not only was the end of the world at hand, but that first they would be attacked and tortured. To avoid such a horrible fate, she directed them to bury themselves alive. At first, 19 of the Believers complied, followed 4 days later by the young woman herself and 6 more terrified believers. The remaining members were arrested and jailed to prevent further deaths, but they immediately went on a hunger strike and so were promptly released from custody. A Russian psychiatrist confidently explained this grisly event by attributing it to "a Slavic tendency to persuasion and strong passivity," in other words, a Russian thing. In another shocking case, a menopausal woman deluded herself into believing that she had been impregnated by the Holy Ghost. Her two daughters, and then the whole neighborhood, became converted to this belief. However, the belief in the sacred nature of her pregnancy was soon replaced by the conviction that her fetus was of the Devil. Directed by the unfortunate patient, three of the neighbors tried forcefully to remove her uterus manually, because they believed it was the seat of all evil in the world.

In recent times we have seen the shocking mass murder/suicides instigated by charismatic messianic cult leaders such as Charles Manson, the Reverend James Jones (Jonestown, cited earlier), and David Koresh and his Branch Davidians. Also illustrated by the Koresh case is the definite tendency for such violence to affect others outside the immediate family.

Currently, in addition to the Jonestown group and the Manson family, there are many other radical religious movements and self-realization cults, indicating the persistent appeal of such close-knit communities. However, these large-scale examples of collective madness are quite distinct from folie à deux. Rather, they can best be understood as a kind of mass hysteria based on the human need for fellowship and family in normal as well as unstable people. Often society is too quick to condemn these outbreaks as pathological. For example, in 1910 the stuffy Dr. Arthur Wilcox called women who were parading and picketing for the right to vote an example of contagious political insanity. We have indeed come a long way.

Following Lasègue and Falret's classical description of folie à deux and an increasing number of case reports, psychiatrists found it necessary to devise the following threefold classification system for a better understanding of the disorder:

1. *Imposed Psychosis* (folie imposée). A well-adjusted person comes to share a psychotic partner's delusions after they have been living together for a long time. Fortunately, the secondary partner's delusions clear up after the two are separated. The definition sometimes includes assertions that the primary partner is more intelligent, dominant, or forceful, and the secondary partner passive, suggestible, and submissive.

2. *Simultaneous Psychosis* (folie simultanée). The partners come to believe in identical delusions. This occurs simultaneously, but independently, between or among closely associated individuals. No one individual is dominant, and therefore separation is not helpful.

3. *Communicated Psychosis* (folie communiquée). The secondary partner eventually develops delusions after a varying period of exposure and resistance. However, even after separation from the psychotic person, the influenced individual retains his or her delusions. For such a disorder to fit this category, some authorities require that the secondary partner's delusions continue to elaborate and expand independently.

Dr. Alexander Gralnick, distinguished psychiatrist and author of a classical review of 103 published cases, has made the only systematic attempt to study the frequency of the different delusional types. He found that there were 61 reports of imposed psychosis, 24 of communicated psychosis, 6 of simultaneous psychosis, and 5 mixed cases. Of the cases reported, there were 40 sister pairs, 26 husband-wife pairs, and 24 mother-daughter pairs. A more recent study, which included Gralnick's 103 cases, reported that 70% were blood related and 30% were not.

The conditions mentioned as favorable for producing psychoses always include both environmental and biological factors. For example, the affected individuals are often very poor and live in remote areas such as farms, dense woodlands, or mountainous regions. Another kind of isolation occurs among recent immigrants without workable knowledge of the language spoken in their new environment. The lack of external social encounters promotes delusional thinking by depriving the individuals of a chance to check their beliefs against reality.

For psychosis to be induced, the association between the partners must also persist over long periods of time, years in most cases. Such prolonged intimate association and isolation are important because these conditions make it easier for the inducer to impose his or her delusional distortions of reality upon a recipient who has few other reality checks or limited access to contrary opinion. Usually the inducer represents authority to the recipient, often because he or she is older, more intelligent, or better educated. The inducer must also be in the early stages of psychosis, so that the distortions and delusions appear to be more plausible, rather than illogical or ludicrous. Coercing the recipient into accepting the delusional system reassures the inducer that he or she is not crazy, since the other person shares the delusions. Finally, adopting the primary partner's distortions of reality must embody some sort of gain or positive value for the secondary partner, perhaps because agreement reduces the tension resulting from continuous haranguing. Some psychoanalytic authorities refer to an unconscious psychological identification between the partners, both sharing the same hidden wishes and desires, which are overt in the first partner and gradually brought to the surface in the second.

In respect to biological factors, investigators regularly point to hereditary predisposition. For example, in 90% of the cases the affected individuals belong to the same family unit, although sometimes by marriage. Furthermore, in many cases the secondary partner never recovers from the induced psychosis even when separated from the primary partner. Poverty, social isolation, and deprivation are seen as the result of a progressing psychotic process. The advance of the disorder can be responsible for the person's being evicted, fired, socially censured, and otherwise rejected and set apart from others. However, only 70% of cases are blood relatives, the rest being spouses and other close associates, making it difficult, as always, to separate the contributions of heredity and environment.

IMPOSED PSYCHOSIS

For a condition to be classified as an imposed psychosis requires that separation of the partners reverses the induced disorder. In both the following cases all of the affected secondary partners recovered their prior levels of adjustment after separation from the dominant primary partners. Thus, the transmitted psychosis and delusional states were of a temporary nature. Even mental health professionals are susceptible to the pressures that induce psychological disorders. One such example was reported by psychiatrist D. H. Ropschitz in the 1957 *Journal of Mental Science.* A manic-depressive doctor affected both colleagues and patients with his delusional thinking.

Dr. Avery is a young physician with a special interest in psychiatry because of his own manic-depressive disorder. Unfortunately, his symptoms began recurring while he was visiting Ms. Burns, an old friend and chief nurse at a large psychiatric hospital. His former therapist was ill at home and unable to see him, and the hospital director, Dr. Jones, was vacationing in Italy. As Dr. Avery entered his manic phase he became loud, talkative, and full of energy. He bragged that no case was too difficult for him, he possessed magical curative powers. He soon took complete charge of the psychiatric unit and began treating patients. Nurse Burns was enchanted and followed him around in a state bordering on ecstacy, observing his miraculous healing gifts. She brooked no criticism from any of the staff, attributing it to petty professional jealousy. Dr. Avery's first case was an ex-airline pilot who had developed a fear of flying. Over a 24-hour period the pilot was implored, threatened, lectured to, and browbeaten into believing his phobia was cured. The next recipient was a man with sexual problems in his marriage who was similarly convinced that he was cured. Now Dr. Avery, the two cured patients, and Nurse Burns became a mutual admiration society, the forerunners of a new era in psychiatry. Nothing would do but for all of them to fly off to Italy to share their new discoveries with the vacationing Dr. Jones. Dr. Jones, aware of Dr. Avery's medical history, immediately arranged with the British Consulate to ship the quartet home. Nurse Burns and Dr. Avery by now were uncontrollably hyperactive, euphoric, and delusional.

Back at the hospital, when Dr. Avery's former therapist was unable to persuade him to sign himself into the hospital voluntarily, the therapist reluctantly signed involuntary commitment papers. Now Dr. Avery was interviewed by a panel of psychiatrists. He talked for a solid hour without pause, denying that he was mentally ill, accusing the panel of professional jealousy, and claiming that his royal blood gave him special powers. He also said he was working undercover for the British Foreign Office, which protected him from being judged by normal standards.

When Nurse Burns was asked her professional opinion, she did not agree that Avery was ill and demanded that the panel contact the Foreign Office. When she was asked whether he would be less mentally ill if he really did work for the Foreign Office, she was silent. Finally, Dr. Avery was sent to another psychiatric hospital, whereupon Nurse Burns, well into denial, claimed that she had known all along that he was psychotic. No longer under the spell of the charismatic Dr. Avery, Nurse Burns and the patients soon returned to their previous selves.

Dr. Maurice Partridge of St. George's Hospital, London, presented another colorful case of imposed psychosis. His article appeared in the *Archives of Neurology and Psychiatry*. The abridged report follows:

Mrs. Farley had been an energetic and productive person all her life. After selling her profitable grocery business, she and husband Harry were enjoying retirement and the quiet country life. This peaceful existence was shattered when she found a small bug on her pillow. Always a meticulous housekeeper, she reacted with typical energy and embarked on a campaign of washing, scrubbing, and cleaning that lasted two full months. With the insect invasion defeated, she took the additional precaution of having the local agricultural authority examine the insect. He thought it was a common garden insect and reassured her that their property was in no danger of a vermin infestation. However, responding to her anxiety, he suggested preventive DDT fumigation. Mrs. Farley carried this out with a vengeance, and the program was hugely successful except for a few bugs she thought she saw in her hair. Now she began repeated hair washings and wound up shaving her head. The varmints were also resourceful, for somehow they had escaped drowning and invaded her ear canals. At this point she was totally involved in the battle against bugs, with the better part of each day spent thinking up new strategies for outwitting them.

At first Mrs. Farley, husband Harry and their daughter thought the insects were so tiny that they were submicroscopic, as no one had ever seen one since the consultation with the agricultural agent. Gradually the family came to believe that they were indeed visible, although authorities assured them that the samples Mrs. Farley presented to them repeatedly were only dust motes. Then Mrs. Farley demanded that the doctors broadcast an appeal for specialists familiar with the rare type of insects that lived only in human hair and ears. Psychiatric hospitalization was recommended, but Mrs. Farley was discharged as unimproved after a month of treatment. At this time Mr. Farley said he didn't really believe that there were bugs in her ears and hair. After her release he changed his mind and expressed complete belief. Their daughter was unsure. During her daily phone chats and weekly visits to her mother she was convinced of the bugs' reality. When her husband came home at night, her doubts became dominant. In fact, during a single interview she could be persuaded to support both positions.

Several months later Mrs. Farley had to be readmitted to the hospital with severe depression and suicidal ideas. Following electroconvulsive shock treatments she gave up her insect delusion, proclaiming that all the bugs had been shocked to death! One year later she had a relapse; the bugs were back and bolder then ever. This time the doctors performed a lobotomy, and the very next day after surgery she reported that all the bugs were gone. With Mrs. Farley fully recovered and the other two affected family members symptom-free, her psychiatrist aptly titled his report "One Operation Cures Three People."

SIMULTANEOUS PSYCHOSIS

In 1986, Dr. Kenneth Kendler of the Medical College of Virginia reported a rare case in which two otherwise normal individuals simultaneously developed a mutual paranoid delusional system.

The patients were well-to-do 81-year-old identical twin sisters who were born and raised in India. Carolyn was clearly the leader, although Marilyn was the firstborn by some 10 minutes. Their childhood was described as very pleasant and uneventful. Early schooling was in India, where they returned after finishing school in Switzerland. Marilyn married first, a happy marriage to a banker which produced a son and a daughter. The family migrated to Ireland. When the husband died, Marilyn moved in with Carolyn, who had also moved to Ireland. Now it was Carolyn's turn to marry, at age 56, but soon she too was a widow.

The sisters lived together for many years in their own house and were well regarded by all. Eventually, because of increasing physical infirmity, they made the transition gracefully to living in an old people's home. However, Carolyn now had a puzzling experience. She heard dogs barking excitedly outside the window. She immediately told Marilyn, and they concluded after several sleepless nights disrupted by the distressing barks, that dogs were being tortured by being tied to the wheels of moving cars. The SPCA and the police were called but were not helpful. Two months later, during a fire drill at the home, they were sure they heard a woman's desperate screams for help muffled by the alarm noise. The very next day a woman in the home was actually found dead, convincing the twins that murder had been done and concealed. They decided that a conspiracy existed, between the staff and certain relatives of other occupants, to murder the occupants for their inheritances. The sisters decided that they were in danger because of their knowledge of the plot. They believed their food was poisoned and the phone was bugged. In bed at night they thought they were being tortured by electric currents and took to huddling all night in chairs or wearing heavy coats to bed. They finally moved out, living in a succession of homes briefly, only to discover the new staffs were part of the original conspiracy. This behavior and the numerous emergency calls to police and other agencies led to their hospitalization. They appeared to be quite normal both physically and mentally, except for their fixed paranoid delusions. They were even well aware that others thought their suspicions crazy, but nontheless denied firmly that their beliefs were imaginary, citing the fact that they had both come to the same conclusions separately but simultaneously. Antipsychotic medication was ineffectual, and the twins were released to relatives, still insisting on their conspiracy theories.

As we have seen, folie à deux often develops in lonely elders sharing a socially and financially impoverished old age. For many of them a dog or cat may be the sole companion, thereby placing the *animal* at risk of folie à deux. The following case is adapted from a letter by Dr. Robert

Howard to the *American Journal of Psychiatry*. In this case, Emily, an 83-year-old widow, and her dog, Bosco, both developed bizarre behavior:

> They had lived together for 15 uneventful years, when Emily began to complain about the noisy tenant upstairs. At first she accused him of moving furniture around at night to disturb her. Then she reported that he was bombarding her flat with "violet rays" to harm her and the dog. This radiation attack not only made her back and chest ache but caused Bosco to scratch himself madly at night, when the rays were strongest. For protection she placed her mattress under the kitchen table and slept there at night. She also fashioned what she called an "air raid shelter" for her four-legged ally from a small table and a pile of suitcases. Now, upon hearing any sound from the flat upstairs, such as a door closing, Bosco would immediately run for the kitchen and dive into the shelter. If restrained in the living room, he reacted to noises from upstairs with agitated barking directed at the ceiling. Emily was diagnosed with late onset schizophrenia, but refused treatment. The dog's diagnosis will have to await a veterinary version of the *Diagnostic and Statistical Manual*. As the psychiatrist in the case observed, psychopathology in nonhuman companions of the mentally ill is probably common but unrecognized.

COMMUNICATED PSYCHOSIS

The following case of *Communicated Psychosis* was reported by Dr. R. D. Goldney in the *Australian/New Zealand Journal of Psychiatry*. Individuals in this category have shown prolonged resistance before surrendering to the inducer's delusional system. In addition, they fail to relinquish their delusions and even elaborate upon them after separation from the coercive partner. Dr. Goldney considered the entire family unit to have been disturbed (folie à famille), even though the children seemed unaffected:

> Pavel was a 42-year-old Czechoslovakian man who had emigrated to Australia as a youth. After working 4 years in a remote area, he

sent for and married a Greek mail-order bride. In time they had a daughter and a son. Pavel and Yolanda both experienced severe culture shock. Although Pavel seemed to adapt well to learning the new language and customs, Yolanda did not. Every place they lived, Yolanda would begin by complaining about the neighbors, how unfriendly they were, how nosy. Invariably these complaints escalated into paranoid delusions. She was diagnosed as a paranoid schizophrenic and hospitalized several times, complaining about the neighbors lurking outside their house at night and voices on the radio abusing her. At first Pavel attributed her complaints to her schizophrenia, but he gradually became convinced that she told the truth. He noted a recent breakdown in their car and a mysterious hole in the dam that held their water supply. Soon he noticed very odd noises in the house, and asked the police to check for a radio transmitter in the walls. Within weeks both the children, at this time 16 and 9 years old, were also hearing threatening noises. Although Yolanda was now living with a sister in a distant province, Pavel continued to hear funny noises in his head as well as in the walls. He developed insomnia, lost his appetite, and had crying spells. His condition worsened suddenly while on a shopping trip with the children. He began driving wildly, stuffed cotton in his ears to muffle the voices, and babbled about being chased by enemies. One hundred miles from home he stopped abruptly and sent the children into a nearby police station for help. He was hospitalized with more paranoid delusions and intense weeping spells. Fortunately, his condition responded well to drugs and electric shock treatment, and he was released in one month. He was then able to convince his wife to return from her sister's, although she remained overtly psychotic.

This family illustrates several of the core features of folie à deux. First is the clearly dominant influence exerted by Yolanda, the primary patient, who insisted on the frequent family moves. In addition, they lived in an isolated community and were further cut off from social life by the language barrier and cultural differences. Given these risk factors, the factual events such as the car breakdown could easily lend themselves to a paranoid interpretation. Finally, even when Pavel was separated from his wife, he continued to produce his own delusions.

THEORETICAL VIEWS

Because of their rarity, bizarre psychological conditions have not attracted much professional attention. Thus it is not surprising that there are a variety of theories as to causes and treatments, but little professional consensus. In folie à deux, the psychoanalytic and biological viewpoints predominate. However, some investigators have looked to sociocultural factors as necessary conditions for instigating and maintaining the shared delusional disorders.

Psychoanalytic View

Psychoanalysts maintain that because of social and psychological isolation, the partners in folie à deux develop an excessive dependency upon each other. This is due to the lack of outside sources of gratification and the stabilizing influence of external reality checks. For some reason the primary partner, the more active one, becomes convinced that the secondary partner is taking advantage and exploiting his or her dependency needs. He or she becomes increasingly resentful, but is afraid to confront the secondary partner directly for fear of being abandoned through driving the other person away. The inhibited, unexpressed hostility is denied by projecting it outward onto others as paranoid delusions. For example, "I am not angry at my sister for getting attention from her social worker, I am angry at the social worker for plotting to murder us and steal our money." The primary partner then begins to pressure the secondary partner to take sides, to accept the paranoid projections. If the secondary partner resists, the primary partner becomes ever more fearful of abandonment and turns up the heat. Now under the gun, the secondary partner feels increasingly threatened and anxious. The situation is resolved only when the secondary partner gives in. It is a small sacrifice indeed to give up reality in exchange for peace of mind and continued dependency. Folie à deux, induced madness, is necessary to restore the psychological balance that was upset by the primary partner's paranoia.

Biological View

The biological view is based on the assumption that the major mental disorders, including folie à deux, are brain disorders. It follows that occurrences of similar mental disturbances in family members are the result of similar biological structures and genetic resemblance. The fact that we actually find a genetic relationship in 70% of the cases of folie à deux provides strong support for hereditary predisposition as a cause. The disrupted family relationships, and the intimate and prolonged contact between the partners, are then said to be the results of the disorder, rather than the cause. Other evidence against prolonged contact and isolation as causes comes from the observation that mental disorders still occur in family members who had left the unhealthy relationship many years before. To explain the fact that 30% of folie à deux cases occur in unrelated partners, hereditarians cite the mechanism of assortive mating. *Assortive mating* refers to the fact that people with mental disorders tend to choose other mentally unstable people for friends or spouses. Therefore, when the primary partner becomes delusional, the secondary partner often is already predisposed to break down.

Sociobehavioral View

From the sociobehavioral perspective, any attempt to study the individual as a separate entity, either unrelated to fellow humans or driven solely by internal forces divorced from relationships, can only have sterile results. Stress arises from societal relations, not from impersonal physical factors alone. Folie à deux is a person's response to the distress arising from dysfunctional relationships. Studies in the Philippine Islands and other non-Western cultures show that mental disorders frequently occur when traditional sources of prestige and security are undermined. A number of other social factors are also implicated. For example, a dependent partner may develop a disorder as a result of seeing the traumatic breakdown of his or her primary partner. Then, too, both partners have been exposed to the same environmental pressures. Other important factors include the emotional climate of family interrelationships, the degree of isolation from nourishing social supports, and the unique personalities of the individuals involved.

BEHAVIOR MODIFICATION

As with a number of other bizarre disorders, there is no specific behavior modification theory for folie à deux. Rather, we assume that both normal and deviant behaviors are explainable by the same principles of learning. Essentially, behavioral excesses, such as hyperactivity, are regarded as the result of positive reinforcement or reward. They can be reduced by either eliminating that reward or by punishing the behavior itself. Peculiar behaviors may also be acquired through reward training in the context of imitation. In folie à deux, the successful therapy outcome produced by separating the partners may be attributable to removing the secondary partner from the model he or she was imitating. It is also possible that when a secondary partner adopts the primary partner's delusions, he or she can escape the primary partner's unpleasant coercive pressure and thereby experience relief (negative reinforcement). The prolonged, intimate relationship between the partners so often mentioned in the literature would provide a closely shared background for the partners and favor the development of similar distortions of reality in both. This would be a possible explanation for simultaneous psychosis. From the behavioral perspective, then, each case is examined for the operation of the same well-established principles of learning and conditioning that govern the development of adaptive, as well as maladaptive, behavior.

Heredity or environment, nature or nurture? We have seen evidence critical of each position and evidence favorable to each position. It is likely that we will increase our understanding of this bizarre behavior disorder more quickly if we assign importance to both factors in all cases and then approach each individual case with an open mind.

TREATMENT RECOMMENDATIONS

Progress in developing treatments has been slow because of the lack of systematic outcome studies and the fact that usually only one of the partners is presented for hospitalization. Even though treatment plans must be based on clinical judgment and case reports, therapists are generally quite optimistic regarding the treatment of folie à deux and its variants. The most important consideration is that we are not dealing with a well-circumscribed behavior deviation such as a phobia but, rather, with complex relationship problems. The traditional therapy recommendation in the past was separation, particularly in the imposed variation in which the secondary partner has not produced independent delusions. Unfortunately, evidence indicates that simple separation may do more harm than good, especially if the secondary partner is mentally retarded, a mother with a small child, or one of two elderly sisters who have lived alone in the same house for many years.

The most common approach currently is to use psychoactive medications to treat the major behavior problems, such as paranoia, anxiety, and depression. When these conditions have improved, then the relationship itself is treated, the specifics depending on the nature of the relationship. Sometimes psychotherapy is valuable in encouraging insight into issues of aggression, dependency, and separation. In general, it has been useful to increase the autonomy of all the partners by providing alternative activities, assertive response training, membership in community support groups, and other social experiences. In any case, we must keep in mind that while some patients will profit from such help, others will not. As an anonymous wise man observed, thoughts are like fleas. They jump from person to person but don't bite everyone.

Suggested Further Readings

Dewhurst, K., & Todd, J. (1956). The psychosis of association-folie à deux. *Journal of Nervous and Mental Disease, 124,* 451–459.

Friedmann, C., & Faguet, R. (Eds.). (1982). *Extraordinary disorders of human behavior.* New York: Plenum Press.

Gralnick, A. (1942). Folie à deux: The psychosis of association. *Psychiatric Quarterly, 16,* 250–263.

Kallman, F., & Mickey, J. (1946). The concept of insanity in family units. *Journal of Nervous and Mental Disease, 104,* 303–315.

Lazarus, A. (1985). Folie à deux: Psychosis by association or genetic determinism? *Comprehensive Psychiatry, 26,* 129–133.

Sacks, M. (1988). Folie à deux. *Comprehensive Psychiatry, 29,* 270–277.

CHAPTER 9

Koro
The Disappearing Penis

A man's penis is the very essence of his masculinity. His penis defines his identity. Of course, we can argue that this is not the way it should be. But in any traditionally patriarchal society, including the United States, that equation does prevail.

The well-publicized case of the Bobbitts of Virginia illustrates both the symbolic and the real significance of the male member as an organ of power as well as sex. In June 1993, Lorena Bobbitt cut off the penis of her husband, John, after, she claimed, he had raped her. She was later thoughtful enough to point out to the police the field where she had thrown it from her car. The police retrieved the penis and delivered it to a team of surgeons, who reattached it to John in a 9-hour operation. Unfortunately for John (and his future partners), only the original one-third of his penis is capable of erection.

Female transsexuals, those biological females who feel that psychologically they are men, insist on having a penis created as part of their sex-change surgeries. Male transsexuals, who are biological males wishing to become females, desire castration and the creation of a vagina as their primary surgical goals. Transsexuals define their identity in terms of their genitals, just as everyone else seems to do.

What if a man believes that his penis is shrinking and disappearing into his body? What could be more frightening? The threat of losing one's penis (nonsurgically) is the essence of the bizarre syndrome of *koro*. The man believes that once it withdraws completely into his abdomen, he will immediately die. The prospect is terrifying.

As rare as koro is in men, the female equivalent of the delusion is even rarer. The woman with koro believes that her breasts, nipples, or labia are gradually disappearing, which makes her just as fearful as the man who feels in jeopardy of losing his penis and his life. When a koro epidemic hit Singapore in July 1967, of the 536 cases that were seen by medical professionals at that time, 521 were men and only 15 were women (less than 3% of the cases).

Epidemics of koro have also been reported in West Bengal, India, in July 1982 and in northeastern Thailand in November 1976. In the latter instance, psychiatric researchers Sangun Suwanlert and Donald Coates estimated that 2,000 people developed the "full-blown koro syndrome." They studied the 350 cases that were treated in the five area hospitals. Those cases consisted of 338 men (96.6%) and just 12 women (3.4%), ranging in age from 6 to 72 years, although most cases were between the ages of 11 and 20. Two other characteristics of those patients are especially noteworthy: 8% were Buddhist monks and none were Chinese, although 10% of the population in that area was Chinese. That absence is very unusual, since koro has traditionally been considered to be a Chinese culture-bound syndrome.

ORIGIN OF KORO

The word *koro* is thought to be of Javanese or Malay origin. The syndrome was first described in Chinese in the *Yellow Emperor's Book of Medicine* as early as 3000 B.C. Undoubtedly, though, males' attention and concerns about penis presence have been occurring ever since the first time two men appeared without clothes in the same place at the same time. The earliest reports of this disorder all came from Southeast Asia and nearby regions.

Other Asian languages have their own names for the koro syndrome. For example, in Chinese Cantonese dialect the term is *suk-yeong,* and *so-yang* in Mandarin. In women the corresponding term is *so-yin.* The terms reflect the disruption of the yin-yang polarity in the unfortunate patient.

The Culture-Bound Controversy

The koro syndrome introduces the concept of "cultural relativism," which suggests that an individual's pattern of behavior or complaint may be seen as abnormal or sick in one culture, but not necessarily so in another culture. In fact, the very same behavior may be especially prized in the second culture and certainly not viewed negatively. Conversely, the concept of "cultural invariance" suggests that some behaviors are so unusual or strange that they should be considered abnormal in all cultures.

The more that individuals deviate from their own cultural patterns, the more likely they will be regarded as abnormal. An interesting illustration of this phenomenon is the different responses shown by British and Indian soldiers during World War II battles in Burma. Combat is stressful, and psychological stress reactions are expected to occur in some men. In this instance the stress-induced responses appeared with equal frequency in the two groups of men, but in strikingly different forms. British soldiers displayed anxiety reactions and talked about them readily. In contrast, the Indian soldiers exhibited hysteriform responses (physical symptoms such as paralysis or rashes brought on by emotional stress) and were quite unwilling to talk about their experiences. In both cases the soldiers were reacting in accord with their own culturally acquired values.

A symptom picture is thought of as *culture-bound* if its unique features arise from beliefs held strongly by members of a particular subculture. For many years koro was defined as a clearly culture-bound phenomenon, because it seemed to affect only Chinese people. Now we have evidence of worldwide occurrences of koro.

Is it because of publicity that koro has in recent years been reported in such diverse cultures as Great Britain, France, Scotland, Cyprus, Israel, Italy, Nigeria, the United States, Canada, Georgia, Yemen, India, West India, Singapore, Hong Kong, and South Africa? This geographical dispersion calls into question the assertion that the syndrome is really so culture-specific. Looking ahead to one of the more interesting and appealing treatments, fellatio, we may better understand the rise in the incidence of koro.

Of course, there can be less tantalizing explanations as well. With the advent of sophisticated technology, relatively inexpensive printing, and television, information becomes readily accessible throughout the world nearly instantaneously. The previously clear distinctions between Western medicine and traditional Chinese folk medicine become blurred. The ability to identify specific, well-defined syndromes, unique to just one culture, is fading.

Koro and other so-called culture-bound syndromes such as *amok, latah, Windigo,* and *susto* reflect a very different perspective on mental disorders than the traditional diagnostic classification system, the DSM IV, which is now in use by U.S. and other Western mental health professionals. These culture-specific syndromes cannot be integrated with the DSM and have no known neurological substrates. They arise from the cultural influences, norms, and personal beliefs of the individual, not from the rigid Westernized standards of normality or test scores.

How Culture Contributes

Culture can contribute to the cause, the form, and the interpretation of various syndromes. In 1982, Dr. Wolfgang Pfeiffer of Münster, Germany, described four ways in which a culture can affect a mental disorder in an individual:

1. *Factors considered to be stressors in a particular culture.* For example, the experience of war, taking university exams, or the family social structure itself can each produce symptom patterns. To illustrate, the traditional arranged marriages in India can produce extreme unhappiness, or even suicide or psychotic possession states.

2. *The form taken by the stress symptom.* The culture can approve patterns of unusual behavior, which show up in trancelike or stuporous states. Examples include the unusual sexual liberties that are taken in conservative Catholic countries during Carnival celebrations (see the discussion on frottage and toucheurism in

Chapter 3) and the amputation of a finger joint as part of a grief reaction by citizens of New Guinea.

3. *The interpreted meaning given to the symptom.* The particular behavior pattern displayed by an individual is structured and understood in terms of the conceptions of the culture. Naming the disturbance is a necessary step before any form of treatment is applied. Koro and other "sperm loss" syndromes are good examples.

4. *The prescribed remedy or treatment.* The culture clearly shapes the healing ritual. Members of the group may participate in treatment rites. Since many of the syndromes are considered to be fatal if untreated, those rites are designed to bring the power that is latent in the patient to its full manifestation, thereby giving the patient new life.

EXAMPLES OF OTHER CULTURE-BOUND SYNDROMES

Culture-bound syndromes are defined by four major characteristics: a rather abrupt onset, a duration of a relatively short time, the absence of a formal thought disorder (nonpsychotic thinking), and a behavior pattern that is reasonably well organized, even if it is bizarre. Thus, the individual is not simply a raving, chronically disoriented madman most of the time. During the episode, though, he or she may show many of our standard stereotypes of psychosis. What is so different is the culture specificity of the syndrome and the influence of the subculture's norms.

To appreciate koro and other sperm-loss syndromes, it is necessary to adopt the perspective of the subculture of traditional Chinese folk medicine.

Chinese Medicine's Concepts and Beliefs

Dr. Keh-ming Lin, a psychiatrist at UCLA, describes the fundamental role of the concepts of yin and yang in traditional Chinese medicine:

These are a pair of polar terms used to describe qualitatively contrasting aspects inherent in the universe. They are relativistic, functional and dynamic. The use of these terms invariably infers a comparison. They are at the same time contradictory, but also complementary and interdependent with each other (i.e., the idea of darkness is necessary for the concept of brightness). The interaction of *yin* and *yang* serves as the basis of all change in the universe, both macrocosmic and microcosmic. Owing to their interaction and the changes that result, temporary imbalance is unavoidable. But ultimately if balance cannot finally be achieved, the result will be a situation of dysfunction.

Briefly described, *yang* signifies not only the apparent, active, excited, upward, forward, aggressive, volatile, hard, bright, hot, but also the abstract and functional. In direct contrast, *yin* signifies not only the passive, inhibited, unclear, inward, downward, retrogressive, cold, dark, soft, unaggressive, but also the material and concrete.

The theory of *yin-yang* has broad application in Chinese medicine. It is used to describe anatomico-physiological relations and pathological conditions. But it also details the nature and phase of disease, as well as the categorization of medication, dietary considerations and other therapeutic measures. The primary concern of diagnosis in Chinese medicine is to delineate imbalance between *yin-yang* and treatment is primarily aimed at the restoration of this balance.

Psychiatrists Keh-ming Lin, Arthur Kleinman, and Tsung-yi Lin draw our attention to the counterpart syndrome to koro, *frigophobia,* which has surfaced in a handful of cases among Chinese patients in Taiwan. Because of their profound fear of cold, these patients put on multiple layers of clothing and stay indoors in stifling conditions, in an attempt to avoid becoming chilled. They ignore symbolically "cold" foods and consume only "hot" foods. Their *yin-yang* balance is upset in the opposite direction to that of koro patients. In koro there is a fear of losing yang, but in frigophobia there is a fear of an excess of the female element yin.

Semen Power

Several additional cultural beliefs and assumptions about health are vital to understanding koro and other Chinese culture-bound syndromes.

Sperm, for example, is the most important bearer of the power of life. Its loss will lead to high anxiety. It is believed that it takes 10 drops of blood to produce one drop of semen. (Some authorities quote a formula requiring 80 drops of blood, which obviously makes semen all the more valuable.) In turn, it takes 10 grains of rice to form each drop of blood. No wonder rice is such an important staple in the Chinese diet!

In India the Ayurvedic medical system, similarly to the traditional Chinese system, teaches that semen loss leads to a loss of good health. Abstinence keeps one healthy. (Note the resemblance to the warnings of American conservative politicians.) The Ayurvedic system's formula is that it takes 40 days of nourishment to produce one drop of semen. This very valuable product must be conserved and not wasted frivolously.

Sexual dissipation and the excessive loss of seminal fluid are believed in many cultures to lead to emaciation and, eventually, death. If the semen loss is involuntary, as might occur in nocturnal emissions, the man becomes especially vulnerable to anxiety. In traditional Chinese society, nocturnal emissions are believed to be caused by evil fox spirits. Those spirits turn into beautiful women who have the power to rob men of their vital bodily fluid (that is, semen).

Similarly, male masturbation is discouraged, because it can lead to the loss of semen if it goes "all the way" to ejaculation. Historically, masturbation has received a bad press in most societies. Western cultures in the nineteenth century even featured antierection devices. One example was a penis ring that displayed four sharp metal points facing inward. Should the penis "inadvertently" become erect, as when self-stimulated, the man's masturbation would be clearly "discouraged"— and all his hard-earned semen would be retained.

Another device was the "erection detector." Again, a band, but without pointed spikes, was fitted over the penis. If and when the penis enlarged, a bell would ring in the adjoining room. It is unclear just who was to respond to the bell and in what way. In any case, we are sure that the erection problem would have been handled appropriately. Could this be another example of "Ask not for whom the bell tolls"?

The alleged harmful effects of masturbation have a long history. Sexologist Edgar Gregersen has listed the following pseudoscientific beliefs that over the years have been associated with masturbation:

[Male masturbation was said to cause] insanity, infantile paralysis, rheumatism, acne, epileptic fits, bed-wetting, round shoulders, blindness, melancholy, impotence, hair growing on the palm of the hands, idiocy, hypochondriasis, tuberculosis, various skin diseases, asthma and suicide. Female masturbation was said to cause rickets, hysteria, hermaphroditism, painful menstruation, jaundice, stomach cramps, falling of the womb, painful childbirth and sterility (among other calamities).

It is a true wonder that anyone would ever take the chance. *Sukra prameha* is the Indian term for sperm-loss syndrome. It typically is self-diagnosed from the following collection of symptoms: urine without color, discharges from the penis, weakness, exhaustion, burning sensations on the surface of the body, joint ailments, disturbances of concentration and learning, and, of course, problems in sexual functioning.

What causes sperm loss? Sexual excesses naturally, including too much intercourse and masturbation. Heated foods, intoxicants, and a "fiery" constitution are cited as additional causes. The appropriate treatment for semen loss follows logically, consisting of rest, sexual restraint, tonics to increase sperm, and a diet and medications which supposedly have a cooling effect.

In the traditional Chinese culture high value is placed on the suppression of negative emotions. It is much more socially acceptable to be physically ill. Therefore, in the face of psychological pressures, the tendency is to hold in the distressing emotions and to express one's reactions in physical symptoms. (In Western medicine this tendency is called *somatization*.) If a man is bothered by sexual anxieties and notices vague or very subtle bodily changes, he could very well develop a full-scale somatic delusion such as koro. What is crucial is that he is aware of and truly *believes* that this syndrome can occur.

Thus, we have a culture-specific variation of the "If you don't use it, you lose it" slogan. Here the concern is "If you believe you'll lose it and die, you won't, but you will acquire a major delusion."

Severe mental disorders, those we would consider psychoses, are, in China, reasons for isolating and avoiding their victims. Such people are considered to be untrustworthy. Treatment is understood to be difficult and expensive beyond the sufferer's means. These attitudes produce a fatalistic outlook for the patients and those around them. In the case of koro, the expectation of death, once the penis has completely disappeared, is the usual outcome.

When a particular symptom pattern makes no sense to the average person with relatively little formal education, one explanation often considered is that of *spirit possession.* A person's unusual behavior is accounted for by claiming that he or she is possessed by a spirit.

Spirits can be good or bad. A person could be possessed by a spirit which gives him or her extraordinary powers, such as the ability to heal or to foretell the future. On the other hand, the spirit could be malignant and create delusions and trance states. In koro the individual falsely believes that his penis (or her labia or breasts) are shrinking and will soon be gone. When that happens, the person will also be gone, via death. There is an implicit belief that when a person's defining sex characteristics have gone, life is over. Even if this shrinkage were really happening, we now know that this unpleasant turn of events would not be fatal. Koro sufferers, however, would not agree.

In sum, koro, according to Chinese medicine, is believed to be caused by a disturbance in the yang-yin balance. More specifically, there has been a great weakening of the yang principle, which can occur as a result of sexual strain. Contributing to the imbalance could be a strengthening of the yin principle, which can happen as a result of extreme chilling or eating cold food.

These features of the traditional Chinese culture, wherein folk medicine is practiced and held in high regard, help create the climate for the development of such a bizarre syndrome as koro. The first cases described in the professional literature were of Chinese men. Then, some occurrences appeared in women and in men in neighboring regions in Southeast Asia. Now that cases have been described worldwide, a new term is offered with less negative cultural connotations—*genital retraction syndrome.*

SYMPTOMS OF KORO

Viennese psychiatrists M. Amering and H. Katschnig have summarized the major symptoms of koro. At the same time, they noted the many similarities of koro to the descriptive symptoms of panic attacks in the traditional Western DSM classification system.

For example, the attacks come on suddenly. Physical symptoms include those typically felt during bouts of high anxiety: breathlessness, heart palpitations, chest discomfort, nausea, abdominal distress, hot and cold sensations, sweating, faintness, trembling and shaking, tingling, and the hallmark symptom of fear of dying. Of course, one individual does not necessarily display every symptom on the list. Surprisingly, during an anxiety episode these physical signs often disappear (but not the penis itself) within a very short time, typically in less than an hour.

Psychiatrists Suwanlert and Coates suggest that the typical clinical picture in koro consists of three phases: (1) the *prodromal phase,* which includes physical symptoms such as dizziness, genital pain or numbness, and diarrhea (which occurred in the Thailand epidemic), after eating the allegedly poisoned food or after smoking tainted cigarettes; (2) the *penile shrinking phase,* during which the patient feels his penis is shrinking or experiences genital numbness, nipple pain, discomfort when urinating, and sensations of panic; in women the complaints include feelings of vaginal dilation; and (3) the *recovery phase,* in which the patients fear continuing impotence, genital shrinkage, and possible later mental illness. (It is unclear why this phase would be called "recovery," since the major symptoms seem to persist.)

The Case of the Genuinely Shrinking Penis

What if a man's penis really did shrink? Psychiatrist Femi Oyebode and colleagues Robin Jamieson, James Mullaney, and Kenneth Davison in Newcastle, England, were faced with a man who met the usual criteria for the diagnosis of koro. They decided to disprove the man's delusion by actually measuring his penis.

The penile plethysmograph is a device that can objectively measure the circumference of a man's penis. It is a standard method of assessing whether various stimuli, *Playboy* pictures, or photos of children, or whatever, are sexually arousing for a particular person. Changes in the "strain gauge" (a loop around the penis that expands when the penis does) are recorded, which indicate the degree of the man's erectile arousal. The results obtained from this machine are actually scientifically more valid than a subject's self-report.

Oyebode and colleagues' case study follows:

> G. C., a 56-year-old man, initially presented . . . with a six year history of recurrent shrinkage of the penis. The first episode occurred suddenly . . . whilst he was out cycling on a cold day; he had experienced a strange sensation in the perineum, and when he stopped to examine his penis, he was convinced that it had shrunk considerably. He had irregular recurrence of this "penile shrinkage" over the years, each episode lasting about 24–28 hours. The shrinkage was associated with the fear that his penis would disappear completely and that it was the sign of a serious illness. However, he never believed that it would prove fatal.
>
> The episode provoked intense panic during which he became restless and agitated; on one occasion, his wife hung onto his penis in order, as he thought, to prevent its total disappearance. The episodes were related to stressful situations such as holidays, difficulties at work, and entertaining at home.
>
> He was born and raised on Tyneside and was an only child, whose mother committed suicide when he was 21 years old; his father died 18 months later, and he perceived these parental deaths as particularly traumatic. He had been married for 26 years, and there were no children by choice. His pre-morbid personality was characterized by obsessional preoccupation with detail and an excessive concern for order and routine.
>
> He was admitted . . . when, in addition to severe recurrence of his conviction that his penis was shrinking, there was also evidence of a depressive disorder with endogenous features. This was his first documented depressive episode. . . . The penile shrinkage had occurred over many years without any associated depressed mood, and appeared to be independent of his depression. . . .
>
> Changes in penile circumference were recorded while the patient imagined shrinkage conditions, sexually stimulating images, and neutral stimuli. . . . Whilst talking about sexual fantasies, he showed rapid fluctuations of penile circumference above the baseline . . . which was indicative of an erection. The greatest increase was caused by voyeuristic fantasies; he was aware of having a partial erection whilst describing these.

> Whilst describing an occasion when he was out cycling in cold
> weather and had experienced his penis shrinking, the plethysmo-
> graph recording showed fluctuations in penile circumference below
> the baseline. . . . He was aware of this as an experience of penile
> shrinkage.

Rather than show the patient that his belief was a delusion, the researchers, with their fancy scientific measuring instruments, actually
proved that his penis was indeed shrinking.

Upon reading this case report, we might fear that the patient's koro
belief had now been permanently installed. The psychiatrists, though,
assure us that G. C. "responded" to a combination of medicines and
that they continue to monitor him. They believe that this patient may
either have been physiologically dysfunctional (that is, his equipment
was not wired exactly right) or that his "obsessional self-scrutiny"
brought on his overreactions to normal changes in penis size.

We tend to favor the second explanation, but also wish to point out
that the doctors had measured G. C.'s penis' *circumference*, when they
should have been measuring its *length*. The fear in koro is not that your
penis is getting too thin, but that it is getting too short—to the point of
disappearing altogether.

Penis Size

Is concern with penis size necessarily a psychiatric problem? If koro is
not just a culture-bound syndrome, as most experts now agree, could it
be a "normal preoccupation"? Or, is that phrase itself a contradiction
in terms?

In American sexual mythology it has long been assumed that longer
penises produce greater sexual pleasure in women and reflect the greater
virility of males. Researchers Mel Poretz and Barry Sinrod attacked this
issue directly in a recent large-scale representative survey of American
households in all 50 states. Their sample of 3,144 people was representative of 89% of the U.S. adult population, with a margin of error of
3%. It included appropriate proportional representations of ethnic mi-
norities. Since their survey is impressive both in terms of its statistics
and its information, we describe their results in some detail.

What do these men feel about the size of their penises? Roughly two-thirds of them are indeed satisfied. Of the 35% of the men who were not satisfied, a sizable group itself, 52% would like a bigger penis, while 12% wanted a *smaller* one. More specifically, 53% would like it to be *longer* and 40% wished for it to be *wider*.

The surveyors asked the women if they were satisfied with their mates' penises. Overall, 86% of them were satisfied, which included a resounding 96% of women in the 18-to-29-year age range. Of those women (14% of the sample) who were not satisfied, 44% wished their mates were bigger and 22% would like them smaller. Regarding further specifications, 48% wanted their mates' members to be longer and 23% preferred wider penises.

Perhaps the 35% of men who are dissatisfied with the size of their penises are especially at risk for developing the koro syndrome. This anxiety over member size could easily lead to excessive self-examination and preoccupation.

One koro patient, described by Drs. John Money and Charles Annecillo at Johns Hopkins University and Hospital, produced drawings that reflected his distorted perceptions of the size of his penis in both the flaccid and erect states. An especially interesting feature of this case is that because of a mass of protruding fat in his lower abdomen, the man, when looking down, could actually see only a portion of his penis. At that angle it indeed did look shorter. His perception confirmed his fears and hardened his delusion.

Because a penis really does shrink (*temporarily* and *normally*) when it and its owner are cold, fatigued, or embarrassed, these already "over-concerned" men might mislabel the retraction as a serious medical problem, which they believe could be fatal.

What is the normal (average) size of the (American) penis? Let's approach this one head on. Sexologist John Money reports that "the average stretched penis length is 6.57 inches with a standard deviation of 0.77 inches." *Standard deviation* is a statistical term expressing the range of sizes. The 1990 *Kinsey Institute New Report on Sex* concurs with Money's figures, but notes that about 30% of American men could not answer this question correctly. Interestingly, but not surprisingly, those who were misinformed were almost twice as likely to overestimate penis size than to underestimate average size. Given men's typical concerns, the Kinsey group found that "American women were almost twice as likely as men to think that the average erect penis is four inches or less or to say they simply didn't know the answer."

The *Report* went on to say, "The average length of the *flaccid* (non-erect) adult penis is approximately 4 inches (measured along the top from the pubic bone to the tip of the penis). . . . Differences in length while flaccid often disappear during erections—men with shorter-than-average flaccid penises have a larger percent of size increase during erection, while larger-than-average flaccid penises increase relatively less with erection."

There is actually a *very* rare medical condition called *micropenis*, but any erect penis that is at least 1.5 inches long can function perfectly adequately for fully pleasurable (to both parties) vaginal intercourse. Men should not be tempted to compare themselves with the record breakers, such as the penis of the blue whale, which measures about 10 feet, or the infamous gentleman of pornography fame mentioned during Supreme Court Justice Clarence Thomas's confirmation hearings, "Long Dong Silver," whose *unverified* penis length is claimed to be 19 inches. Dr. June Reinisch, director emeritus of the Kinsey Institute, lists the longest physician-measured erect penis as a mere 13 inches, the assessment task having been accomplished by a Dr. Robert L. Dickinson early in this century.

PSYCHODYNAMIC THEORY OF KORO

Most of the Western psychological theorizing about koro is derived from the Freudian psychoanalytic perspective. As is so often the case, the problem of koro is ultimately due to the fear of castration. In Freud's theory, the male child fears that his powerful father will retaliate against him for his (unconscious) sexual desires for his own mother (father's wife). That retaliation is assumed to be in the form of castration, a fate that the male child fears (falsely) has already befallen females.

In 1948, psychiatrist Fritz Kobler, then at the National Central University in Nanking, China, suggested that the original cultural punishment for incest, which is the child's desire, was not castration alone, but death, either alone or with castration. This association accounts for the prominence of the fear of death in this disorder, which is even greater than the fear of castration. The patient believes he can prevent death by preventing the disappearance of his penis.

Kobler connects the anxiety concerning the disappearing penis to anxiety about masturbation. In essence, if a boy masturbates, he is to be punished by castration and death. "The symptom also shows a characteristic double meaning by preventing and punishing masturbation on the one hand, but on the other hand leading to the very masturbatory act of holding the penis." The hand that produces the fear can also be the hand that prevents the worst from happening. Hold on for dear life!

Indian psychoanalysts D. N. Nandi and Gauranga Banerjee in Calcutta generally agree with Kobler's description of the dynamics of koro in male patients. They extend their theorizing to explain koro in females as well.

> In the early phallic phase, a child (both male and female) discovers that there is an organ (penis or clitoris) in its body which is highly excitable and full of pleasurable sensations. The child feels that it is much superior to any other part of the body in its capacity for rousing intense pleasurable sensation. . . . All living organisms possess this prized organ. But one group has a manifest organ and the other group has it castrated or hidden.

Nandi and Banerjee acknowledge that "we understand how important is the penis in the emotional life of a man. . . . Turning our attention to the position of the girl we see that during her phallic phase she discovers that her clitoris is the richest source of pleasurable sensation and through which intense gratification can be obtained. However, very soon she also discovers that her clitoris is inferior to the corresponding male organ—the penis. The penis envy starts here and she painfully considers this deprivation as punishment or injustice. This discovery rouses in her an intense sense of loss and narcissistic injury and she attempts to compensate for the inadequacy, with a penis, or the possessor of the penis (the father) or a baby from the father. But she struggles in vain."

They proceed to point out the "great similarity" of the nipple of the breast with the glans penis or glans clitoris. Thereby, they can account for the koro symptoms in women, in which they fear a shrinkage and the eventual disappearance of their breasts or labia. "In the female [the] loss of [the] breast give[s] her an opportunity to get rid of her obvious feminine identity and to satisfy her unconscious wish to be a man." The present authors are very pleased to remind the readers that this theory is not their own.

BEHAVIORAL THEORY OF KORO

The behavioral theory approach to understanding a bizarre disorder is to assume that the unusual behavior or belief has been learned. Other than a few that are the result of biological instincts, most behaviors are learned, even if those behaviors are regarded by most people as "crazy" or abnormal.

With koro, an anxious man may have doubts about his sexual adequacy and may continually check his organ for health and size. Since the penis does shrink temporarily when under conditions of cold or fright, it may indeed become smaller. During the self-examination, the man notices this diminishment and becomes even more fearful, and the penis consequently becomes less sizable. He learns by association that his anxieties are connected to his shrinking penis.

R. Khubalkar and O. P. Gupta of the Mahatma Gandhi Institute of Medical Sciences in Wardha, India, reported a case of koro in a 21-year-old male who complained of "a lack of erection and loss of strength in his penis." He enjoyed pornographic literature and masturbation, but one of the books suggested that "excessive masturbation can lead to reduction in the size of the penis." Even though the authors intended to describe this case from a psychodynamic perspective, they concluded ironically that "development of koro is rather a *learned* [italics added] phenomenon which results in an insecure person by some kind of accidental or occasional exposure of such ideas by reading, hearing or witnessing a case."

The learning theory explanation seems more straightforward and plausible than some of the more convoluted psychoanalytic theorizing. Of course, no known cases have been analyzed and treated from the behavioral perspective. These cases will no doubt be appearing soon, that is, if the problem does not simply disappear.

TREATMENT OF KORO

A variety of treatments have been offered to sufferers with koro, ranging from the pleasant to the painful. At the pleasant end of the continuum is the recommendation that fellatio be practiced immediately, which would serve to help avoid retraction of the organ. Or the patient himself, or a trusted friend, could grip the penis firmly for the same purpose. The application of special wooden or jade clamps or merely tying a ribbon around the penis can serve as preventative measures as well. Some folk medicine prevention techniques have less obvious connections: applying lime to the earlobe or tip of the nose and wrapping the man's big toes in slices of the stem of black arum, a vegetable that is a known irritant.

Since koro represents a disturbance in the yin-yang balance, in Chinese medicine, the prescribed treatment consists of the appropriate diet and medication that can restore the strength of the yang principle. For example, the patient would consume ginseng root, alcohol, lime juice, and lean meat which are considered to be rich in yang. At the same time, he should avoid foods that are thought to contain an excess of yin: cold drinks, fruits, and vegetables, especially if they are uncooked.

Although it is crucial to avoid cold foods and drinks, for some reason it is common to pour buckets of cold water over the head of a koro patient. Perhaps this is the origin of the American folk remedy of a cold shower to abate undue sexual arousal when release is not appropriate or available. Imagined sexual excesses that have led to semen loss are viewed as preceding the koro attack.

Physicians have also provided an immediate injection of calcium gluconate, which produces a feeling of warmth throughout the body. Additional medical treatments that have been tried with koro are electroconvulsive shock therapy and Valium.

During the epidemic of 1982 in India, well-intentioned parents who were concerned that their son's penis was shrinking tied a strong thread to the foreskin of the penis. That thread was then tied to another thread, which had been tied around the boy's waist. Consequently, painful ulcers formed on the foreskin. Doctors measured the penis regularly and reassured the parents that no shrinkage was occurring. Of course, the risk here is that the parents might conclude superstitiously that their own homemade treatment was actually working.

Finally, the friends and family of the patient typically offer their prayers and emotional support for him and the retention of his penis. It certainly could not hurt to seek God's help in such an important matter.

Modern Western medicine views the genital retraction syndrome as an aspect of high anxiety or "acute castration fear." The syndrome is known to appear in association with a variety of other conditions: amphetamine overuse, brain tumor, depression, epilepsy, heroin withdrawal, stroke, schizophrenia, cerebral syphilis, and panic attacks. At this time there is a controversy raging in the professional literature about whether koro deserves its own diagnostic category in the next edition of the official DSM.

Modern treatment of koro is similar to most other psychological disorders: medication, psychotherapy, and behavior therapy. For example, tranquilizers have been prescribed for the patient's intense anxiety and antidepressants for any accompanying depression. To increase the blood flow into the corpora cavernosa of the penis, and to reduce the blood flow out of the same area, yohimbine, a reputed aphrodisiac, has been tried with the koro patient.

Psychodynamic psychotherapy may also be offered as a vehicle to understand the motives underlying the patient's fear that his penis is shrinking into oblivion. It is assumed that once an understanding of the causes of the fear is achieved, then the fear will disappear and the penis will reappear.

We know of no cases in which behavior therapy has been applied to koro thus far. It seems that relaxation training and systematic desensitization to the irrational fear would be the behavior treatment techniques of choice. Of course, some of the Chinese and Indian methods to prevent retraction of the penis are actually behavior-based approaches. The clamps, the gripping, and the fellatio all serve as "response prevention environmental manipulations," in the technical jargon of the behavior therapists. In other words, the devices and the oral sex will keep the penis out, alive, and well.

Our own fear is that if the latter treatment becomes too well known, epidemics of koro will increase!

Suggested Further Readings

Al-Issa, I. (Ed.). *Culture and Psychopathology*. Baltimore: University Park Press.

Gregersen, E. (1983). *Sexual Practices: The Story of Human Sexuality*. New York: Franklin Watts.

Kleinman, A., & Lin, T-Y. (Eds.) *Normal and Abnormal Behavior in Chinese Culture*. Dordrecht, Holland: D. Reidel Publishing Co.

Money, J., & Annecillo, C. (1987). Body-image pathology: Koro, the shrinking-penis syndrome in transcultural sexology. *Sexual and Marital Therapy, 2,* 91–100.

Reinisch, J. M. (1990). *The Kinsey Institute New Report on Sex*. New York: St. Martin's Press.

CHAPTER 10

Savants
Supertalents in the Subnormal

Thirty-eight-year old Bob Simmons (not his real name) is an extraordinarily talented musician. Tall, well built, and bearded, he is an impressive sight as he sits at the piano delivering flawless renditions of classical compositions. He is a pure classicist with the gift of absolute pitch and refuses to listen to anything but masterworks by the most eminent composers. An excellent sight reader, he can also play by ear. He has played private recitals with an impressive list of famous musicians. They rate his musical ability as outstanding. He has even played the piano at rehearsals for a leading chamber music orchestra. In fact, most of the members still visit him and play his latest compositions with him.

Bob also has a marvelous memory. Once he was asked to read selections from Carmer's *Cavalcade of American History* and make an immediate oral report. The articles chosen were about Thomas Edison and George Washington and averaged 2½ pages each. After a single silent reading of the Washington article, he reproduced it perfectly. He refused to repeat the Edison article until he had been allowed a second reading. He then, however, gave another flawless recitation. Asked how he was able to perform such feats, he just laughed and said, "Anyone can do it."

Whenever members of his family are in doubt about a date they ask Bob. He never seems to forget the time or place of family events.

He is delighted to rattle off the dates of birth, marriage, death, and other important events in the lives of heroes from American history. Similarly, he has a large store of information about classical European composers. He can tell where they lived, when they were born and died, the titles of their compositions, and where each composition was first published and played in public.

Ready to trade places with the talented Mr. Simmons? Before deciding, you should know what else goes along with his unusual talents.

Mr. Simmons suffered permanent brain damage at birth and failed to talk until he was 5. He has a mental age of 10 and an IQ score of 67. He makes funny faces and talks to mirrors and to himself continually. Occasionally he will balance objects on his head and launch into peculiar dance steps. He paces the room restlessly, laughs to himself, kisses any object that catches his eye. He sometimes goes out of his way to be rude, pushing people out of his way on the street, belching, and licking his plate and eating utensils after a meal. He is completely unable to care for himself and requires constant supervision by his family. Mr. Simmons's condition is called the "savant syndrome."

DEFINITION AND INCIDENCE

The *savant syndrome* is the modern name for the condition of those rare people who have obvious subnormal intelligence, but who also possess exceptional skills in some special area of functioning. It is difficult to determine the incidence of this condition in the general population. One survey of homes for the mentally retarded, covering 90,000 residents, turned up 54 savants, or about one in every 2,000 residents. Another survey discovered 8 savants in a population of 4,000 residents. However, there are probably many more undiscovered talents in this population than the small number discovered in institutions. A majority of mentally retarded people live at home with their parents, so surveys of institutions will seriously underestimate the general incidence. In any event, more cases of savants have been discovered and studied since 1968 than in all the previous years. The most recent information comes from a major study conducted by the well-known scholar and investigator of autism,

Dr. Bernard Rimland, director of the Institute for Child Behavior Research in San Diego and his associate, Dr. Deborah Fein. They have compiled a data bank containing extensive information on 5,400 autistic individuals and have found that 10% of them have savant abilities, approximately 8% of the boys and 2% of the girls. Dr. Rimland followed up by asking the parents for details of their childrens' savant talents and found that musical ability was most frequent, followed by memory feats and artistic skills. Less frequently reported are remarkable mechanical ability, calendar calculating, and mathematical skills.

Let us return to the definition of the savant as an intellectually deficient person with extraordinary skill in some special area or task. The experts have disagreed about several features defining the condition. For example, should the skill far surpass that of similar people with low intelligence, or should it be outstanding as compared with those of normal intelligence? Perhaps savants seem so unique because a special ability, such as musical talent, stands in stark contrast to the skills of the average mentally retarded person who can scarcely write his or her name or do simple arithmetic. Most authorities now generally agree that to qualify for this definition, the savant's talent must far exceed that of people with average intelligence.

Another thorny definitional problem concerns the level of the savant's subnormal intelligence. Does "subnormal intelligence" merely mean low general intelligence, or does it mean that the person is intellectually deficient as compared with other retarded people? The old-fashioned name for the savant syndrome was *idiot savant,* a French term meaning "wise feeble-minded person," reflecting the puzzling contradiction we see in these people.

Until the early 1900s psychologists and psychiatrists actually used the terms "idiot," "imbecile," and "moron" as technical names for degrees of mental retardation, "moron" being the highest grade. However, these terms have long since been discarded. Modern intelligence testing shows that most savants do not fall into the lowest category, but usually are only moderately retarded. The largest majority have IQ scores between 40 and 70. In only one or two cases did savants test below an IQ of 20, the old borderline for the "idiot" category.

In discussing savant skills it is important to keep in mind that reports of incredible talents may be overenthusiastic. For example, as previously mentioned, the contrast with a person's profound deficiencies in other areas could lead to overestimation, or the individual's degree of retardation might be exaggerated to highlight the contrast with a skilled performance. In the case of musical savants Blind Tom and Leslie Lemke, contrary to folklore, both men had received substantial professional piano instruction before they developed their own unique styles. In addition, some rather cynical professional music critics asserted that the superlative reviews of their concert performances were more attributable to the critics' lack of musical knowledge than to a high quality of performance by the savants. In Blind Tom's case, a more sinister motive was put forward by his biographer, Geneva Southall, author of an exhaustive three-volume study. Tom was born a slave. After the Civil War, unrepentant southerners had a vested interest in portraying blacks as less than human to justify the institution of slavery and the discrimination which succeeded it. Therefore, Tom's talents had to be attributed to mere "slavish" imitation, to diabolical possession, or somehow to a byproduct of his presumed idiocy—anything to avoid acknowledging black musical genius. By keeping these factors in mind, we are in a better position to evaluate the claimed accomplishments of savants.

MUSICAL TALENT

In addition to some more spectacular skill, many savants have special musical abilities. These include perfect pitch, the skillful playing of musical instruments by ear, and the ability to sing whole operatic arias after just one hearing. Trelat, a nineteenth-century French psychiatrist, described one case as follows:

> They had in the Salpêtrière [the asylum for women] an imbecile born blind, affected with rickets and crippled, who had great musical talents. Her voice was very correct, and whenever she had sung or heard some piece she knew perfectly well the words and the music. As long as she lived they came to her to correct the mistakes in singing of her companions; they asked her to repeat a passage which had gone wrong, which she always did admirably. One day, Geraldy

Liszt and Meyerbeer came to the humble singing class of our asylum to bring her their encouraging consolations.

Following the Civil War in the United States, when the nation was ready for lighter things, another savant, the remarkable musical genius Blind Tom, created enormous public interest. Thomas Greene Wiggins, the fourteenth child of an African American woman sold as a slave in 1849 to a General Bethune, was included in the sale at no extra cost since his blindness made him unfit for work. For this reason Tom was allowed to roam the plantation and mansion house freely. He became fascinated by sounds of all kinds—the falling raindrops, the murmuring of the wind in the trees, and especially the sounds of the General's daughters playing the piano. Although barely able to walk or talk until he was 4, little Tom kept time to the music with his body. One day, while seated at the piano, he surprised everyone present by imitating combinations of notes he had heard and improvising little tunes. Late one night the General was awakened by piano music coming from the drawing room. Prepared to scold his daughter for disturbing everyone, he was astounded to see Blind Tom seated at the piano, flawlessly playing a Mozart sonata from beginning to end.

Tom never attended school, partly because of his slave status but also because he was somewhat temperamental except when playing his beloved piano. Within a few years he could listen to a piece of music and then play it through from beginning to end, continuously and without error, note for note. At age 6 Tom began to improvise as well as imitate, and General Bethune, with an eye toward exhibiting Tom as a concert artist, hired world-class professional musicians to instruct the child. Soon his repertoire included Rossini, Donizetti, Beethoven, Bach, Chopin, and virtually all the other major composers old and new. As the prodigy's fame spread, he gave a public concert at age 7. It was such a spectacular success that the General and Tom went on tour, earning more than $100,000 during the first year. Reviews of Tom's performances were superlative, and critics made frequent comparisons between Tom and both Mozart and Beethoven. At age 11 Tom played at the White House for President James Buchanan. However, several suspicious musicians believed that Tom was a charlatan, and the very next day tested him at his hotel by having him play two completely novel compositions. The first, which was 13 pages long, Tom repeated without error from start to finish, and the second, 20 pages in length, was also reproduced flawlessly. As Tom's international fame and repertoire grew, he was regularly tested by unbelieving professionals, effortlessly meeting every challenge. He continued his concert tours until age 53, when General Bethune, his mentor, agent, exploiter, and publicist, died. After the General's death Tom seemed to lose his desire to continue and sank into a deep depression. He died, alone and friendless, in 1908.

Perhaps the most famous modern musical savant, whose development has some uncanny similarities to Blind Tom's, is 33-year-old Leslie Lemke. Leslie Lemke is blind, crippled by cerebral palsy, and mentally functions at the 3-year-old level. He is also a gifted piano virtuoso. His early childhood was a struggle to even stand up, much less walk or talk. His adoptive mother, in her efforts to stimulate his senses, exposed the young child to music very early. She had Leslie touch and feel the vibrations in the piano as she struck each key. Although there was little or no change in the boy, she persisted in her labor of love.

One Sunday when Leslie was 16, his parents were startled from sleep at 3:00 A.M. by music coming from the living room. Leslie was at the piano, skillfully playing a Tchaikovsky concerto he had heard Liberace perform in a TV appearance. At this time Leslie could not speak or even hold a cup. Within the next few years his piano playing improved rapidly, and it became evident that hearing any piece of music only once, he could reproduce it flawlessly on the piano. Soon he began to speak and then began singing and playing a wide repertoire of popular, religious, and classical music. Today he gives concerts all over the United States and has appeared on television numerous times. Although Leslie's talents are unquestionably exceptional, some published accounts inaccurately claim that his 3:00 A.M. recital was his very first performance. In actuality, he had been playing both folk songs and religious music for some time.

Although Leslie's case is widely known, another musical savant has been studied in much greater detail. In the winter of 1966 Harriet Garland, a 40-year-old intellectually disabled single woman, was admitted to Boston State Hospital. Tests in the hospital showed that she had an IQ of 73. She was confused, delusional, and threatening suicide. As her story unfolded it became clear that from earliest infancy well into adulthood she showed the remarkable talents of a musical savant. As a newborn, her music-teacher mother had little time for her. In order to keep an eye on the infant while continuing to give music and voice lessons, the mother placed Harriet's crib directly against the grand piano in the studio. Thus, from the first days of life music was Harriet's most familiar and continuous contact with the outside world. One evening when she was 7 months old her father heard a familiar musical sound from the baby's room. She was lying in her crib humming a famous aria from Rigoletto in perfect pitch, tempo, and phrasing. Within the next year she showed that she could sing all her mother's music students' exercises in all keys, major and minor, with the proper accents, phrasing, and pitch. As she grew and developed it was soon obvious that she also had many serious mental and emotional problems, although her musical talents continued to amaze. When she was 3, Harriet learned to play the piano by watching her oldest sister during piano lessons. At age 4 she could play all the arias her mother's voice students sang, using both hands and proper fingerings and harmony. Before the age of 6, although still not toilet trained and unable to talk, she could read music as well as play the French horn, violin, trumpet, and clarinet, all quite well and with feeling. At 7 Harriet played the piano and violin better than any of her six siblings and could accompany all of her mother's pupils.

Harriet's upbringing outside the world of music was extremely irregular and upsetting. She was in and out of many special schools and institutions for the retarded and emotionally disturbed, returning to her family in between. However, her musical talents persisted and expanded so that by the time she was admitted to Boston State Hospital as an adult, her fund of musical knowledge was described by her psychiatrist, Dr. David Viscott, as "breathtaking." His assessment is as follows:

> She can identify almost any major work in the entire symphonic repertoire, and give the key, opus number, date and place of first performance, and the vital statistics of the composer. Her knowledge of operatic works is even greater than her knowledge of instrumental works. What is most striking is that she knows the works of the lesser composers as well, and is familiar with literally thousands of

compositions, ranging in scope from Monteverdi to Stockhausen! Once she begins to describe a work, she begins to remember details about each performance she has heard, who conducted, and so forth. She has attended every concert of the Boston Symphony Saturday evening series for well over two decades. She knows the name, age, address, family structure, indiscretions, marital problems, and personal musical history of *every member* of the entire orchestra. She rhapsodizes over conductors and can trace their musical genealogy back a hundred years.

She knows the life stories of all the great composers, performers, and conductors, and even of some of the great patrons, and she speaks of these people with the greatest warmth and feeling.

She plays the piano well and tries to imitate orchestral effects and fill in parts which she knows are in the composition but are not written in her piano score. If she is playing an accompaniment that includes a transcribed version of a part usually played by a woodwind instrument, she will try to imitate the instrument's phrasing and tone.

She also plays the violin well although she has not been near the instrument for several years. Her sense of timing is excellent and she sight-reads adequately. She is able to harmonize a melody or improvise a counterpoint or a variation on a theme with ease and facility and with a certain innate musicality. She is able to transcribe parts from memory for her mother's students or for her family.

Her sense of pitch is superior. She has absolute pitch and can recognize the pitch of any sounds, musical or otherwise, including normal conversation. She can name all of the notes in a four-note chord which has been held for less than a half second. She can also identify the chord in terms of key and major or minor mode, and indicate where it would logically progress and resolve. She can name notes struck at random with the fist on the keyboard. She is also able to name the notes struck simultaneously at both ends of the piano with two fists. There does not seem to be any form of decay of pitch sensitivity. She can tune two musical instruments with perfect accuracy.

One of the technical feats which Harriet is able to perform is to change the key of a piece she is playing to any other key asked for upon command, without losing a beat. She can move to the relative minor or major instantaneously. Some of the transitions that I asked her to do were quite difficult, as in some Bach inventions, but she did them cheerfully, sometimes laughing in anticipation of what was asked for. "Oh, that really sounds funny. Let's do another one."

The story has a happy ending. Because of her cooperative attitude, Harriet was given antipsychotic medications and saw a psychiatrist three times a week for psychotherapy. She gradually was able to return to work and continue her musical activities.

MEMORY

Memorization of obscure facts and experiences is often found in savants along with other unusual abilities. However, prodigious feats of memory and rapid mental calculations can also be accomplished by stage performers or anyone else who wants to spend the time learning various rules, shortcuts, and strategies. For example, up until the last century certain Jewish scholars committed to memory the entire Hebrew Talmud (elaborate commentaries on the Old Testament). These legendary memory experts were called *Shass Pollak,* translated as "Polish Talmudists." Incredibly, they memorized not only the thousands of pages of the Talmud's 12 large folio volumes, but also the precise location of each word, phrase, and punctuation mark on every single page. Upon examination they could rapidly and accurately quote the text of any line, verse, or chapter. In fact, this challenge proved much too easy. Should an examiner insert a pin through a word in the text on page 48, for example, the Shass Pollak would unerringly identify from memory the precise word indicated by the pin at the same locus on page 177 or 248 or any other page requested.

While memory feats of intellectually handicapped persons are not quite as astonishing, nevertheless their accomplishments are still startling in contrast to the intellectually disabled person's other subnormal abilities. One such human almanac could repeat from memory the name of the county seat of every county in the United States, the population of every town with more than 5,000 residents, statistics concerning 3,000 mountains and rivers, the names, number of rooms, and locations of 2,000 hotels, and the essential details of more than 2,000 inventions and discoveries. Another man could repeat without error the numbers on all the cars of a passing freight train. Other savants are able to repeat verbatim, immediately after reading, complete pages from books or newspapers, in some cases either forward, backward, or upside down. Harriet Garland, the musical savant, at age 7 knew more than 300 telephone numbers, a list consisting of her mother's pupils, neighbors, relatives, and family friends. Once, as a joke, her father read her the first three pages of the Greater Boston Telephone Directory. For several years thereafter she could give any of these numbers upon request.

Such talents stand in stark contrast to the everyday inadequate personal adjustment these savants show. As extraordinary as their special abilities are, they typically are completely useless in helping them live more satisfying lives.

ARTISTIC TALENT

One of the oldest accounts of an artistic savant is that of the celebrated eighteenth-century German painter Gustav Mind—a rather ironic name in view of his mental deficiency. Mind was a cretin, someone whose intellectual handicap is caused by thyroid hormone deficiency. He was unable to read or write, had no idea of the value of money, and was clumsy and poorly coordinated. His great awkward bulk, large blunt hands, and lurching walk invariably attracted crowds of jeering children in his home village. Despite his ungainly appearance and mental deficiencies, he was a uniquely talented artist. His drawings, woodcuts, and watercolor sketches of cats, deer, rabbits, bears, and children were so marvelously executed that he was known as "The Cat's Raphael." One of his pictures of a cat and kittens was bought by King George IV of England. Other pictures hang in museums in Berlin, Zurich, and Berne. In 1971 one of his works sold for $2,500, and in 1974 another sold for almost $14,000.

In modern times, Japan has produced several talented artistic savants. For example, Kyoshi Yamashita, "the Van Gogh of Japan," is a graphic genius whose paper montages and oil paintings are considered exceptional by the highest standards of professional critics. Born in 1922 in the aftermath of a disastrous earthquake, the offspring of an alcoholic father and a broken home, Kyoshi had an IQ score of 68. Kyoshi wanders all over Japan, sleeping in barns and under bridges and begging for food, when not painting. Another famous Japanese painter, Yamamoto, was born with hydrocephalus, an abnormal accumulation of fluid in the skull often causing mental retardation. Despite an IQ that never exceeded 47 on several testings, his prints, watercolors, and oil paintings have won many prizes. His works have been exhibited at 10 major art shows in Japan, Hawaii, and Los Angeles.

Within the last few years a 19-year-old autistic British teenager, Stephen Wiltshire, has startled the art world with his remarkably precocious artistic talent. Stephen, dubbed the "Child Picasso" in his native London, can draw or paint any building, either right on the spot or from memory. He has done skyscrapers and cathedrals, bridges and castles. With a tested intelligence level of a 10-year-old and unable to count well or use numbers meaningfully, he nevertheless has the uncanny ability to portray the exact number of floors, windows, doors, and other minute architectural details. His use of perspective and space has universally impressed art critics such as Sir Robin Philipson, past president of the Royal Scottish Academy, who says, "I have never stood so much in awe of a marvelous, mysterious gift." When Stephen was 12, Sir Hugh Casson, former president of the British Royal Academy, described him as "possibly the best child artist in Britain." Even more impressive, his use of space and perspective is genuine art and not mere copying of some photographic mental image. His drawings show a deft appreciation of proportion and manage to convey the mood and essence of the structures he draws. In art school he learned the names of various architectural styles, and upon request he can create a fanciful Venetian scene or Gothic cathedral.

Stephen, the son of poor immigrants from the Caribbean island of Santa Lucia, lives with his mother and older sister in central London. His father was killed in an accident when Stephen was 3, and the family receives public assistance. The following year Stephen was diagnosed as autistic, showing some familiar signs such as mutism, temper fits, and withdrawal. He attended a special school, where he was assigned to a small group of children functioning at a more normal level. That improved his behavior problems somewhat, but art class really excited him. As a 7-year-old he commenced to draw everything in sight, and even began to talk. A major turning point came when, as a 12-year-old, he appeared on a BBC television documentary about autism, where he drew impressive pictures of buildings completely from memory. A British news service promptly funded a trip to New York to draw, and other corporate sponsors supported drawing visits to other major European cities.

Thus far Stephen has produced three books, *Drawings, Cities,* and, in 1991, *Floating Cities,* which topped the British nonfiction book lists. Currently Stephen's fee for a pen-and-ink drawing is $1,800, the money going into a trust fund for his future care, since he will always need some supervision. Meanwhile he is maturing as an artist, branching out into pictures of landscapes, cars, and people. Stephen the person and Stephen the autistic savant are finally doing very well.

MECHANICAL ABILITIES

Our account of the savant syndrome would not be complete without mention of J. H. Pullen, the famous British "Genius of Earlswood Asylum." James Pullen was admitted to Earlswood in 1850 when he was 15 years old. He died there in 1916. He was born deaf and spoke his first word, "Muvver," at age 7. He never attended school, but learned to write and spell the names of a few simple objects. Because of an interest in drawing and whittling, he was put to work in the carpentry shop, where he soon demonstrated his mechanical genius.

His masterpiece is a 10-foot-long model of the steamship *Great Eastern.* This model and his other devices were displayed at the institution until recently. The *Great Eastern* took him three years to construct and is completely handmade from careful drawings. The planks are fixed to the ribs by a million and a quarter wooden pins. All these were made by Pullen in a special instrument which he also planned and made. In addition, he devised and built a strong carriage on four wheels for moving the ship. The model is 10 feet long, $18\frac{5}{8}$ inches wide, and $13\frac{5}{6}$ inches deep. It contains 5,585 copper rivets. There are thirteen lifeboats hoisted on complete davits, each of which is a perfectly finished model. The *Great Eastern* is fitted with paddles, screw, and engines, and even contains state cabins, which are decorated and furnished with chairs, tables, beds, and bunks. In fact, the whole ship is complete to the smallest detail.

Pullen invented and attached an arrangement of pulleys by which the whole upper deck could be raised to show the parts below. His other constructions included numerous smaller ships, assorted chairs, tables, bookcases, workbenches, and other handicrafts, as well as a fearsome 13-foot-tall mechanical monster armed with a gigantic sword. As his fame grew, he became more temperamental and independent, a very human tendency also found in many of us non-savants. Once he threatened to blow up the asylum because some request had been refused. On another occasion he took a violent dislike to one of the attendants and rigged a guillotine, the 13-foot-tall sword-bearer, over a doorway to dispatch his enemy—fortunately it misfired. Occasionally he was seen secretly selling some little articles he had made.

Although Pullen may have been difficult at times, he was really no match for his keepers in the dirty tricks department. When he fell in love and demanded to be discharged to marry his lady fair, the supervisors devised a sneaky plot to retain their valuable celebrity inmate. First, they procured a gorgeous blue and gold naval uniform and then invited Pullen to a formal conference in the boardroom. Here he was solemnly given permission to wed. However, the supervisors suggested that if he changed his marriage plans, he could be commissioned an Admiral of the Royal Navy on the spot. The glamorous uniform was immediately brought out of the closet and the enchanted Pullen never again referred to marriage plans, evidently preferring the sailor suit to the role of suitor.

CALENDAR CALCULATING AND MATHEMATICAL SKILLS

What day of the week did July 4, 1776, fall on? On what day will January 2, 2000 fall? What about November 3, 1911? "Calendar calculators" are mentally retarded individuals who nevertheless can instantaneously and correctly come up with the right days to match with such dates. By the way, the correct answers to the preceding questions are, respectively,

Thursday, Sunday, and Friday. How did *you* compare with the calendar calculators?

Charles and George are well-known identical twin calculators in their forties with IQ scores in the 60s to 70s. Their calendar calculations go far beyond the range of other savants. Although Charles is highly accurate for the twentieth century, George is completely accurate for many centuries before and after the limits of our current perpetual calendars. In fact, the perpetual calendar with the greatest range available extends to 2400 A.D., but George is unerring up to 7000 A.D.

Even more astonishing, neither of the men have the slightest idea that there was a change in our method of numbering dates in 1582, the year we changed from the Julian to the Gregorian calendar. Nevertheless, if one allows for the 10-day difference between the calendars, George is *always* right in identifying dates before 1582, and Charles is not far behind. George has a range of at least 6,000 years. Perhaps more noteworthy, the twins are even accurate for backward dates/days. That is, when asked in what years April 21 fell on Sunday, both will answer correctly 1968, 1963, 1957, 1946, and so forth. They will also give you the date of the fourth Monday in February 1993 (the 22nd). Remember, these men are unable to do even simple arithmetic. They can subtract two apples from five apples to get three apples, but cannot do the same for dollars, cannot multiply 3 × 6, or add 20 and 10 correctly. Even more astonishing, a few calendar calculators also show additional talents. One man with an IQ score of 54 was able to play 11 musical instruments by ear and draw elaborate pictures of houses. Steven Smith, in his fascinating book, *The Great Mental Calculators,* describes one such mathematical prodigy as follows:

> Unusual mathematical talents other than calendar calculating are best illustrated by the case of Jedediah Buxton in England. Buxton was an illiterate eighteenth-century alcoholic farmer whose marvelous calculating earned him all the beer he could drink at the local pub. Among the problems he solved easily were the number of barleycorns required to reach 8 miles, the number of times a coach wheel 6 yards around would revolve in traveling the 204 miles to London, and the number of hairs 1-inch long in a cubic mile. He also delighted in converting music to numbers. For example, during a dance he counted the number of steps involved in each rendition. He also

squared a 39-digit number mentally, which took him $2\frac{1}{2}$ months. Although this may seem like a rather long time, he *was* mentally retarded. In any case, we can be confident that he did not cheat and use pencil and paper secretly, since he could neither read nor write numbers.

Because of his illiteracy and lack of schooling he was unaware of the correct names for large numbers such as "billions" and so he invented his own words. He called 10^{18} "tribes" and 10^{39} was called "cramps." He insisted on oiling his calculating machine mind with pints of beer. These he called "winds" because he never took more than one breath to a pint, two to a quart. He kept a mental record of all the free beer he had been given since age 12. It totaled 5,116 pints, which averages out to 5 or 6 ounces per day. This, of course, was beer he was given for calculating and did not include any he might have bought himself. The most curious item on his list was the 72 pints he consumed "at a gathering for his dead cow." This bovine wake must have been quite a moving occasion to have stimulated our Mr. Buxton to drown his sorrows to the tune of *nine gallons* of beer!

THEORETICAL VIEWS

There are almost as many theories to explain the savant syndrome as there are cases. While each theory does explain some aspect of savant behavior, none completely accounts for the range and variety of special abilities as shown in these case reports. The facts that any comprehensive theory must account for are as follows:

1. All savants have measured low intelligence and at least one extraordinary skill.
2. There are six times as many male savants as females.
3. Most savants come from families in which there are no other mentally retarded members, nor family members with any especially prominent abilities or extraordinary talents. However, there is evidence for a tendency toward manic depression in their families.
4. While some of the savants are biologically impaired as a result of congenital syphilis, Down syndrome, hydrocephalus, or cretinism,

in most cases there is no known physiological damage or deficit. For example, J. H. Pullen lived to be a healthy 81 years old.

These facts pretty well rule out *genetic* explanations for the savant syndrome. Older theories frequently mentioned *photographic memory,* a synonym for eidetic imagery, as an explanation. According to this view normal intelligence is not necessary, because the savant can conjure up a mental image and simply "read off" the right answers, or can summon up a visual image and then copy it realistically in watercolors or pigments. While some savants do show an unusual facility for remembering past events in uncanny detail, strangely enough others have very poor memories. Furthermore, one woman calendar calculator had never seen a calendar or numbers, because she had been blind since birth. Recall the twin calendar calculators whose abilities extended well beyond the range of any calendar they may have studied or memorized. Finally, several psychological experiments have been done on memorizing and eidetic imagery. They showed that very few savants have eidetic imagery and that their tested memory spans are not much different from those of other people.

Psychoanalytic View

It is clear that simple and obvious factors are inadequate explanations for these bizarre phenomena. More elaborate explanations are available, which include combinations of different psychological mechanisms such as compensation, concentration, concrete thinking, and sensory deprivation. For example, psychoanalytic theorists regard savants not as mentally retarded primarily, but as mentally ill (psychotic). Their unusual skills are attributed to abnormal concentration in one overspecialized area of functioning. Such concentration is said to be a compensation for their weakness in other areas, a focus on the one skill at which they can excel. The display of this precocious skill, in turn, offsets the emotional deprivation they typically experience at the hands of cold, over-intellectual parents. The rather complicated psychoanalytic viewpoint blends the concepts of concentration, compensation, and deprivation. Psychoanalysis, then, sees the savant syndrome as a bizarre attempt to adjust to overwhelming psychological stress. As children, savants are made vulnerable by their especially intense sensitivity to stimulation. This low threshold for sensory arousal may be inborn. While it gives them an exquisite capacity for differentiating between tiny differences in quality or quantity of sensation, they are easily over-whelmed. That is, what for the average child is just a normal amount of noise, light, or touch becomes for the savant child a painful and over-whelming bombardment of the senses. In defense, they seek protection by resorting to cognitive activities such as counting or memorizing in order to deflect their minds from focusing on such unbearably intense sensations. Naturally, not all mentally ill children develop that rarest of disorders, the savant syndrome.

As previously mentioned, also necessary in this scenario are the cold, perfectionistic parents, who turn the child's precocious ability into a sideshow. Such parents delight in hammering into the child long lists of rhymes, poems, operatic arias, mathematical equations, and other trap-pings of genius. These sensitive children perceive the parents' dissatis-faction with their overall development and learn early that memory feats or musical outbursts bring parental approval. At the cost of more even and balanced mental development, then, these deprived children focus on the production of performances that do generate parental love and appreciation. This strategy is self-defense by the child, a retreat to a safe haven. The overdeveloped skill then becomes an island of security where the savant is competent and in complete control. The result is the savant syndrome, profound deficits side by side with fragments of advanced function developed to substitute for richer and more meaningful ways of relating to others.

Unfortunately for psychoanalytic theory, however, psychotic chil-dren's sensory acuity is no better than that of normal children. In ad-dition, there is scant evidence for the notion of an early emergence of "ego functions," such as an interest in calculation or music before the onset of the illness. Finally, not all parents of savants delight in their child's accomplishments. In fact, some parents are either unaware of the child's abilities or have tried actively to suppress them.

Biological View

The most widely held contemporary view attributes autistic savant skills to some malfunction of the brain. One of the earliest theories postulated that the autistic savant has a damaged capacity for abstraction, an inability to generalize. For instance, after a few experiences adding two apples and two apples, two pencils and two pencils, and two books and two books, the normal child learns that there is a general rule to be applied to any two-plus-two situation. However, the savant child, said to be deficient in abstracting ability, instead concentrates on concrete activities that require only very basic cognitive mechanisms, such as rote memory. Brain damage is the cause most frequently mentioned, because it often produces concrete thinking and a reduced capacity to generalize. For example, an individual with the type of brain damage called aphasia when asked to identify a pencil and a piece of chalk separately might say, "To write with." However, when shown both together, he or she would be unable to say what they had in common.

Yet, biological theory does not take into account that many savants *do* have the ability to generalize. For example, one musical savant could harmonize easily and, upon request, play variations of themes. She could also play a tune with the subtle differences that would be present if it had been composed by different composers. Some critics have pointed out that the special ability often shows itself well before there is any evidence of impaired abstraction. Still other investigators point to research studies that show no differences between savants and other mentally retarded persons on various tests of abstract ability and creativity.

According to Dr. Bernard Rimland, the previously mentioned pioneering investigator in the field of autism, modern research has proposed three possible neural mechanisms that might be responsible for the savants' incredible talents. The first theory proposes that the child has a pathological inability to broaden his or her focus of attention, resulting in the rejection of external stimulation and a consequent intense concentration directed internally. The child's attention becomes focused on a literal reproduction of the purely physical attributes of the stimulus rather than its abstract or conceptual features. The specific regions of the brain involved in attention involve a number of complicated brain systems that are currently of intense interest to researchers, but are not yet well understood.

A second line of neural research suggests that certain brain areas that in the normal child would be responsible for receiving and integrating inputs from a number of sensory sources may have become altered so that they are now dedicated to only one special ability. This ability then becomes enormously overdeveloped, to the detriment of the other functions. For example, the savant's auditory area may become excessively responsive to musical inputs, to the neglect of meaningful speech sounds necessary for language development.

The third promising line of neural investigation implicates that part of the brain involved in shutting out extraneous and irrelevant information and in suppressing distractions. Many autistic children are obsessed with routes and spatial layouts and frequently have exceptional visual memories. When asked to remember a person or event, they may reproduce the entire experience, including items of clothing, the weather, what was playing on TV in the background, and who else was present and where they sat. In other words, they can't see the forest for the trees.

Sociobehavioral View

The preceding theories of the savant syndrome have tried to explain how a superior function can develop from a background of general intellectual retardation. The behavioral approach, on the other hand, explains the savant behaviors as *caused by* retardation, rather than in spite of retardation. This approach attempts to show how mental subnormality might actually be an advantage in fostering special skills. First, there would be less distraction for these individuals, since they often find much of what is going on around them difficult to understand. This would free them to spend more time developing their one special skill. Second, since savants would do poorly in everything except the one exceptional ability, they are rewarded within a very narrow area. Only one activity would consistently produce praise, so that still more interest and motivation become concentrated on the special ability. Third, for the intellectually disabled person there are fewer things to be unlearned or given up in order to devote sufficient time to the special skill. Not having acquired other interests, savants do not have to discard such interests in order to find time for practicing the special skill. Fourth, intellectually deficient children might find it easier to concentrate on a special skill, because fewer other behavioral options are open to them. From early childhood it would be obvious that the child was intellectually limited, so there might not be as much intellectual instruction. The savant would then begin earlier to practice and focus on the special skill and would thus be better at it than peers. What remains to be explained, however, is the preponderance of male savants over females.

Recently Professor K. Anders Ericsson, of Florida State University, has made striking advances in the study of savants and prodigies. Ericsson and his colleagues, in an imaginative and extensive research program, have reproduced in the laboratory many of the special skills shown by savants and prodigies. These investigators conclude from their studies that there is no good evidence for savant giftedness or pure innate talent. Therefore, current research refutes the traditional view of talent that asserts that such individuals have special inborn abilities and basic capacities. Instead, they say, exceptional abilities are acquired, most often under optimal environmental conditions. For example, their experiments showed that calendar calculators produce their answers by using methods that average college students were able to learn in a month of training. The best-established phenomenon linked to talent in music, absolute pitch (AP), is present in approximately one in one hundred of the general population. Although adults are unable to learn AP even after extensive training, research indicates that almost anyone can acquire AP if music instruction is begun during a critical period before the age of 5 or 6. The "gift" of AP thus appears to be the result of training a motivated child on a readily available musical instrument under optimal conditions, during early childhood.

It is very encouraging to see that more attention is being devoted to what surely is one of the most puzzling and fascinating features of human behavior. In fact, the most important aspect of savant skills may be our inability to explain them completely. Based on current innovative research programs such as Ericsson's, we may be close to discovering how to develop such remarkable abilities in anyone.

Suggested Further Readings

Miller, L. (1989). *Musical savants: Exceptional skill in the mentally retarded.* Hillsdale, New Jersey: Erlbaum.

Rimland, B., & Fein, D. (1988). Special talents of autistic savants. In Obler, L., & Fein, D. (Eds.), *The exceptional brain* (pp. 474–492). New York: Guilford Press.

Smith, S. (1983). *The great mental calculators.* New York: Columbia University Press.

Southall, G. (1979). Blind Tom: The post-Civil War enslavement of a Black musical genius. (Vol. 1). Minneapolis: Challenge Productions.

Treffert, D. (1989). Extra-ordinary people: Understanding "Idiots Savants." New York: Harper & Row.

CHAPTER 11

Trichotillomania
Hair-Pulling Compulsion

Mary, a 12 year old girl, was referred because of the symptom of pulling out her eyebrows and eyelashes. This pulling had started suddenly a year previously when her elder brother Harold was about to leave the country. The mother, a widow in her forties, mentioned also that Mary was very jealous of mother's friends, particularly the men, and was afraid that mother might re-marry. The child's father had died suddenly from a heart attack when she was six. Apart from these problems there were no other signs of disturbance. Mary made good progress in school, had girl friends and was well adjusted.

Mary's birth and early development were normal. During treatment mother recalled that at the age of 1–2 years the child had the habit of pinching and scratching her cheeks to the extent of inflicting wounds on herself. This symptom passed, however, and except for sucking her fingers till the age of eight, the child showed no other signs of disturbance in her development.

Mary was much attached to her father who found in the girl, according to her mother, "the love that she herself could not give him." In mother's words: "Father and daughter were in love with each other." Mary would frequently sleep in father's bed and both of them enjoyed this. Mother did not remember if she had talked to Mary about father's death, or what the child's reactions had been.

In any case, after her father's death Mary became very much attached to her eldest brother Harold to whom she had been already very close before. She went to his bed as she had done with father. When Mary was eight, this brother married and Mary developed a very ambivalent attitude towards her sister-in-law. She would occasionally try to separate her from the brother. At the age of eleven, two days before the couple left the country in order to live from now on in Europe, the girl pulled out all her eyebrows and eyelashes. The mother, who was particularly proud of her daughter's looks, lost control of herself and struck the girl hard. From then until the treatment the symptom continued, despite mother's efforts to bring about a change by punishment, promises, threats of cutting the child's nails, and despite the fact that the girl made strong conscious efforts to overcome the symptom. Mother stressed that until the appearance of the hair pulling, apart from the finger sucking up to the age of eight, she felt her daughter to be "perfect."

In the first treatment sessions Mary realized that she pulled her eyebrows and lashes when she was angry with someone and could not express her anger. She complained bitterly that her mother did not allow any expression of opposition. The girl suspected that her mother did not love her. On the other hand she expressed her feeling that mother's criticism of her was justified, and that she was really a bad girl and should be smacked. She also demanded that one should forcibly prevent her hairpulling. Already in this period of strong complaints against her mother, the girl mentioned that her feeling of being bad was probably connected, in some way, with the fact that father had loved her so much.

In one particularly dramatic therapy session, following which the symptom subsided for a long period, Mary stated that she pulls out hairs only when she feels bad or sad. Before the hairpulling period she was in the habit of sucking three fingers on her left hand when she was sad. She demonstrated this and added that simultaneously she used to pluck wool from her blanket or her pullover and rub her nose with it. She liked this very much. When asked if this reminded her of anything, she cried out very excitedly with tears in her eyes: "Oh yes, yes—it reminds me of father. I remember how he used to kiss me in the evenings. I shouted because his cheeks pricked me and I still hear him say: 'After all it's not so bad; even quite nice, isn't it?' and afterwards he brushed his cheek on my cheek and it was awfully pleasant."

Mary continued to tell how at the age of eight she decided to wean herself of the habit of sucking her fingers. She asked mother to give her a slap whenever she saw her sucking, but Mary used to stop the movement of her fingers to her mouth even without mother's slap. Only when Harold, her eldest brother, went to Europe, did she start to pull out her eyelashes, to look at the plucked hairs in her hand and rub the other hand against the hard ends of the lashes which were left on her eyelids. In this session she understood how Harold's departure was for her a repetition of father's leaving her and the hair pulling, like pulling out the wool and feathers before, was bound up with her longing for father and the pleasure she had experienced with him. It was evident that it represented for her a kind of sanction of her libidinal wishes towards father. She asked the therapist to repeat this interpretation and stressed how much relief she felt at hearing it. After a number of weeks there was a chance to go into the aggressive side of her symptom. After she had not pulled out her eyelashes for ten weeks she remembered in treatment how she used to pull them out with strong, aggressive movements, then lay them on the palm of her hand and look at them. She expressed surprise at the strong feeling of satisfaction that this looking used to afford her. Suddenly she cried "Oh, I know why I liked to look at the hairs," and told how she liked to play with Harold's mustache and to twist it around her fingers. With great affect she realized now, how angry she had been with Harold for leaving her and that the eyelash pulling stood for pulling out the hairs of his mustache. (From a case reported by Eliezer Ilan and Esther Alexander.)

Mary's case illustrates some of the common factors found in most compulsive hair pullers: her gender, an associated thumb-sucking habit, a relatively unremarkable developmental history, and some very complex family dynamics. She received 5 months of psychotherapy, after which she chose to terminate the sessions because she felt herself to be free of the hair-pulling symptom.

Although Mary's therapist followed a quite traditional psychodynamic interpretive treatment format, her case history illustrates several points emphasized by both of the major theories to be discussed here. From the psychoanalytic perspective, for example, we note Mary's critical Oedipal experiences (serving as a love interest for her father, who employed her as a substitute for a consenting mother), the symbolic equating of her hair pulling with past pleasurable experiences with her father, and the special aggressive meaning attached to her vigorous eyelash pulling.

Behaviorists, too, find much in the same case history to help explain the development of this bizarre symptom. For example, there had been earlier attention-drawing instances of self-abusive behaviors such as pinching and scratching her cheeks, the experience of learning that hair from her father's beard is capable of producing simultaneous pleasure and mild pain sensations, and the mother's futile use of punishment alone to eliminate Mary's undesired behavior.

However, these two orientations, psychoanalytic and behavioral, are basically incompatible. While both attempt to explain compulsive hair pulling, neither theory can do so in a totally satisfactory or comprehensive way. Later in the chapter we will discuss each theory in greater detail.

As Mary's case history demonstrates, we humans are a puzzling tangle of complexes and contradictions. Even as seemingly simple a natural adornment as hair can become the troublesome focus of complicated motives and habits.

HAIR FACTS

Hair has long been associated with physical attractiveness, sexuality, and strength. Recall the biblical story of the Israelite hero, Samson, allegedly the strongest man in the world. The source of his great strength was his hair. He made the mistake of revealing this secret to his love, Delilah, who subsequently betrayed him and had his hair cut. The weakened Samson was then easily captured by his enemies, the Philistines. Men have viewed hair loss as disastrous ever since.

Hair grows on all parts of the human body, except the palms of the hands and the soles of the feet. Rarely, though, are all of these sites covered on any one person. (That truly would be a hairy sight.)

The average person has about 100,000 hairs on the scalp alone. This number is only an approximate figure, as it is difficult to hire anyone to make exact counts, even at well above the minimum wage. Besides, the definition of an "average person" is also unclear.

We do know that hair grows at a rate of 1.5 to 3.0 millimeters per week. Massaging the scalp, good nutrition, and low stress in your life presumably will help you reach the 3.0 upper limit.

Hair falls out too, at the rate of 30 to 100 hairs a day, with an average daily loss of 75 hairs. These hairs will be replenished unless some abnormal condition intervenes. Baldness has many possible causes. The most common cause, male pattern baldness, has a hormonal and genetic basis. There is still no known effective treatment for this cause.

Women and men can be equally affected by the other possible medical causes of baldness, such as burns, scars, psoriasis, allergy reactions, anemia, high fevers, medication side effects, mercury poisoning, dermatitis, and severe psychological stress.

Baldness can also be self-inflicted. Some people, the vast majority of whom are female and adolescent, compulsively pull out their own hair. They twist it, stroke it, and, ultimately, pluck it. These are the trichotillomanics. This unusual and bizarre syndrome usually begins without their awareness, but eventually leaves them acutely aware, desperately embarrassed, and socially inhibited.

DESCRIPTION OF THE SYNDROME

Trichotillomania is the term coined in 1889 by the French dermatologist Hallopeau to describe a maladaptive behavior pattern of self-mutilation in which an individual compulsively pulls out his or her own hair. Scalp hair is the most common target site, but many of these people also pull hair from elsewhere on the body. In the most extreme cases, all of their body hair is removed. The method is by finger plucking or tweezing, never by shaving or electrolysis.

Trichotillomania has been diagnosed in children as young as 17 months. It can appear at any time from late infancy through adulthood. Most cases are first reported in early adolescence. There is a distinct sex difference with this disorder. The overwhelming majority (80 to 85%) of trichotillomanics are female.

Just how common is this problem? One handbook for therapists estimates that eight million people in America pull out their own hair. Accurate figures on its frequency, though, are especially hard to come by, for several reasons. Only a fraction of the hair pullers come to the attention of a healthcare professional. Patients and their parents are usually quite embarrassed by this behavior and its effects. The availability of wigs, stylish hats, eyebrow liners, and false eyelashes makes it relatively easy to disguise the problem. These cosmetic aids and hairpieces have themselves become quite socially acceptable. However, some serious hair pullers have been known to continue the behavior by pulling the hair from their wigs!

Some parents of trichotillomanic children show a curious attitude in denial of the hair-pulling behavior. Some view it as a temporary "phase" needing no particular professional treatment. Others blindly and unemotionally disregard the obvious reason for the resulting bald spot: "My child's hair was lost" is a typical comment.

When a symptom is embarrassing or socially unacceptable, we often feel more comfortable and less personally responsible if we can claim that it is caused by some biological disturbance. For example, movie stars or well-known sports personalities typically describe their alcoholism or depression as merely an "allergic reaction" or a "biochemical imbalance."

Hair pullers, too, may call on flimsy "physical" explanations for their loss of hair. They may suggest that they have a "congenital weakness of the scalp" or a "circulation problem" that weakens the hair. Sometimes the loss presumably just happens to them in some vague and passive way, "by virtue of the hand being in the hair," as one patient blandly described it.

Several clinical reports have identified one or more close family members who have shown the same hair-pulling pattern. One mother brought her 7-year-old son to a community health clinic for a routine checkup. When asked about the large bald spot on the front of his head, she reported that for the past two years he had been "twiddling out" the hairs there. The psychologist to whom the child was then referred noticed that the mother's own hair was very thin on the sides of her head. Upon interview, he learned that she too had been pulling out her hair ever since she gave birth to twins four years earlier. She described the actual extraction of the hair as a pleasurable sensation, which, in turn, led to a reduction of anxiety. The mother refused treatment for herself, but she did help carry out the therapist's recommendations as part of her son's treatment.

When a psychological or behavioral disorder appears with unusual frequency in the same family, we must remind ourselves that these facts still do not mean that the problem has been inherited. Such a conclusion is tempting. The simple truth, though, is that there is no scientific evidence that trichotillomania can be transmitted genetically or biologically. There are a variety of psychological theories to account for this behavior, two of which are summarized later in this chapter. All of the theories derive from the "nurture" (environmental) rather than the "nature" (biological) camp.

The disorder of trichotillomania is nondiscriminatory. It can be found in individuals of all ages and social classes, of both genders, and at all intellectual levels. Some experts suggest that it is seen more often in brighter people, but it also occurs in 1% of institutionalized retarded patients.

In their study of 288 college students (183 women and 105 men), Dr. Melinda Stanley and her colleagues at the University of Texas Medical School at Houston found 15.3% of them engaged in hair pulling unrelated to grooming, while 58.7% admitted playing with their hair without pulling it. The remainder (26%) denied both behaviors. Women made up 79% of the Pullers, 70% of the Players, and only 40% of the No Symptoms Group.

Many mental health professionals often classify trichotillomania as a type of obsessive-compulsive disorder (OCD). That is, hair pulling is a behavior that the person feels compelled to perform. If something interrupts the behavior, he or she will become upset—usually angry or anxious. Yet Dr. Stanley's group and others find important clinical differences between trichotillomania and OCD. They suggest that it is best not to see them as the same underlying disorder. Clearly, this professional controversy has not yet been decided definitively.

A pulling episode often begins without the person's awareness. Twisting and stroking the hair strands are relaxing activities. Typically, the behavior sequence begins when the person is tense or concentrating intently, such as while reading or watching a dramatic television program or movie. If the stroking should end with one or more hairs being extracted, the puller frequently feels a brief pleasurable sensation. This good feeling must serve as a reward for the behavior.

Compulsive hair pulling has been described as a quirk or eccentricity in an otherwise sane person. Not so. There are usually some other associated psychological symptoms, especially in children. Hair-pulling children are also likely to be thumb suckers, nail biters, anxious, fearful, and socially unskilled. They tend to be introverted and out of favor with their peers. The growing bald spot then elicits more teasing and results in further social isolation.

Adult hair pullers tend to display fewer and less serious associated disturbances than do children. However, some studies report an unusually high correlation with eating disorders, such as bulimia. The pulling behavior, of course, remains an ineffective way to cope with anxiety and daily tensions. The resulting disfigurement produces embarrassment and serious social consequences.

There are possible medical dangers as well, such as infections, scalp damage, and hair follicle damage. If unchecked, the result could be *alopecia capitis totalis* (complete loss of hair from the scalp). Untreated patients can proceed to pull eyebrows, eyelashes, beard, and even arm, leg, chest, and pubic hair. Eventually, their entire bodies are denuded.

While trichotillomanics generally have more than their share of psychological disturbances, most are not psychotic. They remain in contact with reality and can pursue a relatively normal daily existence. Nevertheless, there are a small number of hair pullers who are extremely disturbed and who show additional bizarre behaviors. For example, some exhibit *trichokryptomania*, in which they compulsively hide the pulled hair. Other trichotillomanics engage in *trichophagy*, in which they eat their pulled hair. In September 1986 surgeons in Iran reported removing a 4.4-pound hairball from the stomach of a 24-year-old woman, who had been eating her own hair for more than 20 years. Sometimes trichophagic individuals are diagnosed as schizophrenic, which, of course, is a very serious psychological disturbance.

Dr. Gary Christenson and his colleagues in the University of Minnesota Department of Psychiatry reported on the characteristics of adult chronic hair pullers who had been referred to their trichotillomania clinic. Their sample consisted of 54 females and 6 males between the ages of 18 and 61. The length of time they had been pulling out hair ranged from less than a year to 39 years, averaging 21 years of pulling.

Although hair was pulled from all over the body, the most popular sites were the scalp, from which 75% pulled, eyelashes (53%), eyebrows (42%), pubic area (17%), and the beard and arms (10% each). Most (68%) preferred to pull just one hair at a time. Everyone used his or her fingers to pull, but 43% used tweezers as well.

Interestingly, nearly everyone tried a variety of self-help methods in attempts to resist the hair pulling before seeking professional treatment. The most common procedures attempted (in descending order of frequency) were as follows: placing some barrier on the head, change in activities, keeping hands occupied, wearing mittens or gloves, sitting on hands, taping fingers together, altering fingernails, hiding tweezers, chewing gum, and placing petroleum jelly on the hands or hair.

Nearly half of the patients reported oral behaviors associated with hair pulling. A third chewed or bit off ends of their hair and 10% actually ate their hair (trichophagy), while another 25% merely rubbed the hair around their mouths after pulling it out.

It is reasonable to assume that Dr. Christenson's patients were behaviorally typical of all nonpsychotic adult hair pullers. Clinically, though, they seemed to evidence a fairly high rate of other psychological symptoms, such as mood, anxiety, eating, and substance abuse disorders, which is somewhat contradictory to other studies.

Unless the patients have been observed actually pulling out their own hair, the physician may be uncertain about the cause of the resulting baldness. Some diseases or drug treatments themselves can produce hair loss. To determine whether the loss is indeed due to a patient's own efforts, the physician may administer the *trichotillo test*.

The trichotillo test involves selecting a 5-square-centimeter area within the bald spot and spraying it with plastic bandage. Four layers are applied. The patient (who believes that the test is actually part of the treatment) is advised not to disturb the area. If the problem is true trichotillomania, the area will appear darker within two to three weeks as a result of new hair growth. When the film is removed, there will be hairs of 1/2 to 3/4 centimeters in length. If the hair does not grow back, it is probable that the baldness has been caused by dermatological disease. If the trichotillo test confirms that the person's hair loss is the result of his or her own hair pulling, referral is ordinarily made to a mental health professional. Once a treatment program is initiated, how can the psychiatrist or psychologist determine whether progress is being made? There are several measures of treatment effectiveness they can use. Some are indirect indicators, while others are more direct.

For example, among the indirect indices are the size of the bald spot on the scalp and the length of the remaining hair or eyelashes. Another method is to compare photographs taken before and after treatment. These procedures can be combined with others, such as the patient's self-report and the observations of people who have close contact with the patient, such as parents or roommates.

Obtaining a reliable and valid measure of the problem is critical. The therapist must know whether treatment efforts are helping or whether they may even be worsening the problem. Signs of success may be therapeutic in themselves. When patients are aware of improvement, their motivation for more improvement increases. When others see the positive changes, they, too, will likely be supportive and praising.

The most preferable way to measure how often hair pulling occurs is direct observation of the actual problem behavior. Many therapists ask the patient to count and record the actual number of hairs pulled. The length of time for a hair-pulling session could also be recorded, but this method is not suitable for those patients who pull while sleeping. Counting the hairs in the bed in the morning can work even for these patients.

THEORIES AND THERAPIES

Clinical Classification and Chemotherapy

Chronic hair pulling can be classified in several ways. Whichever system is preferred tends to dictate the type of treatment that will be provided. For example, if the pulling is seen as a learned habit disorder, behavior-oriented treatments will be undertaken. If the pulling is seen as simply an observable symptom of an underlying unconscious conflict, long-term psychodynamic psychotherapy, or even hypnosis, will be offered. If it is seen as some kind of physiological failure, drug treatment (chemotherapy) may be attempted.

The official psychiatric classification system (DSM IV) lists trichotil-lomania as an "Impulse Control Disorder Not Elsewhere Classified," because the person feels tension before and relief after engaging in the critical compulsive behavior. For example, one woman's drive to pull out her hair was so strong that she did not sleep at night so that she could stay up to do so. Nevertheless, great professional controversy re-mains as to whether trichotillomania is simply an aspect of the broader category of obsessive-compulsive disorders or a disease entity on its own.

Regardless of the outcome of that battle, those who adhere to the disease-illness view tend to favor some form of drug treatment. A variety of medications have been tried and evaluated, although the quality of the research has not been high. Most studies include a small group of selected patients who have been on a variety of medications for some time and whose progress is measured simply by the perceptions of their doctors. One recent study, which was scientifically somewhat more rig-orous than most others but included only 13 selected patients, demon-strated the superior effect of one drug (clomipramine) over another (de-sipramine). Nondrug treatments were not evaluated. In other clinical studies certain specific drugs have shown some positive results, for ex-ample, lithium, fluoxetine, trazodone, isocarboxazid, amitriptyline, imipramine, and chlorpromazine. The pharmacological research contin-ues, as it should, while the proverbial medicine chest has been thrown at trichotillomanics in the clinical hope that some of them will stop pulling.

Psychological Perspectives

Feminist author Louise Kaplan has no hesitancy in classifying tricho-tillomania as one of the "female perversions." She considers hair pluck-ing to be "another self-mutilating disorder that brings adolescent girls and women of all ages to the attention of the medical profession."

Kaplan elaborates a complex psychodynamic explanation to account for these women's plucking, which, she says, represents the patient's wish to be both sexes. This is "an uneasy compromise between the young woman's feminine and masculine wishes, strivings that are colored by a persistence into adolescence and adulthood of the infantile equations of castrated-female and phallic-male. . . . She wards off any retaliatory maternal vengeance by demonstrating that she is really a powerless, castrated female who will never actually compete with her mother in the sexual and procreative arenas."

Kaplan's views are certainly provocative, but are less data-based than even those of Freud, who invented, or at least first described, these concepts. In sum, she sees the hair plucking as the forum for the young girl to express her individuality during the conflicts over maturity and gender identity that routinely happen during adolescence. Kaplan's deliberate choice of the label "perversion" is, in our judgment, not helpful in approaching these troubled individuals with the clinical concern and sensitivity that they deserve. We even prefer to avoid labeling these individuals as "trichotillomanics" because of the negative connotation to the term *maniacs.*

There are two major psychological theories to explain trichotillomania: psychodynamic theory and behaviorism. Each of them, in turn, suggests certain specific approaches to treatment.

Psychodynamic Theory.

Freud and other psychoanalytic writers have contributed the major concepts to the psychodynamic understanding of trichotillomania. Hair pulling is seen by this theory as a symptom that reflects the presence of one or more underlying unconscious conflicts within the personality.

However, theorists have shown a surprising degree of variability in exactly how they account for trichotillomania. The hair pulling has been described as a form of masturbation, as an expression of masochism, as self-punishment, as a way to relieve tension, guilt, or hatred, as grief or rage turned inward, and as a forum to discharge feelings of aggression accumulated against an overprotective mother.

The psychodynamic interpretations of the *symbolic* meanings of hair pulling seem especially far-fetched. When some trichotillomanics caress their lips with their torn-out hair, it is considered to be a symbolic substitute for unsatisfied needs for love and tenderness.

Hair itself is considered to symbolize the forces of seduction. To pull out her own hair is a regressive act for an adolescent female. Presumably, without hair the girl will not be "mature" enough to function sexually. She thereby is returning psychosexually to a pre-Oedipal stage (which corresponds approximately to ages 3 to 5), where she will be free from unacceptable, incestuous heterosexual desires. In the Oedipal stage the child, according to Freud, has a desire for sexual relations with the parent of the opposite sex. Getting through this stressful complex satisfactorily, without severe psychic trauma and family disturbance, is a major developmental task.

Psychoanalysts regard the hair as a major battleground for resolving sexuality conflicts. Since hair pulling is so much more common in girls and women, describing the dynamics of their "castration complex" involves an impressive bit of mental gymnastics. Boys are thought to fear castration by father for harboring those evil desires for sexual intimacy with mother. However, girls are said to see themselves as already having suffered this terrible fate. Their mourning the loss of a penis is basic to Freud's very controversial concept of "penis envy." Needless to say, most, if not all, hair pullers would deny any such feelings or incestuous desires. Nevertheless, psychoanalysts present the perfect rebuttal: these processes are all unconscious, and denying them is a form of resistance to treatment. Naturally, then, the patient will be unaware of them.

Hair grows back, but penises do not. Thus, Samson was able to recover his strength. The young girl's unconscious fears, though, cannot be alleviated merely by the passing of time, if psychoanalytic theory is correct.

Family dynamics of adolescent hair pullers have also received considerable attention from the theorists. New York psychiatrists Harvey Greenberg and Charles Sarner have described the pervasive abnormalities in the families of trichotillomanic children. Mother, as usual, receives the bulk of the bad press.

In their study, 84% of the mothers were said to be "highly pathological." Most of them were characterized as "ambivalent, double-binding, critical, hostile, intolerant of aggressive or assertive displays, highly competitive, overprotective and possessive, domineering, alternately infantilizing and parentifying; they had strong, unsatisfied dependency needs and often felt threatened by latent homosexual impulses." These descriptions are of the *mothers* of the patients!

Drs. Greenberg and Sarner further describe a unique mother-daughter mode of interaction—the "hair-pulling symbiosis." Such a relationship is typically marked by mutual ambivalence and hostility. Each person fears separation from the other. When the daughter develops interests in independence and in males, the mother discourages her by severe criticism. At the same time, the daughter represents her mother's own unfulfilled needs and erotic fantasies. It is a genuine love-hate affair, held together by the thin strand of hair pulling.

In case you were wondering about parents sharing responsibilities, the patients' fathers do not escape entirely from the theorists' wrath. The fathers are described as helpless, ineffectual men who are dominated, manipulated, and overwhelmed by their wives. These men can only express themselves in devious and indirect ways at home, even though they may be quite effective and assertive in other social settings. In the home the passive father appears to surrender all significant decision making to the mother, who, in turn, disparages him unmercifully. The psychiatrists further theorize that the father unconsciously feels sexual desires toward the daughter. To cope with those feelings (maladaptively), he simply rejects the child. Treatment for trichotillomania within the psychoanalytic perspective consists of traditional verbal psychotherapy, as previously illustrated in the case of Mary. The therapist helps the patient achieve insight into the symbolic meaning of the symptom. It is assumed that this understanding will be eventually transformed into a reduction and elimination of hair pulling.

Some analytic therapists give special attention to the patient's family dynamics. The symptom serves the symbiotic mother-daughter relationship to the exclusion of their much-criticized father/husband. The patient, typically an adolescent girl, is trying to be self-assertive against her parents' need to keep her in the child state. Hair becomes a phallic substitute for the pubertal girl. Pulling out her hair may be her unfortunate method of getting everyone (her parents, their demands, and male peers) "out of her hair."

Psychoanalytic therapy is necessarily extensive, intensive, and expensive. Unfortunately, the bulk of the objective scientific evidence indicates only a marginal degree of success with this approach. Analytic subtheories about causation certainly are provocative and interesting. For example, some theorists believe that hair pulling is symbolic self-castration, replaces a lost love object, or is a masturbatory substitute. However, the predictions for successful treatment based on psychoanalytic theory are quite pessimistic. Therapies based on behavioral principles, to be discussed next, offer much greater promise as effective and efficient approaches to eliminating this disfiguring activity.

Behavior Theory.

Behavior theorists do not try to explain trichotillomania in terms of family relationships or exotic unconscious processes. Rather, the hair pulling is considered to be simply a maladaptive habit that has been learned.

It is assumed that this behavior, upon its first occurrence, is rewarded, probably accidentally. It then tends to recur. It may begin with hair stroking, likely paired with a pleasant activity such as reading interesting material or watching TV. Pulling the hair is often accompanied by anxiety reduction. Moreover, for many normal people the sensation of plucking a single hair or two is not at all painful and may actually feel rather pleasant. These kinds of experiences become the basis of the original conditions of learning. The hair-pulling habit can thus be acquired unintentionally, without the patient's awareness. (Behaviorists do not believe in unobservable entities such as the "unconscious mind.")

From the behavioral perspective, the exact origins of the habit are not particularly important. Since hair pulling is considered a learned behavior, its treatment must include its unlearning and then the learning of some appropriate alternative strategy for achieving tension reduction.

Behavior therapists have used a variety of techniques to treat patients' hair-pulling behavior. Reports of success have been impressive. However, these reports usually consist of detailed descriptions of the clinical treatments of just one or only a few patients. One reason is that the relative infrequency of the disorder makes it very difficult to form sufficiently large groups for scientific comparisons. Most scientists would prefer to test a particular technique on a group of similar patients. In that way, any extremely unique features of a single hair puller would not be regarded as representative of all such patients.

The use of so many different therapeutic techniques by the behavior therapists implies that no single technique has yet been determined to be the treatment of choice for all cases. Nevertheless, all of the following approaches have been employed successfully with a wide variety of patients.

When feasible, behavior therapists try to transfer the responsibility for therapy to the patients themselves. The techniques are then known as "self-management" procedures. Some examples of self-management for trichotillomania include *self-monitoring, self-instructional training,* and *habit reversal.*

Psychologists have discovered that when you attend to a specific behavior and measure it, the process of observation itself will tend to change that behavior. This process of change is called *reactivity.* The effective therapy procedure that capitalizes on such reactivity is termed *self-monitoring.* The patient is instructed simply to count the number of hairs pulled out each day and to record that number in a diary. Sometimes the hairs must also be mailed daily to the therapist.

In *self-instructional training* the patient is taught that we all behave in ways that are consistent with our thinking styles and our expectancies. Therefore, to modify an undesired behavior, in this instance chronic hair pulling, the patient is taught to tell herself things that will be consistent with eliminating the behavior. For example, when she becomes aware of the urge to pull, she may be told to say "No!" to herself or, "I won't do that." This is the power of negative thinking! These negative self-statements can also be supplemented by positive ones, such as: "I can control my own behavior"; "I am capable of overcoming this problem"; "Keep your fists closed and just relax." (Closed fists obviously cannot be used for hair pulling. In this way, the habit sequence can be broken.)

Self-instructional training can be strengthened by adding positive imaging. In one case a 17-year-old patient was taught to picture herself with a full complement of hair so beautiful that an attractive man would enjoy stroking it.

Habit reversal is another self-management approach, which first emphasizes teaching the patient "habit awareness," a form of self-observation. She must become alert to exactly when the hair-pulling behavior sequence begins. One young patient was advised to wear noisy, jangling bracelets and to put perfume on her fingers to alert her that her hand is approaching her hair. As she becomes aware of the problem behavior, she can then initiate a competing behavior. Holding an object such as a pen or a comb will necessarily preclude using the hand to pull hair. When a behavioral sequence is interrupted, it is weakened. As the hair pulling drops out, instead of the hair itself, compliments and general social support will begin to reward the patient for her attractive improvements.

There are likewise a variety of therapist-managed techniques for treatment of hair pulling. Some of the procedures have simply been forms of punishment for the undesired behavior. For example, a mild electric shock or a whiff of ammonia has been administered when hair pulling occurred. Rubber bands can be snapped on the patient's wrists as the pulling begins. Another shocking method is to show the patient a videotape of herself pulling hair. This visual negative feedback can be quite aversive.

Overcorrection is a therapist-managed procedure that punishes the undesired behavior by requiring the patient to perform the relevant appropriate behavior (for example, brushing or combing her hair) to an excessive degree. However, the overcorrecting behaviors in this instance can themselves contribute to further hair loss and so must be monitored very carefully. *Negative practice* is a related technique that involves instructing the patient to perform the undesired behaviors to the point of fatigue. As with overcorrection, though, this variation can itself worsen the problem.

Finally, an imaginal technique called *covert sensitization* has been used with hair pullers. The patient is asked by the therapist to picture or imagine herself pulling her hair. She is then given some very unpleasant suggestions, for example, of feelings of nausea and experience of vomiting, to feel simultaneously with imagining the problem behavior. Thus, hair pulling will be diminished because of the unpleasant associations it arouses.

Many behavior therapy techniques have been applied to trichotillomanics, all of them generally successful in individual cases. Most can actually be carried out by the patient herself, or by her parents, after only a little training.

An interesting contradiction appears between the psychoanalytic and the behavioral perspectives in the roles that each assigns to the parents of hair pullers. In psychoanalytic theory, the parents, particularly the mother, are seen as being responsible for the child's disorder or, at least, are regarded as coconspirators. In behavioral theory, parents are often expected to function as cotherapists. The issue of causal responsibility is given little attention by the behavior-oriented therapists, except for the presumption that the hair-pulling behavior had somehow been learned at one time.

CONCLUSIONS

Hair on the human body serves several important functions. It helps hold in body heat in cold weather. Conversely, hair insulates the skull from the heat of the sun. The eyebrows serve to prevent perspiration from dripping into the eyes, and eyelashes filter out dust and other foreign materials.

Hair's psychological functions are also critically important to us. Its color, style, length, and degree of curl are essential to our aesthetic self-concept. Perhaps most important, hair is a major aspect of a person's sexual appeal. Note the millions of dollars and hours of time spent on hair care in our society.

On the other hand, some male movie and TV stars (e.g., Patrick Stewart, Yul Brynner, and Telly Savalas) have capitalized on the unique sexiness of their bald heads. Women, usually in the pop-rock or high-fashion subcultures, are also now finding fun in being bald.

Futurists predict that bald men and women will be the norm in 100 years. Maybe the trichotillomanics are simply ahead of their time.

Why would anyone these days compulsively pull out his or her own hair? What possible benefits could there be to this kind of self-inflicted disfigurement? We cannot say for sure. The psychoanalysts have their theories. The behaviorists offer a quite different explanation. Chronic hair pulling is truly a human behavioral phenomenon that goes "beyond the bizarre."

Suggested Further Readings

Azrin, N. H., Nunn, R. G., & Frantz, S. E. (1980). Treatment of hair pulling (Trichotillomania): A comparative study of habit reversal and negative practice training. *Journal of Behavior Therapy and Experimental Psychiatry, 11,* 13–20.

Friman, P. C., Finney, J. W., & Christophersen, E. E. (1984). Behavioral treatment of trichotillomania: An evaluative review. *Behavior Therapy, 15,* 249–265.

Greenberg, H. R., & Sarner, C. A. (1965). Trichotillomania: Symptom and syndrome. *Archives of General Psychiatry, 12,* 482–489.

Ilan, E., & Alexander, E. (1965). Eyelash and eyebrow pulling. (Trichotillomania) Treatment of two adolescent girls. *The Israel Annals of Psychiatry and Related Disciplines, 3,* 267–281.

Stanley, M. A., Swann, A. C., Bowers, T. C., Davis, M. L., & Taylor, D. J. (1992). A comparison of clinical features in trichotillomania and obsessive-compulsive disorder. *Behaviour Research and Therapy, 30,* 39–44.

CHAPTER 12

Necrophilia
Sex After Death

Our difficult task is to find the human core in this, the rarest and most gruesome of sexual disorders, *necrophilia,* sexual arousal caused by contact with corpses. People who engage in such activities sorely test our definition of what it means to be human. Their sex acts may take the form of murder, in order to obtain a dead sex partner, or full sexual intercourse with an already dead body. Their behavior typically includes the whole range of kisses and intimate caresses, or masturbation fantasies involving dead bodies, as well as other less dainty acts. Sex surveys tell us that standards of acceptable sexual conduct have definitely become more liberal over the years. For example, oral sex, formerly an act condemned by the church and polite society, is now a common practice for lovers and spouses. However, even our most modern standards are strongly challenged by this radical form of sexual expression.

Although many people regard necrophilic behavior as the ultimate horror, it actually does little harm to society. When necrophiles are caught by the authorities, if prosecuted, they are generally charged with a minor crime such as "outraging public decency." However, because death remains one of life's great mysteries, our extreme emotional repulsion at the idea of sex with a dead body must certainly reflect an element of sacrilege, as reflected in our use of the word *desecrate.* British murder maven Brian Masters, whose fascinating book, *Killing for Com-*

217

pany, probes the mind of the serial killer Denis Nilson, believes that in civilized societies respect for the dead is an elemental core belief. Illogical as it may seem, the lack of such reverence is a sure sign of insanity to the average person.

Adding to our repulsion is our deodorized society's aversion to decaying flesh, excrement, and rot. To most people, anyone who violates such a strong societal taboo appears capable of any inhuman outrage. However, even though most of us find necrophilia completely alien to our own range of experiences, we must pause to listen to the Master himself, Sigmund Freud, who reminds us that it is the *love instinct* in necrophiles that must be so exceptionally powerful in order to overcome such strong cultural reactions as shame, disgust, horror, and pain.

Criminal corpse snatching and sexual molestation of the dead have occurred throughout history, and many societies with elaborate funeral customs, such as ancient Egypt, had to adopt safeguards against the abuse of corpses. The famous Freudian psychoanalyst A. A. Brill quotes Greek historian Herodotus as follows:

> The wives of men of rank, and such females as have been distinguished by their beauty or importance, are not immediately on their decease delivered to the embalmers: they are usually kept for three or four days, which is done to prevent any indecency being offered to their persons. An instance once occurred of an embalmer's gratifying his lust on the body of a female lately dead: the crime was divulged by a fellow artist.

Evidently, the Egyptians relied on the decay process to deter such indecent attacks. On the other hand, Lord George Selwyn, the well-known eighteenth-century British eccentric, illustrates the more matter-of-fact attitude toward necrophilia prominent for some centuries. Selwyn was famous for his unashamed necrophilic orientation. He was obsessed by executions and was a regular at all the public hangings in London for many years. As a hobby he owned a prized collection of hangman's ropes used in actual executions. He made a special trip to Paris in 1756 just to witness the execution of Damiens, the would-be assassin of Louis XV, who was drawn and quartered. When Selwyn's friend Lord Holland was close to death, he told his butler, "If Lord

Selwyn calls, show him in. If I am still alive I shall be pleased to see him, and if not he will be pleased to see me."

Art historians have known for a long time that many famous painters preferred corpses as models, much valued because they never fidgeted or lost a pose. According to Vasari, a famous art historian of the Renaissance, the painter Luca Signorelli's immediate response upon witnessing the death of a young friend of his was to remove the youth's clothing and begin painting his portrait. Some painters actually cut out the heart of a dead person because it was believed to be the source of a particularly marvelous shiny brown pigment. The painter St. Martin used pieces of the heart of King Louis XIV in his paintings. He also obtained King Louis XIII's heart, which had been preserved in the Church of St. Louis of the Jesuits. (In this instance the king had left his heart in St. Louis, not San Francisco.) When the monarchy was restored to power, he was forced to return the heart, but as a consolation prize he was awarded Louis's gold snuff box.

Necrophilia can be classified in three broad categories:

1. *Violent necrophiles,* who kill to obtain corpses for sex acts, or get a sexual charge out of mutilating dead bodies
2. *Fantasy necrophiles,* who imagine or play-act sexual contact with corpses, often without direct physical contact
3. *Romantic necrophiles,* the bereaved who because of their extreme grief cannot bear to be separated from their loved one, and continue to relate sexually to their beloved much as they did in life

VIOLENT NECROPHILIA

At his court martial in 1849, Sergeant François Bertrand admitted to numerous outrageous attacks on corpses. His confession provides us with the most detailed and personal account of the personality of the violent compulsive necrophile. Born to a respectable French farm family, Bertrand even as a young child was subject to violent, destructive temper fits. He was sexually precocious and began masturbating at age 8. These activities were accompanied by vivid fantasies of torturing, killing, and then sexually assaulting entire rooms full of naked women. When fantasy lost its ability to stimulate the teenage Bertrand, he was ready to move on to genuine flesh and blood. He began to kill and mutilate dogs, cats, and other animals, cutting open the abdomen and tearing out the intestines while masturbating. Soon even this thrill was gone, however, so he then moved on to attack his first human corpse, providing the following account as cited in Krafft Ebing's *Psychopathia Sexualis:*

> At midday I went for a walk with a friend. It so happened that we came to the garrison cemetery, and seeing a half-filled grave I made an excuse to my friend and left him, to return to the grave later. Under the stress of a terrific excitement I began to dig up the grave with a spade, forgetting that it was clear daylight and that I might be seen. When the corpse—a woman's—was exposed I was seized with an insane frenzy and, in the absence of any other instrument, I began to hack the corpse with the spade. While doing so I made such a noise that a workingman engaged near the cemetery came to the gate. When I caught sight of him I lay down beside the corpse and kept quiet for a while. Then, while the workman was away in search of the police, I threw some earth on the corpse and left the cemetery by climbing over the wall. Then, trembling and bathed in cold perspiration and completely dazed, I sat for hours in a small spinney [thicket]. When I recovered from this paralysis I felt as though my whole body had been pounded to a pulp, and I felt weak in the head.

Two days later, this time on a dark and stormy night, like a proper ghoul, he dug up the same corpse with his bare hands. Although his hands were bleeding, he continued to dig in a frenzy until the corpse's abdomen was exposed. He tore it to pieces, then neatly refilled the grave. After this episode, he proceeded to mutilate and destroy corpses with his sword or pocket knife on at least fifteen occasions. On five occasions he masturbated several times while touching the corpse's intestines with his left hand (apparently he was right handed). Then, after six months of abstinence, he unearthed the body of a 16-year-old girl and for the first time had sexual intercourse with a dead body. He recalled that his ecstasy was intense.

I cannot describe what I felt during that time. But all my enjoyment with living women is nothing as compared with it. I kissed the girl all over her body, I pressed her to my heart as though I wanted to crush her; in short, I did everything to her that a passionate lover does to his mistress. Having enjoyed the body for about a quarter of an hour, I cut it up and, as in the case of my other victims, tore out her intestines.

Several months later, he attacked four more women's bodies, expanding his mutilation routine to include slitting the corpses' mouths, cutting off their arms and legs, and lacerating and twisting the amputated limbs into bizarre poses.

In the course of Bertrand's cemetery raids he had accidentally disinterred a great many male corpses, because graves in the potter's field and the suicide cemetery had no markers identifying gender. Once he had to dig up fifteen men before he unearthed a female. This made him furious, and he slashed the male corpses with his sword, but claimed that this nauseated rather than aroused him sexually. It is interesting to note that while conducting his nocturnal escapades, he was still having mutually satisfying sex with women at the many different posts where he was stationed, and several of the women wanted to marry him.

Bertrand's compulsion to dig up, mutilate, and destroy women's bodies occurred at two-week intervals and was preceded by blinding headaches and rapid heartbeat. This may be one of the rare occasions when headaches stimulated sexual activity rather than avoided it. Bertrand's sex drive was so overwhelming that he overcame incredible obstacles in order to obtain gratification. He was shot at by sentries, avoided traps laid for him, and ignored extremes of weather, such as when he had to swim across a freezing cold pond in mid-winter to avoid capture. His luck finally ran out when he was severely wounded by a gun booby trap while climbing over a wall into the cemetery. Nevertheless, he completed his assault, cutting out the female corpse's genitals and slashing her thighs. Several days later a grave digger overheard a soldier say that one of his comrades, a Sergeant Bertrand, had been accidentally wounded a few days before and was in the military hospital. When accused by detectives, Bertrand surrendered and contributed a detailed confession.

Bertrand's is the most widely cited case of necrophilia in psychiatric textbooks. It shows the overpowering nature of the urges that are sometimes associated with this disorder, and the gruesome extremes of mutilation and destruction that humans are capable of inflicting.

FANTASY NECROPHILIA

Fantasy necrophiles range from those timid persons whose only sexual outlet is the thrill and arousal they experience when viewing the dead bodies of strangers in funeral homes or morgues, to more daring individuals who may frequent brothels catering to the rich and famous and deviant, which promise to gratify the most exotic sexual fantasies. According to the famous German sexologist Dr. Magnus Hirschfeld, founder of the Berlin Institute for Sex Science, these luxury brothels typically have dimly lit "mortuary chambers" with walls covered in black cloth. Candelabra with burning candles and other funereal trappings associated with death are arranged near a casket. In a typical scenario the prostitute, dressed in a white Frederick's of Hollywood-style burial shroud, lies motionless on a bier or in a casket. She has previously painted blue death spots on her body and has made her skin feel cold with cold compresses. The necrophile, perhaps dressed as a priest, will kneel before her and recite prayers for the dead, accompanied by faint organ music in the background. The finale comes when he can no longer control his excitement and throws himself on her body, which remains rigid and immobile throughout the act, though, of course, still very much alive.

Although necrophiles are almost all male, according to her biographer the actress Sarah Bernhardt later in life would agree to meet her lovers only while reclining in a coffin. Patricia Bosworth's biography of the late movie star Montgomery Clift quotes him as revealing that he knew a plastic surgeon and abortionist who, as a profitable sideline, occasionally supplied dead bodies to a New York funeral home where, for $50, one could go in and have sex with a corpse.

ROMANTIC NECROPHILIA

Ancient customs and traditions have permitted romantic necrophilia, allowing survivors to display a certain amount of loving attention to a dead lover in order to help them deal with their profound and extreme grief. Some mourners cannot bear to be separated from their loved ones and continue to relate sexually to their beloved after their death. For example, Periandes, one of the Seven Sages of ancient Greece, lived for a year with the dead body of his beloved wife, Melissa. King Herod slept for seven years next to the corpse of his dead wife, Marianna, whom he apparently loved more dead than alive, since he was directly responsible for her murder. In the sixteenth century Queen Johanna of Navarre, in what might be termed "necrotaxidermy," kept the embalmed corpse of her husband, Philip the Handsome, by her side for three long years after his death in 1506. Always insanely jealous, she arranged for the body to travel with her wherever she went, even setting up bodyguards to prevent the late Philip from indulging in a bit of posthumous adultery. She thought of him as just dozing, conversed with him, and insisted that the servants continue to treat him like a king. In some ways, he had been transformed into the perfect husband.

In Central Europe, until the late eighteenth century, if a betrothed woman died before the wedding ceremony, the groom would still be given the opportunity to consummate the marriage by having sexual intercourse with the corpse. In the nineteenth century, Queen Victoria of Great Britain, in mourning for her beloved Prince Albert, had his clothes laid out and his shaving water brought to their chambers daily for several years. Even today, some grief-stricken individuals cannot bear to change a single item in the dead person's room, converting it into a virtual shrine long after the loved one's passing. Still more extreme are those rare instances of frightened and lonely souls who deliberately keep Mommy's body with them at home, for weeks or months, in a crude state of mummification. One of these cases formed the real-life basis for the enormously successful *Psycho* movie, with the fictional Norman Bates as the bereaved son. To psychoanalysts, the Sleeping Beauty fairy tale represents a disguised form of necrophilia, the dead princess aroused from her permanent slumber by the sexual advances of the charming prince. This hidden meaning is made clear, in one version of the story, by the thinly disguised phallic symbolism of his tapping on her "casket" with his "sword." As far-fetched as that spin on the old fairy tale may seem, however, other imaginative psychoanalysts have conjured up the specter of "unconscious necrophilia" to explain the unethical behavior of some male doctors who have sexual intercourse with their frigid (sexually dead) female patients.

Turning now to necrophilia in more modern times, we move to bohemian Key West, Florida, during the closing years of the Great Depression. That necklace of sun-drenched islands has been a tolerant home to all sorts of misfits, strange characters, freethinkers, ex-rumrunners, moonshiners, would-be avant garde poets, painters, and novelists such as Ernest Hemingway. Dr. Alvan Foraker, writing in the Journal of the Florida Medical Association provides us with a case as colorful as the surroundings.

The 60-year-old Count Karl Tangler Von Cosel was strange even by Key West standards. He claimed to be a former World War I German submarine skipper with nine college degrees, now pensioned off and living the good life. He was well known as a tinkerer and inventor and stretched out his meager income by working as an X-ray technician in a local hospital. Suddenly his relaxed life changed abruptly when he was assigned to X-ray an advanced case of progressive tuberculosis in the person of Senorita Elena Hoyos Mesa, a 20-year-old Cuban entertainer. Von Cosel had found his soul mate, only to lose her to the disease shortly after they met. The frantic Von Cosel tried vainly to revive her with a strange electrical device. When this failed, he built an elaborate aboveground burial vault, which he equipped with a specially constructed telephone so that he could communicate with her. He also built a strange airship but refused to discuss its features or function. Two years later, during a recession, he lost his job. He then towed his airship off to a shack he had built in an undeveloped area. He lived there quietly for several years, reading, smoking his pipe, and playing Wagner on a pipe organ he had built. This all changed abruptly one day, when some morbid curiosity seekers revealed that there was no body in the mausoleum. Investigators were shocked to discover Elena's embalmed corpse in Von Cosel's shack, reclining on a large canopy bed curtained with cheesecloth. Autopsy revealed that she had been dead for a number of years. Amazingly, Von Cosel had reconstructed her face, breasts, arms, legs, and trunk, and had even fashioned an ingenious vaginal tube that permitted sexual intercourse. He confessed, revealing that he had cleaned the remains and "rebuilt the lost parts, bandaged the broken parts and the destroyed parts which had to come out I replaced". He went on: "I put in sufficient absorbent material for packing to soak her in solutions and feed her and develop the tissues." He continued to work on the airship, which he said, "would carry [us] both high into the stratosphere, so that radiation from outer space could penetrate Elena's tissues and restore life to her somnolent form." The romantic aspects of a love that conquered death caught the fancy of the Latin American public, even inspiring a sad love song, "Boda Negra," (Black Wedding). The Florida police were much less sympathetic. Von Cosel was jailed briefly, but released because the statute of limitations had expired (in addition to Elena herself). Despite Von Cosel's pleas, the police sealed Elena's remains in a metal cube, which was buried in a secret location.

CLASSIFICATION

It has been very difficult to construct a psychiatric classification system that does justice to the wide range of sexual activities involving corpses. From the Middle Ages we have a simple Roman Catholic scheme that arrived at a definition of necrophilia by elimination. Given the question as to what kind of sex it would be for one to have intercourse with a female corpse, the Church ruled that it was neither whoring (*fornicatio*) nor bestiality, but rather "pollution with a tendency toward whoring." That is, it isn't exactly illicit human sexual intercourse, nor is it animal sex, but rather more similar to masturbation with some resemblance to human sexual intercourse. In any case, the Church was against it.

In 1910, Dr. Erich Wulffen, noted German psychiatrist, made one of the first attempts to classify necrophilia scientifically. He established three degrees of necrophilia:

1. *Necrosadism* (lust murder), in which homicide has the goal of obtaining a corpse for sex
2. *Necrostuprum*, in which a corpse is stolen and then used sexually
3. *Necrophagy*, in which the corpse is mutilated during sex and parts of the body are eaten

A more modern three-category system describes *inhibited necrophilia*, in which the necrophilic behavior is an extension of profound grief over the loss of a loved one. *Pseudonecrophilia* is defined as erotic mastur- bation fantasies without actual physical contact with a corpse, and *sa- distic necrophilia* involves biting, devouring, overtly attacking, or sexu- ally assaulting a dead body.

For the last word we defer to the expertise of two eminent Cleveland psychiatrists, Drs. Jonathan P. Rosman and Phillip R. Resnick of the Case Western Reserve School of Medicine. In 1989 they scoured the entire world of clinical literature on necrophilia and compiled a complete account of all 122 known cases from many countries and spanning sev- eral decades, including 34 rare and previously unpublished reports. Based on the results of their 1989 survey, they divided practicers of necrophilia into *genuine necrophiles* and *pseudonecrophiles,* according to the nature of their behavior with corpses.

Genuine Necrophilia

The genuine necrophile has a persistent and urgent sexual attraction to corpses. His sex acts with corpses are subdivided into necrohomicide (murder to obtain a body for sex), regular necrophilia (sex with an al- ready dead body), and necrophilic fantasy (vivid erotic imagery involv- ing sex with corpses, but no physical contact).

Necrohomicide.

The following case of necrohomicide is illustrative.

In 1982, Denis Nilsen, a 37-year-old British civil servant, was con- victed of killing 15 men whom he had picked up in London pubs and invited to his flat. This horrendous murder spree has been doc- umented in Brian Masters's book, *Killing for Company.*

Nilsen's parents met and married during World War II, but sep- arated soon afterward. His father deserted the family so early that Nilsen does not remember him at all. He was raised by his mother and his Scottish grandparents. He remembers worshiping his sea- faring grandfather and eagerly awaited his return from each of his fishing voyages. One day when Denis was 6, his mother asked him to come see Grandad for the last time. She took him into a large room dominated by a long box resting on trestles, and lifted him up to see the lifeless body of his grandfather. The death was never again discussed, and the taboo against mentioning death forever connected the image of a loved one and a dead body in Nilsen's mind. That event was reinforced by a later sexual experience. When Nilsen was 8 he almost drowned in the ocean but was rescued by a teenager, who then sexually molested the child who was in a semiconscious state.

At school Denis was bright enough but a loner, becoming the class clown to cover his feelings of estrangement. Upon graduation he joined the British Army and served 12 years as a butcher in the Army Catering Corps, a trade that was to come in handy later.

He was a solitary and painfully lonely person, living alone with only a small mongrel dog named Bleep for companionship. Conflicted over his sexual orientation and confused sexual identity, masturbation was his sole sexual outlet well into adulthood. In a typical session, Nilsen would recline nude before a full-length mirror, taking care so as not to show his face, in order to masturbate while pretending that the image was that of a sex partner. When he tired of this game he searched out other young men, usually loners like himself, inviting them to his flat for drinks and conversation. Sometimes, unpredictably, after his companion became drunk and sleepy, Nilsen would slip off his necktie and strangle him. Then, in ritualistic fashion, he would caress the man, bathe and dress the body, and then pose it on the bed, contemplating it lovingly while masturbating. Sometimes he would undress and powder his own body in imitation of the pallor of death and lie down to sleep beside the corpse. He claimed that the body was for him a thing of great beauty, and he denied any premeditation or murderous intent.

After enjoying the corpse for a day or so, he would bury the body under the apartment floorboards or in the garden. Once, when his apartment floorboards were overcrowded, he filleted some bodies into two-inch strips and flushed them down the toilet. This was his undoing. He was caught when the plumbing backed up, which resulted in his arrest.

Nilsen was convicted in 1983 by a jury that was divided down the middle as to his criminal responsibility, that is, whether he was mentally ill and therefore unable to appreciate the nature of his crimes. The jury consulted the judge, who cut to the heart of the issue by declaring, "A mind can be evil without being abnormal."

Nilsen was sentenced to prison and so far has written more than 50 volumes recounting his history, philosophy of life, and similar weighty matters. Unfortunately, the killing did not stop with Nilsen's last victim. During his lengthy interrogation he repeatedly asked about the welfare of his dog, to no avail. The authorities had killed Bleep a few days after his confession.

Three other notorious serial killers fall into the necrohomicide category. John R. H. Christie, the "Rillington Place" murderer of London, killed eight women in order to have sex with them, then disposed of their bodies in the walls and garden of his flat. Edmond Kemper in California killed six young women hitchhikers, and then his mother and her best friend. After strangling his victims he undressed them, took pictures, and then indulged in a variety of sex acts, including masturbating into the mouths of their severed heads. In a 1991 case, the late Jeffrey Dahmer killed 17 young homosexual men whom he lured to his Milwaukee apartment. Dahmer would best be classified as a pseudonecrophiliac, since virtually all the sex acts preceded the death and dismemberment of the victims. Numerous books and popular articles have publicized widely the lurid crimes of Dahmer, Kemper, and Christie.

Regular Necrophilia.

Individuals classified as regular necrophiles perform a variety of sex acts with corpses. They often are found in jobs that afford an opportunity to come in contact with dead bodies, working as hospital orderlies, funeral home personnel, or grave diggers.

A well-known New York case reported by Dr. J. Rapoport involved a 50-year-old single man who was arrested when found kissing the lips and touching the breasts of a female corpse in a funeral parlor. He had been raised by foster parents and was very devoted to his mother, who died when he was 38.

His practice of visiting dead bodies started about six years after his mother's death. It began with the death of his maternal aunt, whose body he saw laid out in a casket. Looking at her body caused an erection, and he felt compelled to go to the bathroom and masturbate. Following this incident he began visiting funeral homes regularly. He would clip death notices out of the newspaper, dress up, and visit the bodies at 9:00 A.M. to avoid encountering relatives of the deceased. Sexual contact with the corpses always involved kissing the lips or fondling the breasts. If unable to do so, he would just stare at the body. All of these activities generated intense sexual arousal, and he would return home to masturbate. He had many undertaker friends, and after his arrest, while on the hospital prison ward, he volunteered that he would be happy to help out as a morgue attendant.

Necrophilic Fantasy.

Individuals who engage in necrophilic fantasy may lust for corpses in their hearts but do not engage in direct physical contact with dead bodies. Modern mental health practitioners are very reluctant to label any kind of fantasy as abnormal or deviant as long as it does not result in self-defeating, harmful, or illegal behavior and does not upset the client. By this standard we would not classify a customer of the previously described funeral brothel as psychologically impaired so long as his mode of sexual gratification fell within those guidelines. It is almost impossible to estimate the incidence of imaginal necrophilia, since such fantasies are subject to strong social taboos and are most likely to be confided to only a very limited audience, such as one's therapist or sex partner.

Pseudonecrophilia

In pseudonecrophilia, sex acts with corpses are generally an unintentional result of the attacker's violent assault. The homicide frequently takes place during a murderous frenzy, and the victim is attacked by throttling or by any means at hand, such as an axe, knife, gun, or club. Although sex acts often follow the death of the victim, it is the momentum of the aggressive attack that is responsible, rather than a basic yearning for a corpse to assault.

Canadian doctors Selwyn Smith and Claude Braun of the Royal Ontario Hospital described a fascinating case involving Darren, a

36-year-old man of average intelligence who was arrested for partially strangling 20 women, the last of whom died during the sexual assault. He continued to have sex with her body several times after her death so as not to waste a golden opportunity.

Darren's mother died when he was a year old, and his life thereafter was a virtual smorgasbord of symptomatology. His alcoholic father remarried and, while drinking, would frequently beat his wife, the patient, and the patient's siblings, sometimes stealing their money to buy liquor. Darren was a sickly child, a loner, habitual truant, and frequent runaway. As a child he tortured animals and attacked his siblings with knives and heavy cooking utensils. Sex was a taboo topic in the home, and during adolescence Darren felt extreme guilt about masturbation. He had a brief marriage to the first woman he had intercourse with, but after the divorce led a life characterized by an astonishing variety of pathological deviations. These included alcoholism, drug abuse, homosexual prostitution, robbery, incest, exhibitionism, autoerotic asphyxiation, and repeated sexual attacks on women, usually while drunk. He was frequently impotent and preferred sex partners who were either unconscious or immobile, in order to avoid critical remarks about his performance. Later he would immobilize them by strangulation. He claimed that he had no difficulty finding these women for his death games, and was charged with partially strangling 20 different women. Several of them apparently not only tolerated his abuse, but actually asked to live with him. In fact, according to Darren, only 8 of his victims were assaulted against their will, and three of the women actually begged him to kill them.

He began these sex practices with his wife, choking her with his legs during oral-genital intercourse and imagining that she was a helpless pawn under his complete domination and control. In that fantasy he could perform any kind of lecherous act on her unresisting body. He progressed to demanding that she play dead during intercourse, and if she refused he would strangle her into unconsciousness and then perform bizarre sexual scenarios with her body. Eventually he graduated to attacking and strangling strange women on the street, and was quickly arrested.

During his trial for murder one psychiatrist testified that Darren did not seem to have had a conscious intent to kill or physically hurt his victims. The psychiatrist cited Darren's many previous involvements in similar kinds of sexual activities (e.g., strangling) that did not result in any deaths. The psychiatrist also testified that Darren was motivated by a desire to obtain an immobile, helpless, and unresisting partner as a laboratory for his sexual experiments, rather than by a compulsion to kill and violate corpses. Darren was eventually convicted of manslaughter and sentenced to a lengthy prison term.

Drs. Rosman and Resnick's survey provides us for the first time with accurate information based on a large number of cases. It allows us to correct several common mistaken ideas about necrophilia. For example, conventional clinical wisdom had long considered necrophiles to be either mentally retarded or hopelessly insane, severely handicapped in their ability to find living sex partners, losing control while drunk, and employed in jobs with easy access to dead bodies. In fact, in Rosman and Resnick's study every necrophile tested had an IQ score above 80, and 69% had scores above 100. As to severe mental illness, only 17% fell into this category. One-half of the necrophiles were diagnosed as having a personality disorder, which is a lesser category of behavior disorder, roughly equivalent to neurosis. In fact, with respect to the necrophiles' previous sex lives, 86% of the genuine necrophiles and 95% of pseudonecrophiles had previously enjoyed live non-necrophilic sex with numerous willing partners.

Traditional wisdom is more accurate in describing the necrophiles' alcohol abuse and access to dead bodies. Drunkenness played a large role in loosening inhibitions, with 80% of pseudonecrophiles and 44% of genuine necrophiles reporting that they drank heavily before their attacks. As to access to corpses, 57% of all necrophiles had jobs such as morgue attendant, hospital orderly, cemetery attendant, funeral parlor employee, or emergency medical technician. These findings indicate that careful employers should definitely screen prospective employees more rigorously, especially if the job involves handling the recently deceased.

THEORETICAL VIEWS

Considering society's revulsion toward the very idea of sex with corpses, it is easy to overlook the advantages mentioned by necrophiles in their uncontrollable attraction to a dead consort. They frequently mention the desirability of a partner who is helpless, unresistant, and completely at their mercy. The dead lover never rejects caresses and is always available when required; makes no demands, is never unfaithful, and never rejects you. This lover does not compare your love-making skills with others', will go along with any sort of kinky sex, and, if things go too far, cannot be harmed and will never file a complaint against you.

Psychoanalytic View

Before the emergence of Freudian psychoanalytic theory, what little was written about necrophilia attributed it to an inborn biological flaw like idiocy or senility. Psychoanalytic interpretations take a totally different tack. Psychoanalysts claim that the need to overcome the *primal scene* trauma is responsible for causing later necrophilia. The *primal scene* refers to the young child's actual or imagined observation of parental intercourse. The child misinterprets the sex act as the father's mounting a murderous attack on the helpless mother, which causes overwhelming traumatic anxiety in the child. This interpretation of parental sex then forms the unconscious foundation for the later emergence of two common types of necrophilia. The sadistic murderer, the necrohomicide type, identifies with the father, the attacker, accomplishing the act of murder during coitus itself. The more timid and repressed necrophile psychologically delays his gratification until after the father has completed his attack and the victim (mother) has been rendered harmless and safely immobile.

A characteristic common to all necrophiles is their lack of self-esteem and deep-seated feelings of inferiority. Unusually sensitive to rejection, they seek out a safe sex partner who is permanently incapable of rejecting them. At first they may be fearful of the dead. However, through the defense mechanism of reaction formation, whereby an unacceptable emotion is replaced by its opposite, they become enamored of the dead and obsessed with them. They develop elaborate fantasies involving corpses, and when environmental or occupational circumstances cooperate, they will act on their hidden desires.

Sociobehavioral View

Most European psychiatrists regard necrophilia as the result of environmental factors, rather than unconscious childhood fantasies. They see the cause to be several factors acting together. These include consistent lack of sexual success with live women, easy access to corpses, and heavy alcohol use, which tends to reduce the natural revulsion toward dead bodies.

From a behavioral perspective, necrophilia is simply another type of problem behavior that is acquired when the proper learning conditions are present. For example, it is common for a man during sexual intercourse to try to delay orgasm while inserted and enjoying the preliminaries. However, this may be hard if his partner is moving very enthusiastically. He may then ask her to slow down or remain motionless before his excitement reaches the point of no return. If having a motionless partner allows him to prolong sexual pleasure, this could be a powerful motive for seeking out other immobile sex partners. In a few rare cases, he could even move on to the ultimate, an unconscious or dead person.

Treatment

There are very few reports of the treatment of necrophilia. Psychiatrists Rosman and Resnick recommend a shotgun approach using a variety of procedures that have proven useful in treating other sexual disorders. These include establishing a noncritical therapy atmosphere, treating any other problems such as stress or depression with appropriate medicines, help in establishing more mature social and sexual relationships, and, for extremely oversexed patients, the use of male-hormone-reducing drugs.

We have seen that necrophilia may range all the way from harmless masturbation fantasies to an unusual kind of kinky sex or even murder. We can now understand how necrophilic behavior might develop, and the advantages for the participants. Our society maintains certain dignified rituals regarding the dead body, but if one's partner only *plays* dead, or if sexual enjoyment is greatly increased when the partners enjoy sex in coffins or cemeteries, are these forms of necrophilia truly beyond the bizarre?

Suggested Further Readings

Burg, B. (1982). The sick and the dead: The development of psychological theory on necrophilia from Krafft-Ebing to the present. *Journal of the History of the Behavioral Sciences, 18,* 242–254.

Hirschfeld, M. (1956). *Sexual Anomalies* (Rev. Ed.). New York: Emerson Books.

Masters, B. (1985) *Killing for Company.* New York: Stein & Day.

Prins, H. (1990) *Bizarre Behaviours.* London & New York: Tavistock/ Routledge.

Rosman, J., & Resnick, J. (1989). Sexual attraction to corpses: A psychiatric review of necrophilia. *Bulletin of the American Academy of Psychiatry and the Law, 17,* 153–163.

Index